Blake and Conflict

Blake and Conflict

Edited by

Sarah Haggarty

and

Jon Mee

First published 2009 by
PALGRAVE MACMILLAN

Palgrave Macmillan in the UK is an imprint of Macmillan Publishers Limited,
registered in England, company number 785998, of Houndmills, Basingstoke,
Hampshire RG21 6XS.

Palgrave Macmillan in the US is a division of St Martin's Press LLC,
175 Fifth Avenue, New York, NY 10010.

Palgrave Macmillan is the global academic imprint of the above companies
and has companies and representatives throughout the world.

Palgrave® and Macmillan® are registered trademarks in the United States,
the United Kingdom, Europe and other countries.

ISBN-13: 978–0–230–57387–1 hardback
ISBN-10: 0–230–57387–8 hardback

A catalogue record for this book is available from the British Library.

Library of Congress Cataloging-in-Publication Data

Blake and conflict / edited by Sarah Haggarty and Jon Mee.
    p. cm.
"The present volume grew out of a two-day 'Blake and Conflict' conference
held at University College, Oxford, in September 2006" – Pref.
Includes bibliographical references and index.
ISBN 978–0–230–57387–1 (alk. paper)
    1. Blake, William, 1757–1827 – Political and social views. 2. Literature and
society – England – History – 18th century. 3. Literature and society –
England – History – 19th century. 4. Art and literature – England – History –
18th century. 5. Art and literature – England – History – 19th century. 6. Blake,
William, 1757–1827 – Religion. 7. Social problems in literature. 8. Politics in
literature. 9. Theology in literature. I. Haggarty, Sarah. II. Mee, Jon.

PR4148.P6B53 2009
821'.7—dc22   2008029928

10 9 8 7 6 5 4 3 2 1
18 17 16 15 14 13 12 11 10 09

Printed and bound in Great Britain by
CPI Antony Rowe, Chippenham and Eastbourne

Contents

Illustrations

Abbreviations

Anns	Annotations
BIQ	*Blake: An Illustrated Quarterly*
BR	G. E. Bentley, Jr, *Blake Records*, 2nd edn (New Haven: Yale University Press, 2004)
E	Reference to page numbers in *The Complete Poetry & Prose of William Blake*, ed. by David V. Erdman, com. by Harold Bloom, rev. edn (New York: Doubleday, 1988)
Experience	*Songs of Experience*
Innocence	*Songs of Innocence*
Marriage	*The Marriage of Heaven and Hell*
Pl.	Plate
Urizen	*The [First] Book of Urizen*

All quotations of Blake's writings, unless otherwise indicated, refer to Erdman's edition. Both plate and line numbers, separated by a colon, are usually given, as well as page numbers.

Acknowledgements

The present volume grew out of a two-day 'Blake and Conflict' conference held at University College, Oxford, in September 2006. The editors are grateful to the staff, fellows and old members of University College for their support. Their thanks are also due to the English Faculty of the University of Oxford for further help with funds.

Sarah Haggarty has been supported throughout the preparation of this volume by the Janice Scott Junior Research Fellowship, based at University College. Jon Mee would like to acknowledge the support of the Leverhulme Trust via the award of a Philip J. Leverhulme Major Research Fellowship.

The editors are especially grateful to their co-convenors, Mark Crosby and David Fallon.

SARAH HAGGARTY
University College, Oxford
JON MEE
University of Warwick

Contributors

Luisa Calè is Lecturer in the School of English and Humanities at Birkbeck, University of London. Luisa's work explores the intersections between the literary and the visual, especially the practices of reading and viewing in the cultures of print, exhibitions and visual entertainments of the Romantic Period. She is the author of *Fuseli's Milton Gallery: 'Turning Readers into Spectators'* (OUP, 2006) and the co-editor of *Dante on View: Dante's Reception in the Visual and Performing Arts* (Ashgate, 2007).

Mark Crosby completed his D.Phil. at Oxford on the three-year period Blake spent in Felpham under the patronage of William Hayley. He now teaches at Oxford and Durham, and is working on a project examining intellectual patronage in the eighteenth century.

Sibylle Erle is Visiting Junior Research Fellow, University of London, and Senior Lecturer in English, Bishop Grosseteste University College, Lincoln. Her academic interests include science, visual culture and Anglo-German cultural relations. She has written a chapter in *The Reception of Blake in the Orient* (Continuum, 2006), a piece in *Blackwell Literature Compass*, a chapter in *Women Reading William Blake* (Palgrave, 2006) and has an article forthcoming in *Comparative Critical Studies*. She is currently completing a book on Blake, Lavater and physiognomy.

David Fallon is a Research Fellow at University of Warwick, working on eighteenth-century and Romantic-period literature. He recently completed his doctorate at University College, Oxford, where his thesis was entitled 'William Blake and the Politics of Apotheosis'. His articles have appeared in *Blackwell Literature Compass* and *Eighteenth-Century Life*.

Sarah Haggarty is Janice Scott Junior Research Fellow in English at University College, Oxford. She has written a monograph, *Blake and the Gift*, and is currently researching an intellectual history of gift-giving in the long eighteenth century. With Jon Mee, she is writing a guide to the criticism of Blake's *Songs* for Palgrave.

Saree Makdisi is Professor of English and Comparative Literature at UCLA. He is the author of *Romantic Imperialism* (CUP, 1998) and *William*

Blake and the Impossible History of the 1790s (University of Chicago Press, 2003).

Susan Matthews is Senior Lecturer in English at Roehampton University. In the 1990s, Susan published work on Blake, the women's novel, and on gender and Romanticism. She has recently returned with a series of published essays (in *The Reception of Blake in the Orient* and *Blake, Nation and Empire*, for example) to work on Blake and the discourses of sexuality. Her new project, *The Female Will: Blake, Sexuality and the Polite* is due to be published by CUP in 2008.

Formerly Margaret Candfield Fellow in English at University College, Oxford, **Jon Mee** is Professor of Romanticism Studies at University of Warwick. He is the author of *Dangerous Enthusiasm: William Blake and the Culture of Radicalism* (OUP, 1992) and *Romanticism, Enthusiasm, and Regulation: Poetics and the Policing of Culture in the Romantic Period* (OUP, 2003), as well as a number of other articles and essays on Blake. He is currently a Philip J. Leverhulme Major Research Fellow working on conversation and controversy in the Romantic period.

Morton D. Paley is Emeritus Professor of English at University of California, Berkeley. He is the author of a number of studies of British Romantic poetry and art, including *The Apocalyptic Sublime*, *Portraits of Coleridge*, *Coleridge's Later Poetry* and *The Traveller in the Evening: The Last Works of William Blake*. He is co-editor of *Blake: An Illustrated Quarterly*. At present he is completing a study of Coleridge and the fine arts with the aid of an Andrew W. Mellon Emeritus Fellowship.

Angus Whitehead is an Assistant Professor at the National Institute of Education, Nanyang Technological University, Singapore. He worked for his thesis, on the immediate living and working environments of William and Catherine Blake, at the Centre for Eighteenth-Century Studies, University of York. Angus has published material on the Blakes in *The British Art Journal* and *Blake: An Illustrated Quarterly*, in which he has another article forthcoming. He is currently writing a book on the last years of William and Catherine Blake. Angus is editor of the *Blake Journal*, the annual journal of the Blake Society of St James. He recently convened the 'Blake at 250' conference in York.

David Worrall is Professor of English and Research Leader in English at Nottingham Trent University. He has published extensively on Blake and on other aspects of the late eighteenth and early nineteenth centuries. His books include *Radical Culture: Discourse, Resistance and*

Surveillance, 1790–1820 (1992) and *Theatric Revolution: Drama, Censorship and Romantic Period Subcultures, 1774–1832* (2006). With Steve Clark, he has edited *Historicizing Blake* (1994), *Blake in the Nineties* (1999) and, most recently, *Blake, Nation and Empire* (2006). From 2004–6, he led an AHRC-funded research project at NTU, on 'East Midlands Moravian Belief Communities, with special reference to William Blake (1757–1827)'. 2007 saw the publication of two of David's monographs: *The Politics of Romantic Theatricality, 1787–1832* and *Harlequin Empire: Race, Ethnicity and the Drama of the Popular Enlightenment.*

Introduction

Jon Mee and Sarah Haggarty

For the majority of William Blake's life, Britain was a nation at war. Countries, ideologies and individuals clashed in the ferment of the American, French and Industrial Revolutions. Britain experienced unprecedented levels of mobilization, chronic food shortages, riots and the repression of civil liberties in 'Pitt's terror'. Blake recoiled with horror from 'the English Crusade against France' and the consequences of living in a militarized state, where freedom seemed to be crushed under 'the Iron Wheels of War' ('Anns. to Watson', E613; *Jerusalem*, 22: 34, E168). Yet Blake's works do not figure conflict simply as a destructive force. If the first plate of the illuminated book *Milton* decried attempts to 'prolong Corporeal War', it also accused 'the Camp, the Court, & the University' of seeking to 'depress mental [War]' (E95). The opening lines of *The Four Zoas* announce 'the march of long resounding strong heroic Verse | Marshalld in order for the day of Intellectual Battle' (E300).

For the combative Blake, the collision of contraries was integral to the creative process. As *The Marriage of Heaven and Hell* has it: 'Without Contraries is no progression' (pl. 3, E34). This principle is obvious in many of the structural aspects of Blake's work: in the dialogue between Devil and Angel in the *Marriage*, or the titanic debates dramatized by the prophetic epics; in the dynamic between Innocence and Experience in the *Songs*, or the competing claims of verbal and visual elements in the illuminated books. Blake has been called a dialectical thinker, although the oppositional processes that animate his works tend not to be resolved into any 'happy state of Agreement'.[1] Due to the heterogeneity and mutual antagonism both between and within each of their component parts, these oppositional processes cannot settle into any just equilibrium. Nor, we think, does Blake represent them as being superseded by any higher synthesis. The kind of conflict that Blake celebrates can be only precariously sustained. Contraries carry with them the risk of irreconcilable difference, and might threaten not just to disrupt progression, but also to prevent transaction of any kind. Progression, to fuel its forward march, might call for contrariness to be smoothed over or transcended, or even for differences coercively to be cancelled out. Conflict, as contrarious progression, is itself conflicted, and highly combustible.

There are several aspects of Blake's works that defy this understanding of conflict as a perpetual struggle, the condition of human life and its spiritual, creative energies. Much of Blake's writing looks towards or finishes with some version of Apocalypse, the conflagration of the last days, when the veil is lifted and the New Jerusalem descends. *Europe*, for instance, ends with the prophetic figure of Los 'in snaky thunders clad', calling 'his sons to the strife of blood' (15: 9, 11, E66). *Jerusalem* closes with a vision of Albion restored; a fourfold humanity apparently reunited 'as One Man reflecting each in each'; and 'All Human Forms identified even Tree Metal Earth & Stone' (98: 39, 99: 1, E258). According to Blake's annotations to Reynolds' *Discourses*, 'Man varies from Man more than Animal from Animal of a Different Species' (E656), but here, in *Jerusalem*, an infinitely various humanity appears to be not just united, but uniform. With this higher unity, it seems, conflict is transcended.

What is lost in this summary suggestion is the dynamism of the eternal human's activity, and the potential for dissonance that remains therein. Even if 'The Four Living Creatures Chariots of Humanity Divine Incomprehensible' are, as it were, singing from the same hymn sheet, they do not sing in unison. Rather, they 'conversed together in Visionary forms dramatic which bright | Redounded from their Tongues in thunderous majesty' (98: 24, 28–9, E257). The envisioning of such bright and thunderous exchanges adds an enthusiastic excitability to the uncertainty attributed by Maurice Blanchot to 'simple conversation'. 'The fact that speech needs to pass from one interlocutor to another in order to be confirmed, contradicted, or developed shows the necessity of interval', he writes, in *The Infinite Conversation*. 'The power of speaking interrupts itself'. Progression, then, is discontinuous and unpredictable; an answer is hoped for, perhaps, in the moment of speaking, but any utterance might be challenged, or met with silence (and even silence, writes Blanchot, 'is still only a deferred speech, or else it bears the signification of a difference obstinately maintained').[2] *Jerusalem*'s visionary conversations, furthermore, open out 'in Visions | In new Expanses, creating exemplars of Memory and of Intellect | Creating Space, Creating Time according to the wonders Divine | Of Human Imagination' (98: 29–32, E257–8). Conflict thus seems not transcended, but transformed through 'regenerations terrific' into a species of mental battle, whereby 'all | Human Forms' are 'living going forth & returning wearied' (98: 34, 99: 1–2, E258). When the veil is lifted at the end of *Jerusalem* what is disclosed to the reader is the ongoing progression of human destiny, an ongoing dispersal of vision into a boundless future.[3] To transpose Jean-Luc Nancy's terms, this 'is not a communion that fuses the *egos* into an *Ego* or a higher *We*. It is the community of others.'[4] Nancy is a thinker who like Blake has worked hard to define what the ideal of community might mean. He is suspicious of the idea of an originary 'communion' as a denial of the kind of 'community' that emerges through communication and even conflict between others. For Blake too, progression is returned to history out of the engagement between contraries played out in the illuminated books.

To understand conflict primarily as a kind of conversation, however, might risk the denial or even the sanction of its violence.[5] This violence has disturbed several critics of Blake, especially as it inflects his handling of conflict between the sexes. A troubling example of specifically male violence comes in the Preludium to *America*, where Orc breaks free of his enslavement and seems to rape the daughter of his gaoler: 'Round the terrific loins he siez'd the panting struggling womb | It joy'd' (2: 3–4, E52). Here, human liberation is imagined in terms of violent male sexual acquisition. The late prophecies, too, seem to make the subjection of what Blake calls 'the Female Will' a necessary part of the progression to Eternity. William Keach has written of the 'fiercely phallocentric and heroically individualistic qualities in [Blake's] revolutionary art'. For Keach and other critics, Blake is guilty of 'the worship of energy as a divinely retributive, ultimately self-validating absolute'.[6] From this perspective the celebration of energy ultimately represents a masculinist will-to-power which is intolerant of difference, for all Blake's investment in contraries. Yet despite the proliferation in the illuminated books of misogynistic images of libidinal power, such images are so variously focalized that it is difficult to align them with Blake's own views.[7] 'The Female Will', moreover, is not the same thing as the will of the female figures in the prophecies. It might rather be understood to be part of a social construction of femininity, which would mean that Blake was participating in the same critique of the delusory power of 'modesty' as was Mary Wollstonecraft. Of course, Blake critics are always susceptible to 'letting him off the hook', but it seems important nonetheless to mark his continually unsettling desire for engagement, his emphasis on 'rouz[ing] the faculties to act', which seems – as Keach claims for Shelley – to insist on 'a dispersal and scattering of the subject's acts of self-representation'.[8] What has come, following Jerome McGann, to be called Blake's textual 'indeterminacy' seems to render conflict not just in terms of 'what Blake is against', but also as a structural principle at work within the illuminated books, one which encourages the reader to create something new from the friction he or she encounters there.[9] To revert again to Nancy's terms, Blake's vision seems less about 'fusion' or 'communion' and more about the kind of community that arises from the communication between differences. The possibility of conflict must be left open if difference is not to be sublated into some prior originary unity.

If Blake explores the idea of conflict in his work, then it also seems to define many of his relationships with his precursors and precursor texts. Even the authors and texts he seems most to have cherished are frequently subject to his corrosive method, that is, Blake often works close to parody, adopting received cultural forms, such as children's poetry, epic, or biblical prophecy, so as to reveal 'the infinite which was hid' (*Marriage*, pl. 14, E39). Even the Bible, constantly rewritten in the illuminated books, is execrated in his notebook: 'The Hebrew Nation did not write it | Avarice and chastity did shite it' (E516). So also *Paradise Lost* is rewritten in *The Marriage of Heaven and Hell*, and Milton himself wrestled into a redeemed form in *Milton*. This agonistic relationship with precursors and precursor texts was described by Harold Bloom as an 'anxiety of influence', although the process in Blake seems more often a matter of engagement – frequently joyous – than war to the death (as Keach's critique seems to suggest).[10] Indeed, the end of conflictual engagement seems a form of death in Blake, the imposition of a Urizenic limit: so, perhaps, the almost compulsive rewriting of his own mythology, and the revision and reprinting of his own books in different forms. Iconoclasm in Blake is a way of keeping faith with the Divine Vision.

The 'unbending deportment' Blake often seems to have shown towards his friends and contemporaries, as well as towards many of the intellectual movements of his times, appears to be both a character trait and, as Jon Mee's essay for this volume elaborates, the product of an intellectual disposition.[11] Blake's pride, as well as his principles, curtailed his involvement with the Mathew circle in the 1780s, and soured his relationship with William Hayley two decades later. '[His] irritability as well as the Association and arrangement of his ideas', wrote John Flaxman to Hayley in January 1804, 'do not seem likely to be soothed or more advantageously disposed by any power inferior to That by which man is originally endowed with his faculties'.[12] While he could sustain it, Blake's reaction to the codes of politeness was one of often contestational engagement, as essays in this collection by Mark Crosby and Susan Matthews suggest. Yet Hayley's notion of friendship as 'Sweet subduer of mental strife' and Blake's own, more oppositional and less regulated model proved irreconcilable.[13] In his disapprobation of what might be the hypocrisy of Hayley's amicable benevolence, whereby 'Corporeal Friends are Spiritual Enemies', Blake appears to cut himself off from all those who do not see the world in the same way that he does.[14] Nevertheless, his triangulation in the later prophecies of 'Contraries' with the idea of 'Negations' prompts an alternative view. The Negation seems to represent blank rejection – the failure to engage with or at least acknowledge the other, even by opposition. 'Opposition' for Blake becomes 'true Friendship' when it acknowledges and engages with what it opposes (*Marriage*, pl. 20, E42). Negation simply denies the possibility of what it negates being possible. It works by prescribing limits and by repressing its others (see *Jerusalem*, 17: 33–47, E162). Eternity seems to be the state in which contraries are allowed the freedom fully to engage and so to change and develop themselves, even if this encounter with difference involves conflict. Indeed, conflict in this regard is a risk inherent in fully engaging with the other. To put too much store in the avoidance of conflict seems, for Blake, to try to determine the limits of community before any communication has taken place.

The essays in *Blake and Conflict* offer an investigation of Blake and conflict across the range of these issues. Many of the essays embrace figurative and structural, as well as historical, interpretations of conflict: as the disruption or sometime reinvigoration of epistemological or ontological dualisms; as a mode of social interaction or of knowledge-production; or as the parodic contestation of verbal and visual genres. The cultural materialist strain that has dominated Blake Studies in Britain at least is inflected in this volume by close readings, empirical detective work and attention to synchronic as well as diachronic heterogeneity.

What is to follow considers Blake and conflict in relation to three main discursive contexts – religion, politics and visual art – although these distinctions are challenged at several points throughout the volume. According to the essay by Saree Makdisi, Blake's concern with the politics of empire is inseparable from his concern with religion. Against recent criticism suggesting Blake is vulnerable to the charge of 'Orientalism', Makdisi recuperates Blake as a prophet against empire, not just during the 1790s, but also throughout his life. Makdisi's Blake is adamantly anti-imperial, hostile to an individualism to which the other falls prey, in Orientalism and empire-building alike. Makdisi sees the same oppressive ontological dualism at work in forging the self-regulating, morally virtuous individualism of State Religion that was anathema to Blake. Through a series of readings, of Blake's Bible as open text, his conquering Rahab and his warlike Pitt, Makdisi brings forth one common enemy: 'the claim to exclusive right, and to exclusion as such as a cultural and political device'. For Blake, all religions are one. For Makdisi, this allows diversity, as well as community: Blakean humanity is 'united in difference rather than in sameness'; Blakean ontology can conceive of 'unity with difference, rather than identity against difference'.

Angus Whitehead's essay is also attentive to the Orient; specifically, to Blake's representations, later in life, of Islam: his mention, to Henry Crabb Robinson, of 'a wise tale of the Mahometans'; his 'Visionary Head' of 'Mahomet'; and his watercolour illustration of Dante's Mohammed and Ali. All religions may be one, but rather than assimilating heathen, Turk and Jew, Whitehead's meticulous reading of Blake's historical circumstances encourages us towards a more precise assessment of his attitude to Islam. His focus is on Blake's minute absorptions of and deviations from the sources potentially available to him: a visible Muslim community in London; George Sale's translation of the Koran; and a wealth of other Muslim and Orientalist publications and manuscripts. Not only, suggests Whitehead, did Blake have a more extensive knowledge of Islam than has hitherto been recognized, but Blake's engagements with Islam were also largely positive.

Aptly, given the genesis of this collection of essays in a conference, David Worrall's essay examines the intricate relationships between another group of conference-goers: those, including 'W.' and 'C. Blake', who attended the Great East Cheap Swedenborg conference on 13 April 1789. Worrall begins by transcribing key evidence from the Swedenborgian archives: a list of those delegates committed to the establishment of a Swedenborgian church. He proceeds to identify many of those present, and to comment on their often diverse ideological commitments. The delegates' interest in, and sometimes first-hand experience of, Africa and colonization, may have informed parts of Blake's illuminated books. They certainly attest to the complexities of Swedenborgian ideas on race and enlightenment.

Blake's position within a complex and shifting cultural debate again comes to the fore in the essay by Susan Matthews. Matthews's emphasis is less on social networks than on Blake's contestation of terms. Her work, on the role of prostitution in the formation of the polite order, is interested in the dynamic processes of conflict – 'the restating and metaphorical shifting of categories' through which 'new meanings are created'. The figure of the prostitute, writes Matthews, was essential to the negative definition of polite society, as well as of the virtuous woman, and yet – especially as prostitutes were visible and audible on the streets of London – was nonetheless destructive to both. In the course of her analysis of the 'harlots curse' in 'London', Matthews attends to Blake's 'impure' diction, the impertinence of his metaphors and the shiftiness of words themselves. Blake's writing, she argues, is transformative; it celebrates female sexuality, rather than reproducing the assumptions of his culture.

David Fallon's essay is likewise alert to the construction of meaning in gendered terms. Fallon's subject is the eighteenth-century discourse of civic humanism, and its permutations in an array of writers, including Blake. He relays how Enlightenment writers such as Gibbon, Hume and Voltaire came, following Machiavelli, to construct a binary opposition between the classical and secular civic humanist as a male figure against the passive and effeminate virtues of Christianity. Blake, however, says Fallon, in line with the English 'Commonwealthman' tradition, had a mingled allegiance to both republicanism and Christianity, even though he often dramatized the clashes between them. Fallon shows how passages of *Europe, The [First] Book of Urizen* and *Jerusalem* resonate with civic humanist discourse. He also elucidates those points at which, increasingly, they diverge. In *Jerusalem*, corporeal war enfeebles rather than invigorates, and the weeping prophet emerges as hero. Women, moreover, seem essential to the renewal of the social body.

The political inflection of Blake's Christianity is again at issue in the next essay, by Sarah Haggarty. Haggarty explores the ambivalence and occasional incoherence of Blake's annotations to Thornton's *Lord's Prayer, Newly Translated*. Recounting the ongoing disagreements in the long-eighteenth century over the nature and proper objects of charity, she traces the increasingly scrupulous separation of virtuous gift-giving from economics and law. It is Thornton's version of this separation, she suggests, that incurs Blake's charge of pecuniarism. Turning to Blake's own marginal rewriting of the Lord's Prayer, Haggarty describes a conflicted text: upholding the gift even as it lambasted voluntary charity; demanding bread as 'due & Right' even as it inveighed against debt and disparaged law. Only an enlarged, relational but still hazardous notion of gift-giving, she suggests, can enable Blake's prayer to sustain such peremptory demands.

Jon Mee's essay draws our attention to the contention at the heart of Blake's notion of conversation. Mee is keen to show the connection between Blakean converse and the 'ongoing reality' of the utopian community it produces. Conversation, he says, is not exhausted by politeness. Godwinian collision and Dissenting candour fostered conversations 'capacious enough to include contention and dispute'. They also admitted of female participants. These freedoms, however, were usually permitted only in a controlled environment. Blakean conversation has an affinity with this conflictual model, argues Mee, but also opens it up, to embrace both women and men in a 'fully social' community. Mee enlarges on these ideas in an extended reading of Book iv of *Jerusalem*.

Dissenting debates about the relationship between mind and matter inform Sibylle Erle's essay about Blake and the science of optics. 'Contrary to what we might expect,' writes Erle, 'contemporary optics extended Blake's range of poetic vision.' Erle views Blake's elaborations of the Creation myth in *Europe* and *Urizen* in the context of the growing philosophical awareness, within optical discourse, of the eye's inherent flexibility. She also assesses the extent to which Blake's vision may have been influenced by George Adams's production of an artificial eye, Swedenborgian ideas of influx and Thomas Young's discovery of lens accommodation.

Mark Crosby's essay also brings together spiritual vision and its technical and material manifestations. Crosby sets the local detail of the miniature portraits Blake produced while in Felpham in the context of the artist's vexed relationship with his patron William Hayley. It was Hayley, mindful of the popularity and potential profitability of the genre, who first encouraged Blake to start painting miniature portraits. He even claimed to have taught Blake its techniques. Crosby's descriptions of Blake's miniatures, however, especially those of Cowper, Thomas Butts senior and Hayley's son, Thomas Alphonso, tell a different story. Comparing and contrasting Blake's techniques with those of other, influential, miniaturists, Crosby emphasizes the disparity between Blake's delicate stippling and the more fashionable technique of hatching. Blake's brush-work thus emerges from Crosby's analysis as a covert form of resistance to Hayley's patronage.

Luisa Calè addresses the conflictual dynamics of Blake's relationship with the field of art. Her essay distinguishes between the robust rivalries of the illustrated book market, and the more liberal competition espoused by the literary galleries. Blake may have felt ambivalent about the galleries' rhetoric of politeness, and excluded from the projects of its printsellers, but his engagement with the book as a medium, as Calè shows, was profoundly influenced by the literary gallery phenomenon. Calè's discussion of the gallery space, and the strategies of viewing, reading and collecting fostered by it, motivates her rethinking of Blake's textual practice. In particular, she argues, our conception of Blake's books as forms radically unbound ought not to displace our realization of those works as books. Rather, 'virtual imaging participates in a dialectical tension with the book as an aesthetic category'. Calè develops her thesis through an extended close reading of Blake's allusions to Fuseli's *Satan Bursts From Chaos*, invoking designs and details from *The [First] Book of Urizen*, and Blake's extra-illustrations to Edward Young's *Night Thoughts*.

In the final essay in the volume, Morton D. Paley considers Blake's Notebook poems about art and artists, both as pugilistic satire and as expressions of Blake's views about fashionable foreigners, pretentious collectors and the art market. Paley also suggests that a major impetus for what we now regard as Blake's characteristic opinions about art was his reaction to the Orléans Sale of 1798, an event that has been little discussed in relation to him. Paley's readings of 'English Encouragement of Art', 'Florentine Ingratitude', 'To the Royal Academy', 'To English Connoisseurs' and 'To Venetian Artists' decode outrageous puns, doggerel rhymes and Blake's special contempt for an artistic pseudo-vocabulary imported from France and Italy.

If the essayists writing in *Blake and Conflict* often disagree about what is worth studying, and how we should go about it, their contention is always generous. It might be objected that this introduction, and the essays that follow, are predicated on good manners and right methods that conspire to forestall true dissonance. But this volume does not pretend to have the last word on the subject of conflict, or indeed on Blake's works. The most we as its editors can hope is that it sparks further engagement and debate.

Notes

1. See, especially, David Punter, *Blake, Hegel, and Dialectic* (Amsterdam: Rodopi, 1982); Blake, letter to George Cumberland, 12 April 1827, E783.
2. Maurice Blanchot, *The Infinite Conversation*, trans. and forward by Susan Hanson, Theory and History of Literature, 82 (Minneapolis, MN: University of Minnesota Press, 1993; first publ. 1969 as *L'Entretien infini*), pp. 75–6. Blanchot's writing about conversation reaches beyond the implication here of a silence that is simply integrated into an enlarged notion of speech. For Blanchot, the tendency of 'simple conversation' is towards unity. Its discontinuities promise exchange (p. 76). It is only 'infinite conversation' that turns away from 'the One' and 'the Same'. Such a conversation is founded on 'an infinite separation' between interlocutors, 'an interruption [...] escaping all measure' (p. 68). Its speech is marked not by simple silences but 'by a change in the form or the structure of language', which might 'allow intermittence itself to speak' (pp. 77–8). Blanchot is not, however, renouncing unity: 'this is the task of each one in working and speaking'. It is in simple conversation that 'we must try to think the Other', and in the simple that infinite conversation might emerge. Yet there is here a grave risk, as well as a fruitful possibility: for

   > when the power of speech is interrupted, one does not know, one can never know with certainty, what is at work: the interruption that permits exchange, the interruption that suspends speech in order to re-establish it at another level, or the negating interruption that, far from still being a speech that recovers its wind and breathes, undertakes – if this is possible – to asphyxiate speech and destroy it as though forever (pp. 67, 78).

3. See Peter Otto, *Constructive Vision and Visionary Deconstruction: Los, Eternity, and the Productions of Time in the Later Poetry of William Blake* (Oxford: Clarendon Press, 1991), p. 217.
4. Jean-Luc Nancy, *The Inoperative Community*, ed. by Peter Connor, trans. by Connor, Lisa Garbus, Michael Holland and Simona Sawhney, Theory and History of Literature, 76 (Minneapolis, MN: University of Minnesota Press, 1991), p. 15.
5. 'All speech is violence – and to pretend to ignore this in claiming to dialogue is to add liberal hypocrisy to the dialectical optimism according to which war is no more than another form of dialogue' (Blanchot, p. 81).
6. William Keach, *Arbitrary Power: Romanticism, Language, Politics* (Princeton, NJ: Princeton University Press, 2004), p. 144.
7. See, for instance, Helen Bruder's account of the complicated relationship between the Preludium and the rest of *America* in her *William Blake and the Daughters of Albion* (Basingstoke: Macmillan, 1997), pp. 123–32.
8. Blake, letter to Trusler, 23 August 1799, E702; Keach, p. 144.
9. See Jerome J. McGann, 'The Idea of an Indeterminate Text: Blake's Bible of Hell and Dr Alexander Geddes', in *Social Values and Poetic Acts: The Historical Judgement of Literary Work* (Cambridge, MA; London, England: Harvard University Press, 1988), pp. 152–72.
10. See Harold Bloom, *The Anxiety of Influence: A Theory of Poetry* (New York: Oxford University Press, 1973). Of the many critiques of Bloom's account of Blake's relationship with Milton, see J. A. Wittreich, Jr, *Angel of*

Apocalypse: Blake's Idea of Milton (Madison: University of Wisconsin Press, 1975).

11. 'Unbending deportment' was J. T. Smith's description of Blake's behaviour in the Mathew circle: see the discussion in Jon Mee's essay below.

12. John Flaxman to William Hayley, 2 January 1804, in *Letters of William Blake*, p. 74.

13. *Poems and Plays by William Hayley, Esq.*, 6 vols (London, 1785), iii, 'Epistle the First', pp. 2–27 (p. 21), ll. 415, 425. This passage is cited by Philip Cox, 'Blake, Hayley and Milton: A Reassessment', *English Studies*, 75 (1994), 430–41 (p. 433). A more oppositional engagement is suggested by the 'Mental Fight' of *Milton*, pl. 1, E95, and the 'severe contentions of friendship' at *Milton*, 41: 32–3, E143, and *Jerualem*, 91: 17, E251, as well as the passage from *Marriage*, pl. 20, cited above in the main text.

14. On corporeal friendship and spiritual enmity, see *Milton*, 4: 26, E98, and Blake, letter to Thomas Butts, 25 April 1803, E728.

1

Blake and the Ontology of Empire

Saree Makdisi

Recent years have witnessed a remarkable surge of interest in Blake's very complicated relationship to British imperialism. Some of the contentions of David Erdman's groundbreaking work *Prophet Against Empire*, which in effect established this field of enquiry, have been criticized and dispensed with, but many others have been substantially altered, augmented, elaborated and improved upon. Work on Blake's even more complicated relationship to religion and the Bible is now beginning to converge with work that has been done on Blake and imperialism, bringing what had been two distinct areas of scholarly enquiry into an ever more productive dialogue. As a result of all this scholarship – and in particular the beginning of the convergence of the work on religion and the work on empire – we are now in a much better position to assess Blake's attitude towards imperialism than we have ever been. Precisely because of the way in which Blake's critique of empire ended up fusing with his critique of what he called 'State Religion', his anti-imperial position can now be understood to have outlasted the radical 1790s to remain one of his lifelong concerns ('Anns. to Watson', E618). In trying to articulate his vision of human freedom from tyranny and exploitation, Blake refused both the logic of imperial domination and that of the religiously ordained supremacy of one people over another. The question of empire in the Romantic period necessarily brings up the question of Orientalism and hence the question of Blake's criticism of – or perhaps, as some have suggested, his complicity in – the discourse of Orientalism. Because of its profound importance for any understanding of imperialism during the Romantic period – especially imperialism in the East, which would become the focal point of the British Empire and would remain so through the nineteenth century and into the twentieth – it is worth spending a little time on this matter before turning to the question of religion and the vast potential it offers for our appreciation of Blake's attitude towards empire. Some of the recent scholarship on Blake and empire has suggested that Blake may not have been so very adamant in his rejection of Orientalist discourse, or as critical of empire, as others have claimed. Edward Larrissy, for example, argues, in a recent assessment of Blake's relationship to the emergence of a properly modern form of Orientalism at the end of the eighteenth century, that many of the negative connotations of the Orient (despotism, cruelty, treachery, benightedness and so on) may have spilled over from that broader cultural and political discourse into Blake's work after all.[1] Others, including Steve Clark, have been arguing that seeing Blake as an oppositional anti-imperial figure involves not only a highly selective reading of his work, but also one restricted to his work from the 1790s. Broaden the focus, they suggest, and we will find a very different Blake, maybe even an outright apologist for empire, which, in effect, is how Clark suggests we read *Jerusalem*.[2]

Although I agree that it's important for us not to idolize Blake by pretending that he could always rise above the imperfections of his period, I also think that it's essential to be very precise about the period's cultural and political dynamics before we determine the extent of Blake's involvement with them. This is especially important given that many of the key structures of feeling in the Romantic period involved not just imperfections, but vast and complex systems, establishing an allegiance to which involves far more than being able to track down scattered individual utterances. Take Orientalism, for example, whose traces some critics have claimed we can find in Blake. Edward Larrissy argues that there is evidence that Blake in *The Song of Los* invokes what had become by the late eighteenth century the classic Orientalist theme of Muslim licentiousness. This claim hinges on Larrissy's reading of the lines on Plate 3 where 'Antamon call'd up Leutha from her valleys of delight: | And to Mahomet a loose Bible gave' (3: 28–9, E67). Antamon, according to Larrissy, represents semen – the fructifying cloud in *Thel*, the 'prince of the pearly dew' with 'lineaments of gratified desire' in *Europe* (14: 15, 19, E66–7). And Leutha, he says, represents the sinful character of sex under the law. Thus that passage in the *Song of Los*, read allegorically, involves, he says, the representative of the male generative impulse, under conditions of repression, calling upon his last remaining hope, the shame-infected sexuality of Leutha. According to Larrissy, it makes sense that Antamon gives a loose Bible to Mohammed immediately following his calling up Leutha because this loose Bible – the Koran – was regarded by Europeans, presumably including Blake, as sexually loose, or in other words, licentious. Thus, on this reading, Blake was participating in one of the best-known Orientalist depictions (really denigrations) of Muslim culture.[3]

I am not persuaded by this reading of *The Song of Los* as an Orientalist text. It is true that classic Orientalism seeks to identify the East – as the West's other – with sexual licentiousness. But sexual imagery, and the expression of various forms of desire, pervade all of Blake's work, not just *The Song of Los*. Texts such as 'The Garden of Love' and *Visions of the Daughters of Albion*, for example, offer visions of freedom from repression (sexual and otherwise) far more excessive than what seems to be allegorically hinted at in *The Song of Los*. Yet neither has anything to do with the East. Clearly, the invocation of sexuality and desire, as in Oothoon's cry, 'Love! Love! Love! Happy happy Love! Free as the mountain wind!' (*Visions*, 7: 16, E50), does not, in itself, necessarily involve Orientalism.

And, as shall become clearer below, the *Song of Los*'s reference to the Koran – really to religious texts in general – has much more to do with Blake's critique of State Religion than with his participation in any recognizably Orientalist form of representation, much less his taking a particular position for or against the Koran or Islam. For Blake, all religions and all peoples have their version of the Bible. The Koran can be thought of as a 'loose' Bible not in the sense that it espouses a sexually or morally degenerate version of Christian doctrine, but in the sense that, according to Blake, all religious texts – indeed, all texts in general – are open to interpretation. As we shall see, the Bible itself is not, on Blake's view of it at least, a 'fixed' as opposed to a 'loose' text. That is, it does not offer a stable normative form from which other religious texts, such as the Koran, can be seen to have 'deviated' or 'fallen'. Rather, the Bible is a text that can be read in different, even mutually exclusive, ways: to authorize conquest and empire, for example – or to contest and oppose them, and to offer up instead a vision of peace and harmony founded on a sense of universal belonging to and participation in a common God, the human form divine.

Not only does the Bible contain both 'normative' and 'deviant' possibilities; Blake was always, if anything, more interested in and sympathetic to the latter than the former. The 'normative' reading of the Bible, after all, is that of the established church and of the imperial state with which it is associated. Deviant readings, even 'disbelief', offer the sole source of hope. To suggest that Blake viewed the Koran as a corrupt and sexually deviant Bible, then, is to recruit him to the ranks of the defenders of State Religion, and to forget that he thought of himself rather as one of the Devil's party, and, like Christ himself, an 'unbeliever' who expressed a faith of his own rather than blindly adhering to faith as dictated to him by the dominant religious and political establishment. Similarly, to assert that he viewed Eastern or Islamic cultures with the disdain of an Orientalist is to assume not simply that he had a negative view of those cultures but rather – much more significantly – that he identified with the normative Western sense of self; a sense of self which could only have been formed through a rigid contrast with the East.

The point of Orientalism, after all, is not that it simply made available the casual denigration of Eastern cultures; it is that it enabled the formation of a contrasting Western culture, and a Western sense of self.[4] In that sense, Orientalism was always more about Western identity than about the Orient – which exists, as an imaginary construct, only to the extent as it provides a foil for the Occident. Thus, Orientalist writing from the Romantic period involves far more than merely various thematic associations, or recycling what had become by 1800 one of the stereotypical depictions of the East, or otherwise making negative or disparaging comments about Oriental or Islamic culture. The primary function of Orientalist discourse at the time (and to this day) concerns the construction of a morally virtuous Western sense of self. Orientalism, in short, provided empire with the language of subjectivity. It helped the West linguistically, philosophically and imaginatively to establish itself *as* the West and, in so doing, to validate its self-appointed imperial mission in the East. Not only is Orientalism, thus understood, inseparable from and indispensable to the ideologies of modern European imperialism: it is also, as I have argued in my own work, inseparable from and indispensable to the elaborations of individualism that emerged alongside and in inextricable association with the new form of empire in the late eighteenth and early nineteenth centuries. What all modern forms of Orientalism have in common is an underlying structural logic distinguishing self from other, the same from the different – at both the individual and the collective level. The consolidation through the Romantic period of the solitary self as the dominant cultural, aesthetic and political category was inseparable from the changing nature of the large-scale European encounter with 'other' cultures. As I argued in *Impossible History*, the imperial politics of otherness in the Romantic period were as essential to the construction and consolidation of the bourgeois sense of self as the latter was to them. Thus the change of mission and self-understanding of Britain's imperial project in the Romantic period would not have been possible, or at least it would not have taken the shape it did, without the category of the individual subject, or selfhood; and the subject, or selfhood, would not have taken the shape it did, without the dramatic alteration of Britain's relationship with its colonial others, above all in the East.

This explains the proliferation, across so many different kinds of writing in the Romantic period – from *Rights of Man* to the *Preface* to *Lyrical Ballads* – of a rigid contrast between a sober, honest, manly self and an indulgent, capricious and feminized or effeminate other: this contrast was essential both to the construction of bourgeois subjectivity and to that Western imperial self judged to be capable of the task of governing a backward and dissolute East. The later imperial understanding of the East that we can detect in the writing of Macaulay, Cromer, or Balfour would crucially depend on the sharp contrast, the binary opposition, of East and West, that was developed during the Romantic period. As Uday Mehta has shown, the opposition between a West (and Westerners) capable of self-government and a dissolute East supposedly not yet up to the task of self-government at either an individual or a collective level, helped to shape and define the contours of classic nineteenth-century liberalism, as we see in the work of John Stuart Mill.[5] And this opposition hinges on the rigid contrast between the vigorous, manly, honest, articulate, sober, active, disciplined Western subject, and the irrational, inarticulate, lazy, weak, degenerate deceitful, disorganized, effeminate and overindulgent Eastern object of his rule. Without this contrast – and without the apparently seamless logical continuity between the sovereignty and organization of the individual self and the sovereignty and organization of the people, the state, the nation – nineteenth-century British imperialism would not have worked, or at least it would have taken an entirely different form, both materially and ideologically, from the one that it actually did.

The point here is that the discourses of Orientalism, imperialism and individual subjectivity merged together and became inextricable from one another in the Romantic period, and they would remain so through the nineteenth century. Again, the role that Orientalism plays in the thinking of John Stuart Mill is only one indicator of this. We in the West are capable of enjoying liberty and representative government, according to Mill; they, out there in the East, where custom holds sway, are not yet capable of self-government – they fundamentally *need* us to teach them how to become self-regulating individuals and nations; the empire is for *their* benefit, not *ours*.[6]

To assess the extent of anyone's commitment to Orientalism and imperialism, including Blake's, then, is also necessarily to assess the extent of his or her commitment to the evocations of individualism that tie together Paine and Wollstonecraft in the 1790s with later nineteenth-century liberals like J. S. Mill. For Blake to endorse wholesale the Orientalist discourse distinguishing between a virtuous, disciplined, productive, sober, rational Western self and a delinquent, undisciplined, unproductive, unregulated and irrational Eastern other, he would have to subscribe to the distinction between self and other in the first place. But not only is such a rigid contrast between self and other not something that we can find anywhere in Blake's work, early or late: it is also the very antithesis of all of his work, one of the notions, along with empire and state religion, that he struggled to resist and subvert.

This is why Blake refuses Orientalism: because he utterly refuses the logic of individualism predicated on an opposition to otherness – the logic that Orientalism fundamentally requires as its motive force. Whether in the work of poets or radical pamphleteers, Romantic-period Orientalism sought to authorize a modern – and morally virtuous – Western sense of self against what it perceived to be an Oriental culture supposedly incompatible with its own values (liberty, freedom of commerce, etc.). Blake was not part of that programme because he was never invested in the concept of the self that provided Romantic radicalism, and so much of Romantic poetry, with its point of departure. Moral virtue – especially moral virtue as the foundation for self-regulating individuality – was simply *not* something he was interested in.

Quite the contrary, in fact. For, as against what he called 'Philosophic & Experimental' knowledge (*There is No Natural Religion* [b], E3), with its class- and race-defined requirements for what must be recognized as a stable Western subject (adequately learned, prepared, disciplined and cultivated), and with its quest for moral virtue over what it took to be a culturally dissolute other, Blake proposes the prophetic power of those excluded and marginalized by the discourse of a morally virtuous individual subjectivity. Jesus, he writes, 'supposes every Thing to be evident to the Child & to the Poor & Unlearned Such is the Gospel'. For, he adds, 'The Whole Bible is filld with Imaginations & Visions from End to End & not with Moral virtues that is the baseness of Plato & the Greeks & all Warriors The

Moral Virtues are continual Accusers of Sin & promote Eternal Wars & Domineering over others' ('Anns to Berkeley', E664).

As I said at the beginning of this essay, the Bible turns out to hold the keys to understanding Blake's attitude to empire, and I will turn to the Bible and the question of religion in a moment. First, however, I want to register the fact that Blake sought to undermine and subvert the notion of a morally virtuous individual subjectivity because he saw it as inimical to the form of being in which he was, for his part, much more interested – a form of being which recognizes that 'God is Man & exists in us & we in him' and that 'all must love the human form, | In heathen, turk or jew. | Where Mercy, Love & Pity dwell, | There God is dwelling too' ('Anns to Berkeley', E664; *Innocence*, E13). For if the world of Blake's illuminated books precludes the simple juxtaposition of self and other which was essential to modern Orientalism, what it reveals instead is a decentred network made up of common and shared elements; putative selves and others are shown to be themselves constituted by and within this network of shared elements, so that, as Giordano Bruno put it, anticipating both Spinoza and Blake, 'we ourselves and the things pertaining to us come and go, pass and repass; there is nothing of our own which may not become foreign to us, and nothing foreign to us which may not become our own'.[7] For Blake too our being is not fixed in a definite and intermeasurable form, in opposition to otherness; instead, we exist as ever-changing bundles of feelings, relations and emotional bonds articulated together by our infinite desires. For Blake, then, the ultimate horizon of our affective relations and our infinite desires – and hence the ultimate horizon of our being – is not a narrow formal selfhood, a self as opposed to others, but rather our participation in the 'Divine Body' of which 'we are [...] Members' (*Laocoön*, E273).

Blake's conception of an open God is, of course, essential to his attitude towards other peoples and cultures. The conception of God as offering a divine dispensation for the conquest and brutalization of others is anathema to Blake. Here, ironically, Blake finds himself in an alliance with the very man many of whose rational and liberal positions he otherwise found deeply problematic, namely, Tom Paine, and specifically the Tom Paine of *The Age of Reason*. Florence Sandler points out that Paine's critique of the punishing God of the Bible in *The Age of Reason* is in part a critique of the Terror in France, where, as Paine says, 'the intolerant spirit of church persecution had transferred itself into politics; the tribunals, stiled Revolutionary, supplied the place of an Inquisition; and the Guillotine of the Stake'.[8] But there is clearly an excess in Paine's reading of the Bible, which is what Blake found compelling about it when he approached it via Bishop Watson's 1798 *Apology for the Bible*. 'Like Voltaire,' Sandler argues:

> Paine is revolted by the accounts in Judges of the Israelites' wholesale massacre of Canaanite cities – men, women, and children offered up as a 'devotion' and 'sacrifice.' He is appalled by the story in the Book of Kings of the two baskets of children's heads, seventy in number, exposed at the entrance of an Israelite city (2 Kings 10), and the story of the Israelite king, Menachem, who rips up all the women with child, in his capture of the city of Tiphsah. (2 Kings 15)

Paine's indictment of the Bible's punishing God, Sandler continues, 'left no doubt that the Bible was indeed in essential features the product of political interest and State Religion, and that it showed a God who ruled by War and Terror, whose miracles were the means of his imposition of his arbitrary power'.[9]

In reading Paine's *Age of Reason*, Blake reconfirmed his sense of the Bible as a deeply divided text, or perhaps a text split between what might be considered 'perverted' and 'unperverted' readings. As E. P. Thompson argues, this is because the Bible could be read to authorize both grace and the moral law. From Blake's perspective, Thompson writes, 'The Ten Commandments and the Gospel of Jesus stand directly opposed to each other: the first is a code of repression and prohibition, the second a gospel of forgiveness and love.' Hence the profound ambivalence about the Bible expressed in Blake's annotations to Watson, where Blake oscillates between two uses of 'the Bible' which are directly opposed. He writes as 'one who loves the Bible' (E611), but while, as Thompson points out, on the one hand he cites the authority of the Bible against Bishop Watson's argument, on the other 'he is stung to fury by the Bishop's complacent endorsement of the Bible's authority for the divine justice of massacring the Canaanites'.[10] Building on Thompson's reading of the annotations to Watson, Stephen Prickett and Christopher Strathman argue that on this view Blake read the Bible as a book 'stretched over an immense abyss separating "the gospel" and "moral law" – and that in reading the Bible for the truth of "love" and "forgiveness" one is always somehow in danger of being drawn back over to the side of the "law"'.[11] In this sense, as many other scholars have argued, the Bible is for Blake the ultimate unfinished, infinitely open – or 'loose' – text. Blake's task, then, in steering clear of what he considered the Bible perverted, is to rediscover and reclaim the unperverted parts. As Florence Sandler argues, this was an immense task. She writes:

> After Paine's grand objections, Blake is left with only shreds of the Bible littered around him – or rather, to use Paine's own figure, with only the treetrunks that Paine had uprooted, boasting that, though propped back into the ground, they could never be made to grow again. The recognition of the extent of the ruin and the attempt to see what might be grown again is, one might say, the whole subject of Blake's major poems of the next decade – *Milton* and *Jerusalem*.[12]

What needs to be added here, however, is that Blake's task of recovering the unperverted Bible – the gospel of love and forgiveness – was partly predicated on recovering an anti-imperial Bible, to be set up in intellectual warfare against what G. A. Rosso has recently termed 'the religion of Empire' that one also finds in the Bible.[13] It turns out, in other words, that Blake's anti-imperialism was not merely, as some critics have suggested, a passing fad of the 1790s, but rather an integral component of the entire programme of the illuminated books, from the *Songs* through *Jerusalem* itself – and hence that Blake's concern with empire was inseparable from his profound concern with religion.

Rosso's reading of Blake's critique of the religion of Empire, which ties the *Four Zoas* to *Milton* and *Jerusalem*, centres on Blake's highly unorthodox use of the biblical figure of Rahab, who appears in the Bible in two distinct and differently gendered figures, first as the chaos dragon destroyed by God at the creation and, second, as the harlot of Jericho in Joshua chapters 2 to 6 who shelters Israel's spies and enables the capture of the city by the Israelites and hence the conquest of Canaan and the massacre of the Canaanites. According to Rosso, the two biblical Rahabs are not ordinarily tied to each other in most readings of the Bible, but Blake establishes just such a connection. 'His reading is unique and based on a profound grasp of the turning points of biblical history,' Rosso argues, and shows 'an apocalyptic sensibility rooted in antinomian dissent and nourished in the revolutionary currents of his age.'[14]

Jericho's Rahab is normally given very positive treatment in both the Old and New Testaments and in various exegetical commentaries. Rosso points out that Blake breaks with the long tradition of praising Rahab and actually places her at the crucifixion scene, where she takes part in Jesus's trial and death:

Blake construes Rahab's behavior – her sacrifice of the Jericho people to the Israelite conquerors – as a negative type of Jesus or the Lamb's sacrifice in the New Testament. Since Blake defines Joshua's Rahab by her complicity with the conquerors, and since he defines Jesus by his act of self-sacrifice, the two figures form a clear and dramatic opposition in his works. Indeed, Rahab is brought into Night 8 of the *Four Zoas* as the Lamb's mortal opponent. She oversees his crucifixion.

According to Rosso, then, Rahab is for Blake the ultimate embodiment of empire, and 'symbolizes the collusion of religion (the harlot) and empire (the dragon) that Blake encapsulates in the phrase "Religion hid in War"'. Seeing Rahab this way, Rosso argues, involves applying 'the anti-empire, anti-harlot polemic of prophetic tradition to Joshua's Rahab in order to critique Israel's theology of conquest'. And by extending this critique from the Old Testament onwards, and combining the so called 'good harlot' of Joshua into the harlot-dragon symbolism of the Book of Revelation, Blake, according to Rosso, is able to 'repudiate the whole ideology of Judeo-Christian conquest'. On Rosso's reading, Blake continues this line of thought to *Jerusalem*, where he champions 'the willing sacrifice of Self' against the 'sacrifice of (miscall'd) Enemies | For Atonement' (28: 20–1, E174), and where he contrasts the 'spiritual deaths of mighty men | Who give themselves, in Golgotha, Victims to Justice' (34: 53–4, E180–1) with the death sentences required by 'the System of Moral Virtue, named Rahab' (35: 10, E181).[15]

Blake's rejection of the enslaving system of Moral Virtue as enforced by religiously ordained violence against others was already registered, of course, in his Annotations to Watson of 1798, a year when, as he famously wrote, 'to defend the Bible in this year 1798 would cost a man his life', because 'the Beast & the Whore rule without controls' (E611). His defence of the Bible is thus announced as an explicitly anti-imperial gesture, a refutation of the Beast of empire and the Whore of what he called State Religion. In his annotation to the passages where Watson writes approvingly of the Israelite destruction of the Canaanites, Blake fulminates: 'To me who believe the Bible & profess myself a Christian a defence of the Wickedness of the Israelites in murdering so many thousands under pretence of a command from God is altogether Abominable & Blasphemous' (E614). Believing in the Bible in this context is obviously a highly selective proposition: the belief that is being affirmed here is a particular reading of the Bible, rather than the Bible as such, which can't meaningfully be said to even exist as such, since it is internally divided between the gospel of love and the Moral Law which Blake saw subtending the 'System of Moral Virtue', and of which Rahab was the ultimate embodiment. If Christ died as an unbeliever, it is, on Blake's view, precisely because he sought to abolish the Old Testament's endorsement of massacre, pillage, war and empire. The moral precepts of the Old Testament are, he continues, 'the basest & most oppressive of human codes. & being like all other codes given under pretence of divine command were what Christ pronounced them The Abomination that maketh desolate. i.e. State Religion which is the Source of all Cruelty' (E618). Christ was murdered, Blake writes, because he taught that God 'loved all Men & was their father & forbad all contention for Worldly prosperity' (E614), a message distinctly incompatible with the Bible set up as a 'State Trick' and used to authorize massacres, executions, conquests and wars – the essential components of empire as defended by someone like Bishop Watson (E616).

What is problematic about making what is supposed to be a unique claim to the protection of God is precisely that such a claim – almost inevitably imperial – is designed to exclude others, to authorize their conquest and destruction. In that sense, the claims of exclusivity that Blake found in the Bible he could also detect among the proto-imperialists of his own age. Modern Orientalism did not (and does not) entirely depend on religious distinctions, but it is also obviously predicated on a rigid distinction between self and other, on to which religious distinctions could readily be superimposed. The objections that one could make against the biblical invocation of divine authority to perpetrate the massacre and conquest of the Canaanites are the same objections that one could make against modern injunctions to conquest and empire, even if they seem to have secular rather than expressly religious justifications. (As current controversies remind us, the distinction between the religious and the secular is not always easy to make.)

The real enemy here, in any case, is the claim to exclusive right, and to exclusion as such as a cultural and political device. Blake's conviction that all religions are one is set up precisely against claims of exclusive right. 'The antiquities of every Nation under Heaven,' he notes in the *Descriptive Catalogue*, are 'no less sacred than that of the Jews. They are the same thing as Jacob Bryant, and all antiquaries have proved. [...] All had originally one language, and one religion, this was the religion of Jesus, the everlasting Gospel' (E543). That original religion manifests itself differently in different languages, cultures and peoples: the *actual* expressions of a *virtual* poetic genius which Blake thinks of in immanent terms (in other words, it is virtual in that it exists only in its actual manifestations rather than as something antecedent to them). 'The Religions of all Nations,' as he writes in his first illuminated book, 'are derived from each Nations different reception of the Poetic Genius which is every where called the Spirit of Prophecy'. Thus, he concludes, 'As all men are alike (tho' infinitely various) So all Religions' (*All Religions*, E1–2). This conception of humanity united in difference rather than in sameness recurs throughout Blake's work, most perfectly, perhaps, in 'The Divine Image' in *Songs of Innocence*, which exhorts us all to love the human form, 'in heathen, turk or jew' (E13).

Blake's openness to other cultures – precisely the opposite of what was demanded of Englishmen, and Europeans in general, by the modern Orientalism emerging in his day – is perhaps best explored in that other entry of the *Descriptive Catalogue*, the one accompanying the painting 'The Spiritual Form of Pitt, Guiding Behemoth'. The entry acknowledges the artist's indebtedness to what it refers to as the mythological apotheoses of 'Persian, Hindoo, and Egyptian Antiquity', which, we are told:

are still preserved on rude monuments, being copies from some stupendous originals now lost or perhaps buried till some happier age. The Artist having been taken in vision into the ancient republics, monarchies, and patriarchates of Asia, has seen those wonderful originals called in the Sacred Scriptures the Cherubim, which were sculptured and painted on the walls of Temples, Towers, Cities, Palaces, and erected in the highly cultivated states of Egypt, Moab, Edom, Aram, among the Rivers of Paradise, being originals from which the Greeks and Hetrurians copied Hercules, Farnese, Venus of

Medicis, Appolo Belvidere, and all the grand works of ancient art. (E530–1)

Strikingly, Blake is claiming to derive inspiration not from ancient Greece and Rome but rather, on the contrary, from their ancient Asiatic predecessors. Moreover, the Asiatic republics – and it is interesting indeed that he specifically singles them out as *republics*, in addition to monarchies and patriarchates – that Blake claims to derive inspiration from do not seem to have been chosen at random. Egypt, Moab, Edom and Aram are consistently deployed in the Old Testament as Israel's enemies, and hence as subject to plagues, floods, massacres, invasions and conquests. By Blake's time, of course, one of the standing national allegories involved reading Israel as a stand-in for England: Milton had his version of this, so did Dryden (most obviously in *Absalom and Achitophel*), and so did others through the eighteenth century. One of the ideological justifications for the British Empire could certainly be located in such affirmations of England as a new chosen nation.

In the painting and catalogue entry for Pitt, however, Blake is in effect turning the long-standing national allegory on its head. Viewers and readers with republican sympathies would presumably have seen the depiction of the godlike Pitt as their enemy, rather than the Prime Minister to whom they owed their unquestioning loyalty. What is most impressive about the painting of Pitt, in other words, is that it seems to transform the figure of the former Prime Minister beyond all recognition. Pitt reappears here not in mere mortal guise, but in spiritual apotheosis as an angel of war and destruction, 'that angel who, pleased to perform the Almighty's orders, rides on the whirlwind, directing the storms of war' (E530). David Fallon argues that this bizarre renditioning of Pitt could be taken by loyalists simply to refer to the Prime Minister as the angel of God's chosen nation (England). But Fallon also points out that the image and the accompanying catalogue entry could also be read 'as a critique of the rhetoric of the chosen nation, led by a self-appointed representative of the Almighty'. Based in the lands that were subject to the jealous Old Testament God, Fallon argues, Blake's visionary models:

> appear to suggest Pitt as an angel of death. Blake hints at this beneath the former premier's left hand, where he depicts the escape of Lot and his daughters from the destruction of Sodom (Genesis 18–19). The justice wielded by Pitt the legislator is that of Old Testament

moral judgment; the destructive results are suffered by Lot's wife and in [the] burning cities behind.[16]

In this brilliant gesture, Blake fuses together his criticisms of the violent exclusivism of ancient religion – the kind of exclusivism that would justify the destruction of Canaan – and the equally violent exclusivism of modern empire-building. Blake's attack on what he calls the perversions of the Bible converges with his attack on modern-day imperialism. In both cases, what Blake opposes is the logic of monolithic and centralizing power, of which, of course, the concept of a punishing God is one of the most formidable embodiments. And he is reasserting his belief in forms of life, modes of being, that are inherently open and multitudinous, that can imagine and conceive of unity with difference, rather than identity against difference – which, as I was trying to suggest in the first part of this essay, is the conceptual foundation of modern Orientalism, and hence the great imperial project that began in Blake's time and carried on through the nineteenth century and on into the twentieth.

Blake's understanding of being as open, variable, dynamic, infinite, was opposed to a sense of being as closed, fixed, definite, ordered, disciplined and governed by a punishing God. If what he was opposing was what Rosso refers to as the religion of empire, what he proposed instead was surely a religion of liberty – genuine liberty. This would be for Blake a continuing, enduring and necessarily anti-imperial project. Far from ending in the 1790s, Blake's engagement with politics and empire carried on into the era of *Milton* and *Jerusalem*.

Notes

1. Edward Larrissy, 'Blake's Orient', *Romanticism*, 11 (2005), 1–13.
2. See *Blake, Nation and Empire*, ed. by Steve Clark and David Worrall (London: Palgrave, 2006); esp. Steve Clark, 'Jerusalem as Imperial Prophecy', in *ibid.*, pp. 167–85. Also see *The Reception of Blake in the Orient*, ed. by Steve Clark and Masashi Suzuki (London: Continuum, 2006), for approaches to the question of Blake and what was once called the 'far East', i.e. East Asia. Most of the work on Orientalism has been concerned with the 'middle East', i.e. West Asia, and also South Asia, the primary sites of European imperial investment.
3. See Larrissy, esp. pp. 9–11. See also the essay by Angus Whitehead in this volume.
4. The definitive work on this topic remains Edward Said, *Orientalism* (New York: Pantheon, 1978). Also see, however, Raymond Schwab, *The Oriental Renaissance: Europe's Rediscovery of India and the East, 1680–1880*, trans. by

Gene Patterson-Black and Victor Reinking (New York: Columbia University Press, 1984).

5. See Uday Mehta, *Liberalism and Empire: A Study in Nineteenth-Century Liberal British Thought* (Chicago: University of Chicago Press, 1999).

6. See John Stuart Mill, 'Considerations on Representative Government', in *The Collected Works of John Stuart Mill*, ed. by John M. Robson, 33 vols (Toronto: University of Toronto Press; London: Routledge, 1963 ff.), pp. xix, *Essays on Politics and Society Part II*, ed. by John M. Robson (1977), pp. 372–580.

7. Giordano Bruno, quoted in Frances Yates, *Giordano Bruno and the Hermetic Tradition* (Chicago: University of Chicago Press, 1979), p. 242.

8. Tom Paine, *Age of Reason*, quoted in Florence Sandler, ' "Defending the Bible": Blake, Paine, and the Bishop on the Atonement', in *Blake and his Bibles*, ed. by David Erdman (West Cornwall, CT: Locust Hill Press, 1990), p. 46.

9. Sandler, p. 46.

10. E. P. Thompson, *Witness Against the Beast: William Blake and the Moral Law* (New York: New Press, 1993).

11. Stephen Prickett and Christopher Strathman, 'Blake and the Bible', in *Palgrave Advances in Blake Studies*, ed. by Nicholas Williams (London: Palgrave, 2006), pp. 109–31, esp. pp. 116–17.

12. Sandler, p. 64.

13. See G. A. Rosso, 'The Religion of Empire: Blake's Rahab in its Biblical Contexts', in *Prophetic Character: Essays on William Blake in Honor of John E. Grant*, ed. by Alexander Gourlay (West Cornwall, CT: Locust Hill Press, 2002), pp. 287–325.

14. Rosso, p. 292.

15. See Rosso, esp. pp. 301–8.

16. David Fallon, ' "That Angel Who Rides on the Whirlwind": William Blake's Oriental Apotheosis of William Pitt', in *Eighteenth Century Life*, 31 (2007), 1–28 (esp. p. 20).

2

'A wise tale of the Mahometans': Blake and Islam, 1819–26

Angus Whitehead

Curiously, in an era in which conflicts worldwide between 'East' (the Islamic 'Orient') and 'West' dominate news headlines, William Blake's literary and graphic responses to Islam have received scant attention from scholars.[1] In particular, the context of Blake's responses – the Muslim texts and designs available to him, and the evidence of an established and visible Muslim community present in London in the early nineteenth century – has been overlooked. In this essay, I suggest the ways in which Blake's references to Islam in his writings, designs and 'table-talk' from the 1820s are likely to have been informed by the wealth of Muslim and Orientalist publications and manuscripts accessible to the artist throughout his life, as well as by his encounters with London's Muslim community. Blake, it emerges, may not have considered Islam to be exclusively a religion of 'the East'. His references to Islam might also have been informed by George Sale's translation of the Koran, a widely available work that privileged Oriental sources over Orientalist ones. Careful, nuanced and balanced discussion of Blake's engagement with Islam is long overdue; I hope here to begin to remedy this neglect.

'A loose Bible'?

In *The Song of Los* (1795), the eternal prophet recalls how 'Antamon call'd up Leutha from her valleys of delight: | And to Mahomet a loose Bible gave' (E67). On the basis of Blake's fleeting reference to Islam on plate 3 of this illuminated book, Percy H. Osmond, in *The Mystical Poets of the English Church*, a 1918 publication for the Society for the Promotion of Christian Knowledge, described *The Song of Los* as 'a eulogy of Mohammedanism at the expense of Christianity'. For Osmond the poet-artist's positive portrayal of Christianity's rival Islam was clear evidence that 'by [1795] Blake's mind was becoming unhinged'.[2] Harold Bloom, however, suggests a converse allegiance: the adjective 'loose' suggests, to him, that Blake deemed the Qur'an 'a poor reflection of the Bible' (E905).

There are further analogues of 'loose Bible'. W. H. Stevenson suggests that 'Koran' means 'a collection of loose sheets'. Indeed, the Qur'an is commonly referred to as the *mushaf* meaning a 'collection of pages'. It was collated in its present written form during the caliphate of Uthman, c. 650 CE, approximately eighteen years after Muhammad's death.[3] Another possible influence on Blake's 'loose Bible' may have been Thomas Boston's book of popular theology, *Human Nature in its Four-fold State*, 12th edn (Edinburgh, 1761), which, according to David Groves, Blake encountered. Blake could therefore have read the following sentence: 'The light of glory will be a compleat commentary on the *Bible*, and loose all the hard and knotty questions in divinity.'[4]

Saree Makdisi has helpfully reminded us that Blake was 'the *only* major poet of the period [...] who categorically refused to dabble in recognizably Orientalist themes or motifs':

> nowhere in Blake's work [...] do we see the turbans, harems, genies, seraglios, sultans, viziers, eunuchs, slave girls, janissaries, snake charmers, fakirs, and imams made familiar by two or three generations of European Orientalist myth-making and found irresistible by most of Blake's romantic contemporaries.[5]

In his essay in this volume, Makdisi recuperates Blake's 'loose Bible': by his reading, a text positively 'open to interpretation'. In *Blake and the Impossible History of the 1790s*, Makdisi's discussion of the term is implicit. He suggests that the text of plate 3 of *The Song of Los*, in which Los compares and demonstrates interactions of Eastern and Western cultures, reflects Blake's reversal of a pervasive Hellenocentric model of Western European identity emerging in the 1790s, which involved the repudiation and denial (as 'other') of the Afro-Asiatic sources of the earliest European cultures. According to Makdisi, Blake's emphasis upon the Afro-Asiatic source of all cultures is part of the poet-artist's attempt to resurrect a lost common being in order to reunify mankind.

Makdisi maintains that for Blake such a common being does not make all men the same, but rather acknowledges difference.[6] He cites the final stanza of 'The Divine Image', in *Songs of Innocence*, as 'a radical challenge to the emergent cultural policies of British imperialism [...] written at a moment of intense political and military interest in foreign cultures':

> all must love the human form,
> In heathen, turk or jew.
> Where Mercy, Love & Pity dwell,
> There God is dwelling too.
>   (18: 17–20, E13)

Makdisi believes that the word 'Turk' is synonymous with 'Muslim', but the term may not be as all-embracing as he suggests.[7] According to the writer of *The Morality of the East* (1766), Turks are 'not the only mussulmen [muslims] [but] the most distinguished part of them [...]'. Elsewhere, the writer distinguishes Turks from other Sunni Muslims ('Tartars, Arabians, Africans, and the greatest part of the Indian Mahometans'), as well as Shia Muslims ('the Persians, and followers of the Grand Mogul').[8] Having said this, Makdisi's reading of Blake remains, to my mind, largely persuasive.

A recent essay by Edward Larrissy, however, challenges Makdisi's conclusions, and argues for a Blake in thrall to Orientalist attitudes. In the *Song of Los* passage, says Larrissy, 'Blake evokes Muslim licentiousness'. 'The Koran', he explains, 'is "loose" in the sense of "licentious" [...] It is sternly concerned with submission to the law, but countenances polygamy, including marriage to slave girls.'[9] Larrissy's interpretation derives principally from a far more traditional, textually based approach to the poem, keyed to a system of 'Blakean' concepts. Larrissy takes it as read that all readers of the *Song of Los* are in 'broad agreement' that Leutha is 'the sinful character of sex under the law'; that Antamon signifies the 'male seed' is 'surely correct, for the reason that it makes sense of the few references there are to him'. Larrissy's interpretation of Islam is also markedly traditional. In fact it is unclear whether his representations of Islam and the Qur'an (just cited) are supposed to stand merely for Blake's take on Islam and its holy book, or also our own widely accepted and 'surely correct' early twenty-first-century understanding of Islam. The historicized readings of Blake's allusions to Islam in the present essay question Larrissy's doubly reductive reading of plate 3 of *The Song of Los* and, I believe, lend substantial support to Makdisi's contention that Blake's representations of Islam differ widely from those of the majority of writers in the late-eighteenth and early-nineteenth century. In addition, by building its own detailed position, this essay opens up new areas for discussion regarding Blake's encounters with and responses to Islam.

S. Foster Damon deduces from Blake's reference to a 'loose Bible' in *The Song of Los*, and details of his description of the Last Judgment in Night Nine of *The Four Zoas*, that the poet-artist might have encountered the work of George Sale.[10] Sale's translation of the Qur'an was first published in 1734, and regularly republished thereafter for well over a century – for example by Joseph Johnson, still at this stage one of Blake's main employers, in the mid-1790s. Including exhaustive explanatory footnotes as well as a 'Preliminary Discourse', the volume provided an unprecedented, thorough and objective overview of Muslim belief and practice. Sale's *Koran* also reflected a heightened level of European scholarship and understanding of Islam as a more complex, liturgical (and less legalistic and libidinous) belief and value system than earlier Western writers had allowed.[11] Significantly, in both Sale's 'Preliminary Discourse' and footnotes, Islamic sources, notably the authoritative Qur'anic commentaries by the medieval Mu'tazilite (rationalist) scholars al-Beidâwi and Zamakshari, were privileged over European ones. As Edward Said observes, Sale 'let Muslim commentators on the sacred text speak for themselves'.[12] It was such revolutionary, balanced, and thorough Qur'anic scholarship that prompted Edward Gibbon to refer to Sale as 'half a mussulman'.[13]

Sale was not a lone voice. The anonymous editor of *The Morality of the East, Extracted From the Koran of Mohammed*, a compilation of excerpts from Sale's Koran published in 1766, suggested that: 'Surely while we revere our Bible, we must believe there is some truth and meaning in passages [of the Qur'an] which extend the mercy of God as far as the sun extends its rays, or the flowers refresh the earth.'[14] If, as Damon suggests, Blake did encounter Sale's translation of the Qur'an, the 'Preliminary Discourse' may have informed Blake's identification of 'Mahomet' with the Biblical figure of 'Ishmael' in the manuscript Notebook description of his design for *The Last Judgment* (1810): '[Beneath] <Ishmael is Mahomet>' (E566). Here Blake appears to be alluding not only to the Judaeo-Christian-Islamic idea that the Arabs descended from the patriarch/prophet Abraham through his eldest son Ishmael, but also to the Muslim belief that the Qur'an received by Ishmael's descendant Muhammad derives from the same divine source as the Torah of Moses, the Psalms of David and the Gospel of Jesus.[15]

By 1820 it is unlikely that Islam could still be considered solely a religion of the East. The first recorded English conversion to Islam, that of John Nelson, dates from the second half of the sixteenth century.[16] An anonymous pamphlet, published in 1641, provides the first recorded reference to an identifiable settled Muslim community in London, 'led along with a certain foolish belief of *Mahomet* which professed himself to be a *Prophet'*. The community is named alongside twenty-eight other 'most damnable and wicked' sects, such as the Antinomians and the Family of Love, present in seventeenth-century London.[17] In the May 1805 edition of the *Gentleman's Magazine*, an anonymous contributor recorded the following:

April 11 MAHOMMEDAN JUBILEE

Last Saturday, Monday, Tuesday and this day, the Lascars of the Mohammedan persuasion at the East end of the town had a grand religious festival. The first day they went in slow procession along the New Road, St George's in the East, Canon Street, Ratcliff Highway, Shadwell and other streets with drums and tambourines. Part of them were selected, performing pantomime dances, with drawn swords, cutting the air in various directions; then followed four blacks in long white robes, holding emblematical figures in their hands. Another held a vase in which was a fire, and a man in a white vestment, treading backwards, threw incense into it; another, with a handkerchief, fanning their faces; when at every turn of the streets, a groupe of the same lifted up their heads and hands to the canopy of Heaven, humming some passages out of the Koran. They conducted themselves with great propriety, *although a multitude of people followed them* [...] We understand this was a kind of jubilee in honour of the commencement of their new year, and of the translation of Muhammad into paradise, and imploring him to give peace to the suffering world, and them a safe return to their own country.[18]

So as well as examining manuscript copies and published translations of the Qur'an, Blake may also have heard passages of the sacred book recited in Arabic in the streets of London. It is clear, then, that during the first three decades of the nineteenth century a Muslim community was present and visible in the British metropolis. Furthermore, at trials at the Old Bailey during the eighteenth and nineteenth centuries it was customary and acceptable for Muslims to swear to the truth of their statements on a copy of the 'alcoran' rather than the Bible.[19] About 1820,

The Koran Society, an organization based at 5 Water Lane, Fleet Street, in association with the supporters of the imprisoned radical publisher Richard Carlile, published cheap pirated editions of Sale's Koran, without its scholarly apparatus and significantly renamed the *Holy* Koran.[20]

The presence of this Muslim community, as well as Blake's possible access to carefully researched Western scholarship regarding Islam, provide contexts for his allusion to the Qur'an as a 'loose Bible' still to be properly investigated by Blake scholars. However, in the rest of this essay I want to focus on three allusions to Islam made by Blake during his last years: an observation recorded by the diarist Henry Crabb Robinson, one of the 'Visionary Heads', and an illustration to Dante's *Divine Comedy*. In these allusions Blake concerns himself not with the Islamic world of his own time, but rather with world of what Sale described as the 'primitive Moslems',[21] the period of the sahábah or companions of the Prophet, traditionally regarded by Muslims as the first and best Muslim generation.[22] Blake's responses suggest a positive engagement with Islam, at least during the 1820s, a period in which this religious faith was still regarded by many in Britain as 'the Devil's Methodism'.[23]

Blake's 'wise tale of the Mahometans' (1825)

Of Blake's three late engagements with Islam, I will begin with his observation to Henry Crabb Robinson made at a dinner held by patrons of the arts Karl and Eliza Aders in Euston Square on 10 December 1825. Robinson records that:

> Perhaps the best thing [Blake] said was his comparison of moral with natural evil – [']Who shall say what God thinks evil – That is a wise tale of the Mahometans – Of the Angel of the Lord that murdered the infant (alluding to The Hermit of Parnell I suppose)[.] Is not every infant that dies of disease in effect murderd by an Angel ?['].[24]

Robinson's transcription of Blake's remarks on the 'wise tale' is open to interpretation. Does the second part of this passage, beginning 'Of the Angel of the Lord that murdered the infant', introduce a different subject, or continue the same one, as both Bentley and Damon believe?[25] Is the 'wise tale' primarily of the infant's murder, or of 'what God thinks evil'? What is clear is that Blake is drawing upon what he perceived to be a Muslim tradition to reflect upon natural evil, during a period in which he regarded himself as a Christian (albeit a Christian who – according to Robinson – rejected the necessity of Jesus's crucifixion and the doctrine of atonement).[26] Robinson's revision of this account in February 1852, in his manuscript 'Reminiscences', suggests a more certain relation of the 'wise tale':

> Not everything was [...] absurd and there were glimpses and flashes of truth & beauty As when he compared moral with physical Evil[.] 'Who shall say what God thinks Evil? That is a wise tale of the Mahometans Of the Angel of the Lord who murderd the Infant' – The Hermit of Parnell I suppose – Is not every Infant that dies of a natural death, in reality slain by an Angel?[27]

Robinson's later version of Blake's comments implies that the 'wise tale of the Mahometans' refers to 'the Angel of the Lord that murdered the infant'. In Fountain Court, Strand, the location from 1821 of William and Catherine Blake's final residence, the death of an infant was a common occurrence.[28] Burial records for the parish church of St Clement Danes regularly note the deaths of the children of Blake's neighbours between 1821 and 1827.[29] Robinson rather suggests a specific literary source for the 'tale': the early eighteenth-century poet and essayist Thomas Parnell's widely known poem 'The Hermit'. In this poem a hermit encounters and accompanies a fair youth (who is in fact a disguised angel) on a journey, during the course of which the latter surprises and horrifies the hermit by a series of incomprehensible acts. These include the murder of a child:

> Before the pilgrims part the younger crept
> Near the clos'd cradle where an infant slept,
> And writh'd his neck: the landlord's little pride,
> O strange return! grew black, and gasp'd, and dy'd.

Finally, the angel, revealing his true nature, explains that the deed was done to turn the doting father back to God:

> ([...] 'twas my ministry to deal the blow).
> The poor fond parent, humbled in the dust,
> Now owns in tears the punishment was just.[30]

'The Hermit' contains no explicit reference to Islam, and yet Blake identifies a Muslim provenance for the 'wise tale', suggesting, perhaps, that Robinson was wrong to connect Parnell's poem to Blake's 'tale'. It is possible that Blake was aware of Oliver Goldsmith's *The Life of Thomas Parnell* (1770), in which Goldsmith observes of 'The Hermit's plot: "I have been informed by some, that it is originally of Arabian invention." '[31] Alternatively, Blake could have encountered the same story in the Qur'an, identified by Damon as the source of Parnell's poem.[32]

Although Damon provides no specific Qur'anic reference, it is possible that the plot of 'The Hermit' derives from one of the more esoteric passages in the Qur'an, to be found in surah, 'al-Khaf' ('The Cave'), 18: 61–83. The passage records Moses' encounter with a mysterious spiritual being whom the Qur'an describes as 'one of Our [i.e. God's] servants [...] whom We had taught Knowledge from Our own Presence'. According to Sale's annotation:

> This person, according to the general opinion, was the prophet al Khedr [the green one]; whom the Mohammedans usually confound with Phineas, Elias and St George, saying that his soul passed by a metempsychosis successively through all three.[33]

Al Khedr reluctantly agrees to take on Moses as his pupil and companion on his journey. However, Moses, despite repeated efforts and al Khedr's repeated warnings, only has patience to learn limited knowledge, due to his inability to contain his outrage at a series of incomprehensible acts, perpetuated by al Khedr, including the murder of a boy. In Sale's translation the passage reads:

> they [...] proceeded: until they met with a youth; and [al Khedr] slew him. MOSES said, Hast thou Slain an innocent person, without *his having killed* another? Now hast thou committed an unjust action.

Finally al Khedr dismisses Moses, but before he does so, he explains his reasons for his seemingly unjust actions, including the killing of the youth:

> As to the youth, his parents were true believers; and we feared lest he, *being an unbeliever*, would oblige them to suffer *his* perverseness and ingratitude: wherefore we desired that their LORD might give them

a more righteous *child* in exchange for him, and one more affectionate *towards* them.[34]

Whether Blake derived a 'wise tale of the Mahometans' from Parnell's 'Hermit', the Koran, or some other Islamic 'wise tale', Robinson's account is intriguing, because it shows Blake supplementing Christian beliefs with a Muslim insight into the esoteric spiritual realities that lay behind 'natural evil'.

'Visionary Head' of 'Mahomet' (1819–25)

Blake's two other late engagements with Islam both feature portraits of Muhammad. Since the controversy over a series of Danish cartoons of the prophet erupted in January 2006, and the appearance of an Italian cartoon published in *Studi Cattolici* in March 2006, the issue of the pictorial representation of Muhammad has become a sensitive topic.[35] While for non-Muslim viewer-readers, Blake's images may at first glance seem neutral portrayals of Muhammad, the works have the potential to offend especially Sunni Muslim sensibilities.[36] Nevertheless, I wish to suggest that Blake's portraits of Muhammad may be read, by the standards of Britain in the 1820s, as positive engagements with Islam.

The Visionary Head of 'Mahomet' belongs to a series of drawings that Blake executed between 1819 and 1825, in the presence, and probably at the behest, of the landscape artist and astrologer John Varley. According to Martin Butlin, in Blake's portrait of the Prophet, Muhammad is 'shown [...] as of strong, forthright character but with no specific attributes or signs of approval or disapproval'.[37] For David Fuller, the portrait reveals 'an attractive, open face which implies no criticism'.[38]

Morton Paley suggests that although the Visionary Heads were 'perceived rather than invented' – in other words, that rather than merely making them up, Blake in some sense saw the figures he drew – 'the facial features and costumes of his human subjects must also have derived from Blake's own prior visual experience'.[39] In several respects, Blake's Visionary Head of 'Mahomet' corresponds to traditional Muslim descriptions of Muhammad in which the Prophet is described as having large wide luminous eyes, long lashes, extensive, slightly arched but not joined brows, an aquiline nose, a wide and finely shaped mouth, tanned white skin and 'a light on his face [...] especially apparent on his broad forehead'. The same sources, however, also record details which do not feature in Blake's portrait, including hair reaching midway between the lobes of his ears and his shoulders, and a beard of similar length.[40] Nonetheless, Blake's atypical portrayal of a clean-shaven, fairly youthful Muhammad seems significant. According to Muslim tradition, the first verses of the Qur'an were revealed to Muhammad when he was forty years old.[41] Blake may therefore have consciously portrayed a younger Muhammad, perhaps at the outset of his fifteen-year spiritual quest prior to his initial encounter with the angel Gabriel and the first Qur'anic revelation. Alternatively, Blake may have recalled a passage from Sale's 'Preliminary Discourse':

> [the inhabitants of Paradise] will enjoy a perpetual youth; that in whatever age they happen to die, they will be raised in their prime and vigour, that is, of about thirty years of age, which age they will never exceed.[42]

Blake's execution of the Visionary Head may also have been influenced by his evident interest in phrenology during this period. Anne K. Mellor suggests that by the 1820s both Johann Caspar Lavater's theories on physiognomy and Johann Gaspar Spurzheim's theories concerning phrenology had become part of Blake's visual language.[43] Blake's visual language may also have been informed by a study by his neighbour and associate, the amateur phrenologist James De Ville. That De Ville made a life cast of Blake's head for phrenological purposes about August 1823 is widely known.[44] My own research has revealed that De Ville's Phrenological Museum and consulting rooms at 367 Strand were directly opposite the mouth of Fountain Court.[45] The fact that Blake and De Ville were virtually neighbours may have facilitated the creation of this phrenological cast. In 1821 De Ville wrote a phrenological manual, *Outlines of Phrenology: An Accompaniment to the Phrenological Bust*. The manual was reprinted in expanded editions in 1824 and 1828 (Figure 2.1). Since Blake was a neighbour to and sitter for De Ville, it is likely that the two men discussed De Ville's developing phrenological theories at some point during the period 1819–25. According to De Ville, the upper central forehead, upper temple and brow are the location of a number of prominent mental organs or faculties. These include the organ of comparison, located in the centre of the forehead and present in 'persons, who in order to convince others, ha[ve] recourse to similarities, examples, and analogies; and but seldom to philosophic reasoning [...] It is generally said to be found in the heads of good artists, and in popular preachers.' The organ of hope, located between the upper temple and

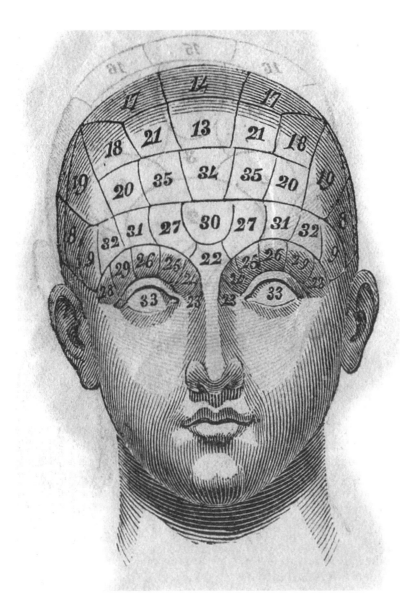

Figure 2.1   [James De Ville], *Manual of Phrenology, as an Accompaniment to the Phrenological Bust*, frontispiece (1828). Courtesy of Angus Whitehead.

the top of the head, is found in persons 'disposed to admit the immortality of the soul'.[46] According to De Ville's expanded 1828 edition of his manual, the organ of marvellousness, situated between the upper temple and outer forehead:

> contributes a good deal to the faith in religion, by the belief in mysteries and miracles [...] The works of Jacob Behmen, Swedenborg and the mystical writers, are dictated by the feelings given by the activity of this organ [...] [which], when large, gives strong feelings for the Deity, and [...] makes the devotee to religion.

Benevolence, located in the centre of the upper forehead 'give[s] a disposition to acts of benevolence and compassion [...], a mildness and cheerfulness to the temper, and a charitable mode of judging of the characters of others'. Of the organ of veneration found at the upper part of the head, De Ville notes:

> Those having this organ [i.e. Veneration], Benevolence, Hope, and Marvellousness, largely developed, are inspired with a sensation of respect, and when directed to a Supreme being, leads to adoration. [...] Numerous observations now prove that when this organ, Marvellousness, and Hope are large, and the sentiments fully developed, persons so organized manifest strong dispositions of religious feeling, and will be seen constantly attending to its devotions and places of worship.[47]

Significantly, in Blake's portrait of Muhammad, who as a prophet might be expected to have possessed many of these qualities described, the central forehead and upper temple are particularly prominent. So Blake, possibly informed by Sale and probably by early nineteenth-century British phrenological theory, appears, in his visionary portrait of 'Mahomet', to have created an atypical, positive representation of the Prophet of Islam.

Blake's illustration to the first section of Dante's *Inferno*, Canto 28

At first glance, in his watercolour illustration of Dante's *Inferno*, Canto 28 (Figure 2.2), 'The Schismatics and Sowers of Discord: Mohammed and Ali', Blake faithfully reproduces Dante's seemingly hostile response to Islam's most prominent adherents.[48] One might expect that Blake would

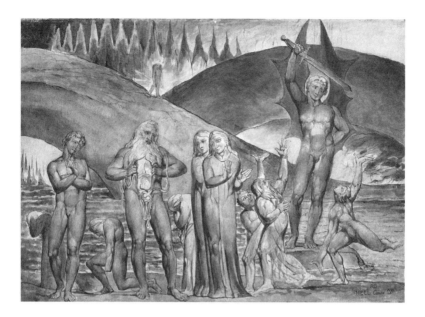

Figure 2.2 William Blake, Illustration to Dante's *Divine Comedy* (1824–7) *Hell*, Canto 28; *The Schismatics and Sowers of Discord: Mahomet*, pen and watercolour over pencil, 37.3 x 52.7 cm. Reproduced with kind permission from the National Gallery of Victoria, Melbourne, Australia.

have used this opportunity to subvert the Italian poet's portrayals of Muhammad and his nephew and son-in-law Ali subjected to merciless vengeance: held, as schismatics and heretics, in the ninth gulf of Hell, and punished by a fiend who splits them open perpetually, as they heal. Yet most discussions of this image have concurred with David Fuller's perplexed assertion that 'Blake simply depicted what we know he deplored.'[49] Careful comparison between Blake's watercolour and the first section of *Inferno*, Canto 28, though, reveals several subtle but significant deviations from Dante's text. Blake's positioning of Dante and Virgil with respect to Muhammad and Ali differs from Dante's description. Dante describes Virgil and himself having a privileged panoramic view as they look down on Muhammad and Ali from what Dante describes as 'scoglio'. This Italian word, as seemingly polysemous as Blake's most difficult illuminated books, can be interpreted as either a bridge, a cliff, or, as in Henry Cary's translation, which we know Blake consulted, a rock.[50] In contrast, Blake places Dante and Virgil at ground level and in close proximity to Muhammad and Ali. Blake's positioning suggests an intimacy and sympathy between the pagan and Christian poets and the Muslim prophet and first Shia Imam.

In his portrayal of Muhammad, Ali and the punishing fiend, Blake exploits Dante's brief and vague descriptions of these figures, and introduces details which appear to subvert the poet's description of the punishments of the prophet and his nephew. Dante gives a sustained account of Muhammad's wound:

> torn from the chin throughout
> Down to the hinder passage: 'twixt the legs
> Dangling his entrails hung, the midriff lay
> Open to view, and wretched ventricle,
> That turns the englutted aliment to dross.[51]

Dante does not, however, provide any further description. Blake, on the other hand, endows Muhammad with a distinct appearance. William Michael Rossetti suggested that Blake's representation of Muhammad 'retains some symptom of the traditional likeness of the prophet'.[52] However, this image bears even less resemblance to Muslim or Orientalist descriptions and representations of Muhammad than the Visionary Head just discussed. According to Albert Roe, Blake's Muhammad 'has the bearded countenance of Urizen [...] display[ing] his wound as though demanding vengeance'.[53] But the image of Muhammad, whose dignity seems enhanced by the rudimentarily drawn fellow sufferers surrrounding him, bears an equally close resemblance to other designs such as Blake's representations of a suffering Job, or the old man led by a child in 'London' of *Songs of Experience*, and *Jerusalem*, plate 84.

Dante provides even less description of Ali, noting merely that 'before [Muhammad] | Walks Ali weeping, from the chin his face | Cleft to the forelock'.[54] However, as Roe observes, Blake portrays Ali in the act of making a gesture, not described by Dante. Roe suggests he is 'mak[ing] a gesture of blessing'.[55] But Ali's folded left arm and partially raised right hand may indicate a teaching posture, perhaps reminiscent of a figure in a medieval Christian devotional illuminated manuscript such as a Book of Hours.[56] From his reading of Sale, Blake is likely to have known of both Ali's piety and his revered position, especially in Shia Islam, as fourth caliph, first imam, martyr and a repository of esoteric knowledge.[57]

Blake also adds details not found in Dante's text in his portrayal of the 'punishing fiend'. In Canto 28, Mohammed merely says that,

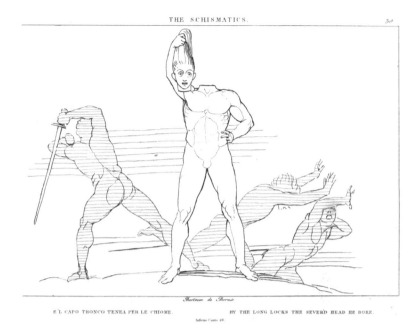

THE SCHISMATICS.

E 'L CAPO TRONCO TENEA PER LE CHIOME.   BY THE LONG LOCKS THE SEVER'D HEAD HE BORE.

Inferno Canto 28 .

Figure 2.3 John Flaxman, Illustration to Dante's *Inferno* Canto 28, in *Compositions [...] from the Divine Poem of Dante Alighieri, Containing Hell, Purgatory and Paradise* (London, 1807), George Smith Collection, University of York Libraries and Archives, Special Collection. Reproduced with kind permission from the Borthwick Institute for Archives, University of York.

'A fiend is here behind, who with his sword | Hacks us thus cruelly'.[58] In his illustration of a later section of *Inferno*, Canto 28, John Flaxman portrayed the same fiend enthusiastically chasing after and attempting to poleaxe victims with his enormous broadsword (Figure 2.3). In contrast, Blake's representation has prompted Milton Klonsky to suggest that this seemingly debonair 'avenging demon [...] stands nonchalantly upon a ledge with his hand on his hip'.[59] Yet Klonsky's reading fails to account for the demon's seemingly angelic appearance, noticed by Bindman.[60] Blake's statuesque 'demon', his sword frozen above his head, appears reluctant or unable to mete out vengeance on Mohammed, Ali, or any of the other inhabitants of the ninth chasm. Blake's comment to Robinson (10 December 1825) may be pertinent here: '*Dante* saw devils where I see none – I see only good [...]'.[61] Such a reading seems confirmed by the fact the demon's eyes are, like Ali's, filled with tears.[62] The angel-demon, and Muhammad and Ali, punisher and punished, are represented by Blake as nobly suffering figures enslaved by Dante's system of cruel vengeance.

This essay has discussed Blake's later engagements with Islam. The apparently informed and positive nature of those responses suggests Blake's exposure to as yet untraced images and texts in Islamic and Orientalist publications. As Keri Davies has observed, Blake may have encountered Arabic manuscripts and Orientalist scholarship in the collections of Alexander Tilloch and Rebekah Bliss.[63] Other collections of Oriental works such as those of William Beckford and William Hayley, Blake's patron while at Felpham, may also have been consulted by the poet-artist.[64] Hayley, a pioneer Danteist, owned early editions of Dante, commentaries and illustrations of which may have informed Blake's illustration of the first section of *Inferno*, Canto 28.[65] G. R. Sabri-Tabrizi and Marsha Keith Schuchard have discussed briefly Blake's probable reading of Emanuel Swedenborg's writings on Islam.[66] In the light of Davies's and Schuchard's recent discoveries concerning Blake's mother Catherine's membership of the Moravian church,[67] Moravian writings on Islam also merit examination.[68] Parallels might be drawn between Muhammad's and Blake's conceptions of themselves as 'prophets', their reported encounters with the angel Gabriel and the form and polysemous content of the prophecies dictated to them.[69] Such research will provide the informed context required for a balanced, if belated, exploration of Blake's explicit and implicit engagements with Islam.

Notes

For help of various kinds during the writing of this essay I am indebted to Craig D. Atwood, Keri Davies, Ziad Elmarsafy, Kurt Johnson, Ruqaiyyah Waris Maqsood, Vito Polito, Alex Watson and David Worrall.

1. Interestingly, Helen Bruder, when discussing so far 'neglected non-Western spiritual traditions' in Blake Studies, does not mention Islam: see her 'Blake and Gender Studies', in *William Blake Studies*, ed. by Nicholas Williams, Palgrave Advances (Basingstoke: Palgrave Macmillan, 2006), p. 151.
2. Percy H. Osmond, *Mystical Poets of the English Church* (London: Society for the Promotion of Christian Knowledge, 1919), p. 281.
3. See *Blake: The Complete Poems*, ed. by W. H. Stevenson, 3rd edn (Harlow: Pearson Educational, 2007), p. 248; Cyril Glassé, *A Concise Encyclopedia of Islam*, 2nd edn (London: Stacey International, 1991), p. 230.
4. See 'Blake, Thomas Boston and the Four-fold Vision', *Blake: An Illustrated Quarterly*, 19 (Spring 1986), 142 (p. 142); Boston, *Human Nature*, 12th edn (1761), p. 386.

5. Saree Makdisi, *William Blake and the Impossible History of the 1790s* (Chicago: University of Chicago Press, 2003), pp. 209, 210.
6. See Makdisi, pp. 204–59.
7. Makdisi, pp. 247–8.
8. [Anon.], *The Morality of the East, Extracted from the Koran of Mohammed* [...] (London: 1766), pp. 33, 22. In this context, one might ask how we are to read Blake's reference to 'the Wild Tartar that never knew Man [who in response to Hand's furious march east from Albion] | Starts from his lofty places & casts down his tents & flees away' (E243).
9. Edward Larrissy, 'Blake's Orient', *Romanticism*, 11 (2005), 1–13 (pp. 9–10). In fact, only about 10 per cent of the Qur'an is concerned with religious and social law; the remaining 90 per cent can be described as liturgy: see Angelica Neuwirth, 'Form and Structure of the Qur'ān', in *Encyclopaedia of the Qur'ān*, ed. by Jane Dammen McAuliffe (2007), available at: <http://www.brillonline.nl/subscriber/entry?entry=q3_COM-00070> (accessed 29 August 2007). Although Larrissy cites no specific Qur'ānic source for his last remark regarding Islam and polygamy, he is probably referring to Surah 4 verse 3 (see *The Koran, Commonly Called the Alcoran of Mohammed*, trans. by George Sale (London: 1734), p. 60.
10. See S. Foster Damon, *A Blake Dictionary: The Ideas and Symbols of William Blake*, rev. edn (Hanover: University Press of New England, 1988), pp. 236a and 259c.
11. See, for example, Humphrey Prideaux, *The True Nature of Imposture Fully Display'd In the Life of Mahomet* (London: 1708).
12. Edward W. Said, *Orientalism* (London: Penguin, 2003), p. 117.
13. Edward Gibbon, *The History of the Decline and Fall of the Roman Empire*, ed. by David Womersley, 3 vols (London: Allen Lane, Penguin Press, 1994), iii, *Volume the Fifth (1788) and Volume the Sixth (1788)*, p. 333.
14. [Anon.], *The Morality of the East, Extracted From the Koran of Mohammed: Digested Under Alphabetical Heads* [...] (London: 1766), p. 32. See also [Anon.], *Reflections on Mohammedanism* (London: 1735).
15. See Genesis 25: 16–18, and Glassé, pp. 72–3, 193.
16. See Captain Thomas Sanders, *The Voyage Made to Tripolis in Barbarie in the Yeere 1583 With a Ship Called the Jesus, Wherein the Adventures and Distresses of Some Englishmen are Truly Reported*, cited in Nabil Matar, *Islam in Britain, 1558–1665* (Cambridge: Cambridge University Press, 1998), p. 34.
17. [Anon.], *A Discoverie of 29 Sects Here in London, All of Which, Except the First, Are Most Devillish and Damnable, Being These Which Follow, Protestants, Puritans, Papists* [...] (London: 1641), p. 3.
18. 'Mohammedan Jubilee', *Gentleman's Magazine*, 75 (May 1805), 479 (my italics). The writer appears to be describing celebrations commemorating Islamic New Year (1 Muharram). Indeed, 1 Muharram 1220 AH fell at the beginning of April 1805. However, the reference to 'the translation of Muhammad into paradise' sounds like a reference to the Isra, Muhammad's miraculous Night Journey from Mecca to Medina, and the Miraj, the prophet's journey to the heavens and encounters with other prophets and Allah. These events are celebrated on 27 Rajab, over six months after Muharram. Perhaps the writer has confused Isra and Miraj with the Hijrah, Muhammad's migration from Mecca to Medina in 622 CE/1 AH. This event

marks the first year of the Islamic calendar and is celebrated especially by Sunni Muslims on 1 Muharram. However, the fact that the worshippers are described as 'Lascars', 'with drawn swords' and 'drums', suggests that this group were East Indian Shia Muslims commemorating the martyrdom of the prophet's grandson Husayn at Kerbala, Iraq in 680 CE. See Glassé, p. 220; see also 'Interment of a Lascar', *Gentleman's Magazine*, 93 (January 1823), 80. See further Diane Robinson-Dunn, 'Lascar Sailors and English Converts: The Imperial Port and Islam in late 19th-Century England', *History Co-Operative's Conference Proceedings* (2003), available at: <http://www.historycooperative.org/proceedings/seascapes/dunn.html> (accessed 29 September 2006).

19. See for example 'John Ryan, Jeremiah Ryan, Mary Ryan, Theft: Specified Place, 27th February, 1765' [t17650227–5], and 'Levy de Sizer, Theft With Violence: Robbery, 5th July, 1832 [t18320705–3], *Old Bailey Proceedings Online*, available at: <www.oldbaileyonline.org> (accessed 7 June 2007).

20. See [George Sale], *The Holy Koran: Commonly Called the Alcoran of Mohammed* (London: 1822). As Edward Royle observes, the society also printed and sold Sale's translation in a series of three-penny installments (Royle, *Victorian Infidels: The Origins of the British Secularist Movement* (Manchester: Manchester University Press, 1974), p. 33).

21. *The Koran*, trans. by Sale (1734), p. 168.

22. See Linda L. Kern, 'Companions of the Prophet', in *Encyclopaedia of the Qur'ān*, ed. by Jane Dammen McAuliffe (2007), available at: <http://www.brillonline.nl/subscriber/entry?entry=q3_COM-00038> (accessed 29 August 2007).

23. *The Gentleman's Magazine*, 98 (January 1828), 342–3 (p. 343).

24. *BR*, p. 425.

25. See *BR*, p. 425n, and S. Foster Damon, *A Blake Dictionary: The Ideas and Symbols of William Blake* (Providence, Rhode Island: Brown University Press, 1965), p. 259.

26. See *BR*, pp. 421, 453.

27. Cited in *BR*, p. 698. The speech marks in this version of Blake's conversation appear to suggest that the 'wise tale' does refer to Parnell's poem.

28. From a window of his first-floor flat in Fountain Court, Blake pointed to a group of children at play outside and observed to a friend, probably Samuel Palmer: 'that is heaven' (Alexander Gilchrist, *Life of William Blake*, ed. by Ruthven Todd (London: Dent, 1945), p. 301).

29. See Richard Angus Whitehead, 'New Discoveries Concerning William and Catherine Blake in Nineteenth Century London: Residences, Fellow Inhabitants, Neighbours, Friends and Milieux, 1803–1878' (unpublished doctoral thesis, University of York, 2006), i, 196–214.

30. 'The Hermit', in *The Poetical Works of Dr. Tho. Parnell* [...], in 2 vols (London: 1786), i, pp. 64 –72 (ll. 150–3, 231–3).

31. Oliver Goldsmith, *The Life of Thomas Parnell, D. D. Archdeacon of Clogher [...]* (London: 1770), p. 47.

32. See Damon, p. 259.

33. *The Koran*, trans. by Sale (1734), pp. 245, 245a.

34. Qur'an 18: 74, *The Koran*, p. 245 (Sale's italics); Qur'an 18: 81, *The Koran*, p. 246 (Sale's italics).

35. See David Rennie, 'Outrage and Defiance Over "Shocking" Cartoons', *Daily Telegraph* (3 February 2006), available at: <http://www.telegraph.co.uk/news/main.jhtml?xml=/news/2006/02/03/wcart103.xml> (accessed 4 June 2007); *Studi Cattolici* (Milan) (March 2006); Malcolm Moore, 'Muslims Outraged by New Cartoon of Prophet in Hell', *Daily Telegraph* (17 March 2006), available at: <http://www.telegraph.co.uk/news/main.jhtml?xml=/news/2006/04/17/wcart17.xml> (accessed 4 June 2007).

36. Blake's images of Muhammad have been cited in defence of the Danish cartoons. See, for example, Ayesha Akram, 'WHAT'S BEHIND MUSLIM CARTOON OUTRAGE: Muhammad's image: Revered prophet of Islam has been depicted in art for hundreds of years', *San Francisco Chronicle* (11 February 2006), available at: <http://www.sfgate.com/cgi-bin/article.cgi?file=/c/a/2006/02/11/MNGRCH6UQK1.DTL> (accessed 4 June 2007).

37. Martin Butlin, *The Paintings and Drawings of William Blake* (New Haven: Yale University Press, 1981), p. 720. William Michael Rossetti recorded that the head was 'Something like Mrs Blake, according to Mr Linnell; there is a kind of hint too of the semi-nude Dr Johnson in St Paul's. The mouth has a grim smilingness in it; the forehead is very retreating, but powerful. Fine' (quoted in Alexander Gilchrist, *Life of William Blake*, rev. edn, 2 vols (London: Macmillan, 1880), ii, p. 244).

38. David Fuller, 'Blake and Dante', *Art History*, 11.3 (1988), 349–73 (p. 358).

39. Morton D. Paley, *The Traveller in the Evening: The Last Works of William Blake* (Oxford: Oxford University Press, 2003), p. 303.

40. Martin Lings, *Muhammad: His Life Based on the Earliest Sources*, rev. edn (Cambridge: Islamic Texts Society, 1991), p. 35.

41. See Glassé, p. 280.

42. See *The Koran*, trans. by Sale (1734), p. 99.

43. See Anne K. Mellor, 'Physiognomy, Phrenology and Blake's Visionary Heads', in *Blake in His Time*, ed. by Robert N. Essick and Donald Pearce (Bloomington: Indiana University Press, 1978), pp. 53–74 (p. 57).

44. See *BR*, p. 387.

45. Earlier scholars such as Bentley interpreted De Ville's address, written on the back of one the casts of Blake's head, as '17 Strand'. Using contemporary trade directories I traced De Ville's residence and Phrenological Museum to '367 Strand': see Angus Whitehead, ' "My present precincts"; A Recreation and Exploration of the Last Living and Working Space of William Blake: 3 Fountain Court, Strand, 1821–7' (unpublished MA dissertation, University of York, 2002), pp. 17–21.

46. [James De Ville], *Outlines of Phrenology: An Accompaniment to the Phrenological Bust* (London: 1821), pp. 27, 58.

47. [James De Ville], *Manual of Phrenology, As an Accompaniment to the Phrenological Bust* (London: 1828), pp. 59–60, 48, 51.

48. Morton D. Paley omits this image from his discussion of Blake's illustrations to the Divine Comedy (see *Traveller*, pp. 101–77). Hugh Haughton's account does not name who is being punished, merely referring to 'another of the damned': see 'Purgatory Regained?: Beckett and Dante', in *Dante's Modern Afterlife: Reception and Response from Blake to Heaney*, ed. by Nick Havely (New York: St Martin's Press, 1998), pp. 140–64 (p. 153). In composing the *Divine Comedy*, Dante was clearly influenced by Muslim accounts of

Muhammad's night journey through the levels of paradise and Hell: see Miguel Asin Palacios, *Islam and the Divine Comedy*, trans. by Harold Sutherland (London: Frank Cass, 1968).

49. Fuller, p. 358. Albert Roe notes that Dante's face as he witnesses Muhammad and Ali's punishments 'reveals rather more feeling than usual' (Albert S. Roe, *Blake's Illustrations to the Divine Comedy* (Princeton: Princeton University Press, 1953), p. 113).

50. See *BR*, p. 426.

51. *The Vision of Dante Alighieri; Or, Hell, Purgatory and Paradise*, trans. by H. F. Cary (London: Dent [1908]), p. 118.

52. Gilchrist (1880), ii, p. 220.

53. Roe, p. 113. However, as Morton Paley suggests, 'the hermeneutics of the Dante series is a contested subject' (*Traveller*, p. 116).

54. *The Vision of Dante Alagheri*, p. 118.

55. Roe, p. 113.

56. Blake had certainly seen such manuscripts: see Anthony Blunt, *The Art of William Blake* (London: Oxford University Press, 1959), p. 48.

57. See Sale (1734), pp. 149n., 473n.

58. *The Vision of Dante Alagheri*, p. 118.

59. Milton Klonsky, *Blake's Dante: The Complete Illustrations to the Divine Comedy* (New York: Harmony Books, 1980), p. 150. According to Roe, p. 113, the demon is 'a young, handsome figure with fair hair. While his wings are of the type which Blake associates with devils, they are elongated and raised majestically over his head. These features combine to suggest the dual nature of the "angel" who in the name of law, order, and justice, metes out all sorts of cruelty without pity.'

60. William Blake, *The Divine Comedy*, ed. by David Bindman (France: Biblioteque de l'Image; Maidstone: Amalagamated Book Services, 2000), p. 168.

61. *BR*, p. 424.

62. At least, this is how it appears to me, examining the image under magnification using *The William Blake Archive*: see <http://www.blakearchive.org/exist/blake/archive/object.xq?objectid=but812.1.wc.59&java=yes> (accessed 13 September 2007).

63. See Alan Philip Keri Davies, 'William Blake in Contexts: Family, Friendships, and Some Intellectual Microcultures of Eighteenth- and Nineteenth-Century England' (unpublished doctoral thesis, St Mary's College, University of Surrey, 2003), pp. 92–186.

64. For Blake's possible association with William Beckford, see *BR*, pp. 571, 730.

65. By 1821 Hayley's library included sixteenth- and seventeenth-century Italian editions of Dante, Henry Boyd's *A Translation of the Inferno of Dante Alighieri in English Verse, with Historical Notes, and the Life of Dante* (1785), and other English and French translations of the Italian poet: see *Sale Catalogues of Eminent Persons*, vol. ii, *Poets and Men of Letters: Lady Blessington, Thomas Day, Thomas Gray, William Hayley, Samuel Rogers*, ed. by Alan Noel Latimer Munby (London: Mansell with Sotheby Parke Bennett Publications, 1971), pp. 107, 109. Hayley's library also contained a 1734 edition of Sale's Koran, and John Haddon Hindley's *Persian Lyrics; Or, Scattered Poems, From the Diwan-i-Hafiz* (London: 1800): see Munby, pp. 163, 187.

66. See Gholam Reza Sabri-Tabrizi, *The 'Heaven' and 'Hell' of William Blake* (London: Lawrence and Wishart, 1973), p. 168; Marsha Keith Schuchard, *Why Mrs Blake Cried: William Blake and the Sexual Basis of Spiritual Vision* (London: Century, 2006), pp. 148–9.

67. See Keri Davies and Marsha Keith Schuchard, 'Recovering the Lost Moravian History of William Blake's Family', *Blake: An Illustrated Quarterly*, 38 (2004), 36–43; Keri Davies, 'The Lost Moravian History of William Blake's Family: Snapshots From the Archive', *Literature Compass*, 3 (2006), 1297–319; Keri Davies, 'Jonathan Spilsbury and the lost Moravian history of William Blake's family', *Blake: An Illustrated Quarterly*, 40 (2007), 100–9.

68. For Moravian encounters with Muslims in the Middle East, as well as Moravian writings on Islam during the eighteenth century, see Joseph Edmund Hutton, *A History of Moravian Missions* (London: Moravian Publication Office [1923]), pp. 160–4. During the 1750s Dr Frederick Wilhelm Hocker, a Moravian physician, tried three times to travel to Ethiopia via Egypt. On the final trip, John Antes accompanied Hocker and later published an account of his travels: see his *Observations on the Manners and Customs of the Egyptians* (London: John Stockdale, 1800). It is possible that Blake would have known about Hocker's Egyptian adventure through David Cranz's *Ancient and Modern History of the Brethren* (London: W. and A. Strahan, 1780) – see especially sections 193–4, 232–3 – published as part of a PR campaign for the Moravians. As a member of the Moravian church in the 1750s Blake's mother Catherine Blake would have heard reports of Hocker's efforts.

   During the mid-1750s as part of the major revision of their litanies the Moravians added a prayer for the 'children of Isaac and Ishmael', possibly the first regular prayer in Christian worship regarding Muslims. In this prayer, Muslims are depicted as people of the covenant. The prayer as featured in the 1759 *Collection of Hymns, Chiefly Extracted From The Larger Hymn-Book of the Brethren's Congregations* (London: [no publisher], 1759), p. 48, reads: 'Deliver the ten Tribes of Israel from their Blindness [...] O that Ishmael also might live before Thee! (*Gen. xvii*). Hear us, O dear Lord and God!' The inclusion of a prayer for the Muslims was almost certainly in response to the Moravians' repeated failures to establish a missionary beachhead in the Near East.

69. See Glassé, p. 136, Lings, pp. 43–5; *BR*, pp. 234–5, 599.

3

Blake, the Female Prophet and the American Agent: The Evidence of the 1789 Swedenborg Conference Attendance List

David Worrall

This essay announces for the first time the identities of the people William and Catherine Blake met at the Great East Cheap Swedenborg conference on Monday, 13 April 1789. The argument is founded on the supposition that the Blakes' experiences approximated to a series of encounters familiar to modern delegates attending professional or academic conferences. In other words, while they wouldn't have talked to everybody, they would have conversed at length with a few people, chatted with several more and listened to and watched many others. The Blakes met an extraordinary set of individuals, including a female prophet, an eminent mystical composer, an entrepreneur with a scheme to appropriate native American lands and a number of people deeply implicated in a project to establish a Swedenborgian colony in Sierra Leone. While the Blakes' encounters at the conference are likely to have been coincident rather than necessarily signifying earlier networks of sociability, a number of the other delegates had contacts with each other which clearly preceded the event and continued for some time afterwards. To what extent the Blakes were a part of these connections it is impossible to judge. This essay can do little more than suggest the context and some of the implications of the extraordinary range of personalities gathered together that spring morning in 1789. Nevertheless, it is difficult to imagine the Blakes encountering this particular group without experiencing a number of profound challenges to their own political, religious and social beliefs. The origins and experiences of their fellow delegates were not only geographically and economically diverse but also likely to have been fractured by markedly divergent personal temperaments. This notwithstanding, the conference itself (convened to decide on the establishment of a Swedenborgian church) was held in a convivial atmosphere, the event's historian recording that 'the members dined together at a neighbouring tavern in Abchurch Lane, to the number of sixty or seventy, male and female; at which repasts the most cordial unanimity and brotherly affection were observable'.[1]

The key document located in the Swedenborg archives is a nineteenth-century copy of a lost original never transcribed before.[2] In it the Blakes are simply recorded as 'W. Blake' and 'C. Blake'. While the second edition of *Blake Records* (2004) notes the presence of the Blakes, no account of the names and identities of the other delegates has ever been given.[3] The following is a transcription of the entry:

Fol. 69
General Conference
Monday April 13, 1789 – 10 Oclock in ye Morn.g
          – The Conditions of Admission, were to
          subscribe the following Paper – viz

We whose Names are hereunto subscribed, do each of us approve of the Theological Writings of Emanuel Swedenborg, believing that the Doctrines contained therein are genuine Truth, revealed from Heaven, and that the New Jerusalem Church ought to be established, distinct and separate from the Old Church. – Persons who subscribed, besides ye 77 who signed ye circular Letter

Augustus Nordenskjold. Charles Harford
John Child. Frederick von Walden Daniel Banham
Benj. Carpenter
C. Barrell Josh Richards H. S.
Barthelemon Thom. Carter Jno. Aspinshaw R. Beatson
W. Blake. C. Blake Dor. Gott John Haywood
                    – Thomas Scott – Harman[4]

The note that those listed were 'besides ye 77 who signed ye circular Letter' refers to a document entitled 'Reasons for Separating from the

Old Church' printed some weeks earlier under Robert Hindmarsh's direction and distributed to sympathizers in London and Manchester.[5] The people who attended were not casual passers-by. The presence of 'Conditions of Admission' makes it clear that endorsement of Swedenborgian doctrine was required.

Of those present, I have been unable to identify several delegates, including Frederick von Walden, Daniel Banham, John Haywood and the person listed simply as 'Harman'. A number of others remain obscure. Robert Beatson, for example, is identified elsewhere as being from Rotherham, Yorkshire, and acted as Secretary. Others, like the Blakes themselves, fall into pairs suggestive of kinship bonds such as husbands and wives, fathers and children, or brothers and sisters. For example, John Child was presumably a relative of William Child, one of the 778 signatories of the original circular announcing the conference (noted in a photocopied list at the Swedenborg Society filed in the context of the minute book). Other identifiable kinship groups include John Frederic and Elizabeth Okerblom, John and Mary Sudbury, John and Margaret Morley, Samuel and Elizabeth Bembridge, Benedict and Charles Harford and John and Elizabeth Citizen.

Out of these individuals, perhaps one person more than any other suggests the importance of the conference's potential impact on Blake's poetic development in the 1790s. Entered directly after the Blakes is the name of a female prophet, Dorothy Gott, who had just published her extraordinary *The Midnight Cry, 'Behold, the Bridegroom Comes!'; or, an Order from God to Get Your Lamps Lighted [...] This is My Experience* (1788). The meeting of Blake and the Quaker visionary ex-servant Gott must have been formative, occurring immediately before he embarked on producing his major illuminated poems in relief etching generally termed 'Prophecies'. In other words, the poems in which Blake ironizes several contemporary prophetic rhetorics was preceded by his meeting a woman who already commanded the prophetic mode ('I saw myself as laying at the Beautiful-gate [...] it seemed as if a great light (to the view of my mind) came out at the gate, and raised me up on my feet').[6] As Jon Mee has shown, Blake carefully modulated and differentiated his discourse from that of his contemporaries.[7] It is now possible to posit the moment when that process first began. Notably, Blake's encounter with Gott predates the French Revolution and suggests the extent of his absorption in a set of issues specific to the fortunes of the Swedenborgian movement in the late 1780s.

Gott's narrative in *The Midnight Cry* of her Bedlam visits and religio-sexual displacements may have alerted Blake to the eccentricities of the prophetic mode she exemplified but her presence there may have been stimulated by her fascination with the feckless Scottish ex-soldier, John Murray, and his development of a 'camera' or 'solar microscope'.[8] Murray's solar microscope (also known as a lucernal) was an image projection device which Gott had deployed as a metaphor to describe how God's glory could be magnified 'even as the solar microscope enlarges the smallest mite … as large as St Paul's'.[9] While a similar instrument had been notoriously used in the mid-1780s by Dr Gustavus Katterfelto to theatricalize 'a great Variety of New Occult Secrets' in popular displays held in Piccadilly, it was also in use prior to 1791 by the experimentalist scientist Joseph Priestley at his Birmingham 'Elaboratory'.[10] However, the solar microscope also formed part of an effort by Swedenborgians to use new technologies to inform their understanding about the mechanics of vision and their relationship to the visionary.

George Adams's *An Essay on Vision, Briefly Explaining the Fabric of the Eye* (1789) had announced that he was using 'New Church principles' to explain 'the secret mechanism by which the eye communicates so many diversified and animated perceptions to the soul'.[11] Adams, who is also discussed by Sibylle Erle in her essay in this volume, was a central Swedenborgian figure at this time, collaborating with Hindmarsh and William Spence in coordinating the printing of Swedenborg's works.[12] As the son of a noted scientific instrument maker, Adams had written a number of illustrated scientific textbooks. His *Essay on Vision* perfectly exemplifies how an understanding of Newtonian optical principles and a knowledge of the physiology of the eye was frustrated by the contemporary inability to fathom 'the secret mechanism' which appeared to convert retinal images into perception. For Adams, the implication of Swedenborgian belief was that the doctrine of influxes provided this divine mechanism of conversion. An early eighteenth-century invention, the solar microscope projector provided an instrument which not only embodied a metaphor for religious illumination by using light to make images communally visible, it could also be deployed to display the scientific discoveries partially enabled by its use such as those conducted by the Royal Society concerning the circulation of blood.[13] The solar microscope had renewed topicality in the late 1780s because of its coupling to Ami Argand's vastly improved oil lamp, a device whose immediate impact on the representation of the theatricalized sublime can be glimpsed in Fuseli's iconic *The Three Witches* (oil on canvas, 1783, Kunsthaus, Zürich).[14] As Adams's publisher and future Swedenborgian historian, Richard Hindmarsh can be identified as a pivotal figure mediating contacts between these disparate sets of people.

Whatever the Blakes thought about Gott, they would certainly have become aware of the international nature of the conference. Curiously, August Nordenskjöld's Swedish countryman, Carl Bernhard Wadström, is not listed, but as the conference's principal organizer he may not have bothered to sign himself in. Wadström was a major motivating figure behind the contemporary Swedenborgian Sierra Leone colony project, a plan which had much of its genesis at the conference, coinciding with Wadström's *A Plan For A Free Community Upon The Coast Of Africa* (1789).[15] As much as shared spiritualities within friendship circles, the colony project may also suggest a rationale for attendance in bringing together prospective colonists. Indeed, the importance of the abortive colony can be judged by Nordenskjöld's subsequent fate. Barely three years after the conference, Nordenskjöld died in Africa. Not least, Wadström along with his companion, the ex-Cook voyager Captain Anders Sparrman, had given evidence to the 1789 Board of Trade inquiry into the slave trade (to which Olaudah Equiano had been summoned).[16] With Wadström having visited Guinea in 1787–8, this means that by the time Blake was commissioned in 1793 to produce engravings for John Gabriel Stedman's *Narrative of a Five Years' Expedition* (1796) he had met someone who had directly witnessed the effects of slavery in an African context.[17] After the Swedenborgian colony project was abandoned, Nordenskjöld sailed from Bristol to Sierra Leone in January 1792. Following Schuchard, Deirdre Coleman suggests that this expedition combined his expertise in mineralogy with his new interest in alchemy, implying that his journey was motivated by a quest for African gold.[18] However, this probably underestimates the depth of Nordenskjöld's involvement with the spiritual meanings of Africa then circulating within contemporary London Swedenborgianism. In the account related by Wadström, 'much weakened by a dangerous illness', Nordenskjöld had set off to 'attempt an incursion into the interior [of Africa], before the rains were over'. Having penetrated eighty miles 'attended by one or two free blacks', 'he was taken ill', became 'delirious', returned to the coast and 'died in a few days'.[19] Although Coleman places the Swedenborgian colony into the general context of European ambitions to commandeer and subdue Africa, her argument does not take sufficient account of the group's complex spiritualities. Wadström recounted that, despite his illness, 'and before his recovery was perfected [...] [Nordenskjöld] signified an ardent desire to penetrate immediately into the country, where he always hoped to find an innocent, hospitable people, among whom he could pursue his researches'.[20] In other words, ignoring the best advice of friends, illness and bad weather, Nordenskjöld headed off on a virtually suicidal journey.

He was probably motivated by contemporary speculation about Africa being the location of the Bible's lost prophetic books. The specific biblical lost book, until then known only in fragmentary form, was the book of Enoch, a work described in James Bruce's *Travels to Discover the Source of the Nile* (1790). Coleman does not mention Bruce's *Travels* or its impact on the London Swedenborgians, but Susan Matthews has detailed the implications of Bruce's Enoch discovery for Blake's knowledge about Africa.[21] These Swedenborgian networks of sociability should not be underestimated nor the shared beliefs in potentially recoverable books of the Bible. For Blake the moment was a significant one, occurring at the beginning of his cycle of illuminated books on continental themes in prophetic formats. Within the next five years he produced *America: A Prophecy* (1793), *Europe: A Prophecy* (1794) and *The Song of Los* (1795), with its subsections on 'Africa' and 'Asia'. Furthermore, *The [First] Book of Urizen* (1794) and *The Book of Los* (1795) must also be counted as contributions towards a wider contemporary debate, initiated by Paine's *The Age of Reason* (1794), about the authenticity of biblical texts. As Matthews points out, the idealization of a pristine African reception of God was standard Swedenborgian doctrine, and Nordenskjöld clearly anticipated being assisted in his travels by the 'innocent, hospitable people' of the interior.[22]

However, something of the context of early 1790s London Swedenborgian circles may be judged by the account given in William Spence's *Essays in Divinity and Physic [...] and the Spiritual Sense of Scripture: In Refutation of Dr J. Priestley, and the Socinian System* (1792). Spence's *Essays* were part of an attempt to regroup Swedenborgian fortunes after the Sierra Leone debacle and the high-profile attacks mounted in Joseph Priestley's *Letters to the Members of the New Jerusalem Church, Formed by Baron Swedenborg* (1791), notwithstanding Priestley's own persecution at the hands of loyalist rioters in July 1791.[23] Amidst the intricate mentalities of contemporary nonconformity existed a network drawn from the quasi-scientific professions. As well as the Fleet Street scientific instrument maker George Adams, Nordenskjöld was a mineralogist and alchemist, Robert Beatson was a 'Chemist', Spence and Henry Peckitt (a conference co-organizer) were surgeons and another prominent Swedenborgian, Peter Provo, was an apothecary.[24]

Spence specifically directed his comments at Priestley's scepticism about the reception of God in Africa: 'What you quote out of Swedenborg concerning Africa and the gentile [...] is proving every few years to be more and more fulfilled. Abyssinia is not the centrical part of Africa spoken of; yet even there, Mr Bruce has proved that they have ideas of the Lord's human divine.' Spence particularly wanted to emphasize how 'Mr Bruce has been the means, under God, of bringing to Europe [...] the long lost book of Enoch or Chanoch according to the Hebrew. According to all the quotations I have seen of it, it truly answers Mr Swedenborg's description.'[25] For Spence, Bruce's location of Enoch in Abyssinia, precisely because this was not Swedenborg's 'centrical part of Africa', reawakened the possibility of finding other lost books of the Bible. Spence wrote of 'three other books of the ancient Word' in 'Great Tartary [...] described by Swedenborg to be preserved there, one the book of *Jasher*, another the *Wars of Jehovah*, and the third called *Enuntiata* or *Prophetic*, all partly quoted by Moses'.[26] Such residual notions of Swedenborg's claims about the inherent divinity of Africa and Asia clearly lie behind Blake's *Song of Los*. In other words, Nordenskjöld's ill-fated journey into Africa's interior was perfectly cognate with contemporary Swedenborgian beliefs about retrieving the Bible's lost prophetic books.

Given this range of spiritualities, not only was Blake's meeting with Nordenskjöld a remarkable conjunction, but also the unusual trajectory of Nordenskjöld's life can be compared and contrasted with the larger range of religious perspectives present among the delegates. Although evidence for the identities of two delegates, Benjamin Carpenter and Thomas Scott, remains circumstantial rather than forensic, the suggestions made here about their backgrounds are cognate with several others present. Carpenter was possibly a Dissenting minister from Stourbridge who, if correctly identified, came from a liberal tradition, openly addressing to 'persons of different persuasions' his *Difference of Sentiment No Objection to the Exercise of Mutual Love: A Sermon* (1780).[27] Like Blake, Carpenter had an interest in how the Christian ministry encountered children, publishing *An Abridgment of Dr Watts's Psalms and Hymns* (Birmingham: *c.* 1790), and, moreover, becoming engaged with another backwash of Priestley's maltreatment in the English Midlands in his pamphlet, *A Letter to the Rev. R. Foley* (Stourbridge: *c*.1792). Carpenter's *Letter* not only referred to Priestley's allegation about Stourbridge's 'High Church Spirit', but was also concerned with how children at a local Dissenters' school at Lye-Waste were obliged to make monthly visits to the local parish church to receive religious instruction.[28] The intensity and intricacies of such disputes created unexpected eruptions of meaning. One of the charges against the Stourbridge Dissenting school was that it had supplied 'cloathing' for its children.[29] A possible meaning implicit in Blake's 'Holy Thursday' of *Songs of Innocence* (1789), where children process into St Paul's cathedral wearing 'red & blue & green', may refer not only to the annual charity thanksgiving service held since 1782 but also to these contemporary undercurrents where school uniforms held significant cultural meaning (E13).[30]

Although the identification is once again circumstantial, another person possibly present was Thomas Scott (1747–1821), a significant and complex figure. Scott, who had early acquired a reputation as an 'Enthusiast, or a Methodist', had been curate in a Buckinghamshire village near Olney in the 1770s where he came under the influence of the charismatic ex-slaver and Church of England minister, John Newton (1725–1807).[31] Scott's *The Force of Truth: An Authentic Narrative* (1779, rev. ed. 1789) is a remarkable confessional, recording his thoughts about Methodists, including that 'when I preached against them, I was as one fighting with my own shadow', and tracing his struggle with various kinds of unorthodox religious influence.[32] Not least, his proximity to Olney suggests a very early transmission route for Blake's knowledge of William Cowper who had assisted Scott in preparing *The Force of Truth* for publication.[33] By 1785 Scott had moved to London to become morning preacher and visiting chaplain at the Lock Hospital, founded in 1746, a charity specializing in the treatment of venereal disease and the recuperation of female prostitutes. Scott's work at the Lock Hospital, described in his *Thoughts on the Fatal Consequences of Female Prostitution* (1787), brought him into contact with the 'poor Creatures [...] not above Thirteen, or Fourteen Years of Age', who are 'in a Community, an Evil, not dissimilar to a Person infected with the Plague'.[34] Again, it is tempting to trace back to Scott a possible source for Blake's remarks in 'London' about 'How the youthful Harlots curse [...] blights with plagues the Marriage hearse' (E27). Certainly Scott's position at the Lock Hospital continued to give him a platform from which to express his carefully modulated positions about his past unorthodoxy, abhorrence of prostitution, and the slave trade alongside concerns about 'the general prevalence of scepticism and infidelity' and 'loose antinomian tenets'.[35]

If Scott and Carpenter remain only circumstantially identifiable, there can be little doubt about several others. 'C. Barrell' can be positively identified as Colborn Barrell. Two months later, on 24 June 1789, he signified his native country as 'America' and endorsed himself, along with Wadström and Nordenskjold, as a signatory to *A Plan For A Free Community*.[36] Five years later, Barrell subscribed to Wadström's *Essay on Colonization Particularly Applied to the Western Coast of Africa* (1794), where he gave his occupation as 'American Agent', at the same Threadneedle Street address which also appeared in the anonymous *The American Kalendar; or, United States Register* (1796).[37] The nature of his work can be deduced from *The American Kalendar* where his name appears in a commercial partnership with the Swedenborgian Henry Servanté, a signatory of *Minutes of a General Conference of the Members of the New Church [...] Great East Cheap* (1789), and senior clerk in the Excise Office, Broad Street.[38] According to *The American Kalendar*, by the mid-1790s Barrell and Servanté had both become 'Agents for the Purchase and Sale of American Funds, Lands, etc'.

Colborn Barrell's presence is significant. Not only does this make Barrell the first American who can be positively identified as having met Blake before he printed *America: A Prophecy* (1793), but Barrell and Servanté's partnership also gives credence to Deirdre Coleman's general argument in *Romantic Colonization and British Anti-Slavery* (2005), that Swedenborgian utopian agendas were marked by capitalism and colonialism. Whatever their commercial objectives, Barrell and Servanté would have known that *The American Kalendar* had reminded its readers that the 'Western Territory' beyond the ex-British colonial states 'is yet claimed and occupied by the original natives'. There can be little doubt that Barrell and Servanté were involved in facilitating colonization projects aimed at displacing native Americans – particularly, as *The American Kalendar* put it, from those areas, south and 'north-west of the river Ohio'.[39] By 1796 Barrell and Servanté had become agents for five land funds, including the 'Ohio-Company' ('*Fifty Townships* [...] *Six Miles square*'), the 'Ohiopiomingo' company ('120,000 Acres') and the Ohio Company, all projects with greater potential following 'Confirmation of Peace with the Indians'.[40] Their 'North-American Land-Company' was instituted in Philadelphia in 1795, although it clearly received enough criticism in London for them to write a lengthy pamphlet of vindication published by Joseph Johnson.[41] An indicator of the advanced state of development of the Kentucky-based 'Ohiopiomingo' project is testified by extant contracts signed by Servanté and a kinsman of Barrell now deposited in an American slavery archive.[42] By contrast, Gilbert Imlay's *A Topographical Description of the Western Territory of North America* (1793) similarly made extensive reference to Ohio but commented on the problem of slavery and the displacement of native Americans.[43] Both Barrell and Servanté cite Imlay's *Topographical Description* as an authoritative source of information.[44] In other words, by the time Blake came to write *America* and *Visions of the Daughters of Albion* (1793) he would not only have met the American, Colborn Barrell, he would also have known about his land acquisition aspirations and how these involved the Swedenborgian Servanté. It may be these circumstances that inform not only *America* and *Visions*, but which are ironized in Blake's Notebook lines, 'Tho born on the cheating banks of Thames | [...] The Ohio shall wash his stains from me | I was born a slave but I go to be free' (E473). Although it would be a mistake to underestimate the role of Nordenskjold's piety in travelling into the African interior in 1792, there clearly developed a different set of interests for Barrell and Servanté with reference to America. Certainly, the American focus of *Visions of the Daughters of Albion* now looks to be meaningfully contextualized in an array of influences encompassing Imlay, Barrell and Servanté, and specifically related not only to slavery but also to the land ownership hinted at in *Visions* ('Thy soft American plains are mine'), all presented alongside residual notions of Swedenborgian sexuality continued from *The Book of Thel* (E46).

If Barrell and Servanté were situated on the entrepreneurial fringes of London society, then another person present had a much wider public profile. The delegate listed as 'H. S. | Barthelemon' probably marks a simple transcription error for the 'native of France' and *Essay on Colonization* subscriber, François Hippolyte Barthélemon (1741–1808). Barthélemon was a well-connected violinist, conductor and Freemason; his wife was a composer; and both of them were associated with the King's Theatre opera house and Marylebone and Vauxhall pleasure gardens. They both wrote Swedenborgian hymns including at least one on an African subject.[45] The further presence of 'Benjamin Banks, of Salisbury', as a signatory of the East Cheap minutes of 17 April 1789, provides another link to eighteenth-century music in identifying a significant violin maker, many of whose instruments still survive.[46] Less than a year later, Barthélemon became violin master to George Augustus Polgreen Bridgetower (1780–1860), the Polish born half-African violinist who gave the first performance of Beethoven's 'Kreutzer' sonata.[47] Again, the implications of Blake's meeting with Barthélemon appear to have been significant. Barthélemon's *Oithóna: A Dramatic Poem* (1768), with its ravished heroine ('Loose and dishevell'd was her dark-brown

Hair [...] | Blood stain'd her snowy Arm [...] | Perdition on the Ravisher')
confined to a cave markedly recalls the frontispiece to *Visions of the
Daughters of Albion* ('There, all in Tears, I sit within the Cave, | Nor do I
sit alone, Oh! gallant GAUL, | The gloomy Chief of CUTHAL sits
beside [...] | [...] oh, what! Can poor OITHÓNA do?'). Similarly, Blake's
inclusion of a recurrent chorus in *Visions* ('The Daughters of Albion
hear her woes. & echo back her sighs' [E46, 48, 51]) appears borrowed
from the unusual strophic and antistrophic structure of respondent
choruses used in *Oithóna*, and quite alien to James Macpherson's prose
Fingal, An Ancient Epic Poem (1762).[48]

If Barthélemon's influence on Blake clearly impacted on his poetics,
another common thread to these 1789 East Cheap connections are their
intricate links to abolition, Africa, colonization projects and the presence of black people. Something of the complexity of how this
Swedenborgian group reacted to slavery is exemplified by the Jamaican
merchant and East Cheap conference organizer, Robert Jackson, who
was ordained as a Swedenborgian minister in September 1790 and
returned to the island as a missionary.[49] Prior to this, *The New Jamaica
Almanac* for 1787 reveals that Jackson held office in Jamaica as an assistant judge, implying his jurisdiction over the slave plantations as well as
his European ethnicity. Also listed in the *Almanac* was Colonel Edward
Marcus Despard who had been sent to Jamaica in 1780 to fight the
Spanish before becoming Superintendant of the Bay of Honduras in
1787.[50] Whatever his personal or spiritual motives, like Wadström and
Nordenskjold, Jackson provides another example for how Blake could
have encountered before his meeting with Stedman direct testimonies
as to the conditions of Atlantic slaving.

There is also a possible link through this group to Olaudah Equiano,
author of *The Interesting Narrative of the Life of Olaudah Equiano, Or
Gustavus Vassa, The African* (1789), published just three weeks earlier
in late March 1789. The connection between Equiano and the conference delegates – including the Blakes – comes through two routes. The
first is 'Jno. Aspinshaw', a Holborn 'smith' of 60 Leather Lane, who
had been recommended by Hindmarsh for entry to the Society two
weeks earlier and who is signed in alongside the Blakes (Folio 68–9).
Although the minute book records Aspinshaw simply as a 'smith', a
case heard at the Old Bailey in 1797 discovers him as a gold or silver-
smith working at the Mint and confirms not only his address but also
that there were at least two other male members of the family.[51]
Despite a spelling discrepancy, this is almost certainly a relative of the
'Joseph Ashpinshaw' who is listed as a subscriber to the first edition of

the ex-slave Equiano's *Interesting Narrative*. Crucially, Wadström was also a subscriber to Equiano's book.[52] In turn, in 1794 Equiano (under the name of 'Gustavus Vasa, a native of Africa') subscribed to Wadström's *Essay on Colonization*. Since the publication process of Equiano's *Interesting Narrative* required the payment of money in advance, Wadström, Aspinshaw and Equiano must all have been mutually acquainted before the conference because Equiano needed to receive their subscriptions.[53]

Colborn Barrell the American agent, Robert Jackson the Jamaican judge, John Aspinshaw the Holborn smith and Equiano subscriber, Barthélemon the French masonic Swedenborgian violinist and hymn writer, Wadström the Swedish conference co-organizer: those present indicate the diversity of the spiritual community the Blakes encountered, all of them with distinctive backgrounds and agendas but all associated with intricate notions about Africa. Not least, this diversity suggests these individuals were not disingenuous agents of collective imperialist zeal since their own national identities were so clearly fragmented. A crucial case is that of Peter Panah, a youth kidnapped into slavery from West Africa, redeemed by Wadström's intervention and put to school in Croydon in the late 1780s. Whether this is the specific black boy alluded to in 'The Little Black Boy' of *Songs of Innocence* (1789) it is impossible to say. Although there is no evidence to suggest he attended the conference, the Swedenborgian background of 'The Little Black Boy' was noted by Professor S. E. Ogude writing in the Ghanaian journal, *Asemka*, in 1976 and there can be little doubt of the song's Swedenborgian context.[54] Nevertheless, the circumstances of Panah's redemption are worth exploring further since they personalize the sets of interventions required to rescue kidnapped blacks in late eighteenth-century Britain and illustrate the complex nature of contemporary piety.

The account Wadström gave in a document filed among Colonial Office papers (not noted by Coleman) refers to a 'Mulatto-merchant, a Mr Johnson, at Grenada', who supposed Panah to be a king's son capable of commanding a high price if returned to Africa. While it is not certain who transported him back to England, the role in Panah's capture of the owner of 'an English slave-vessel, (Capt. Fraser)' gives a clue as to the probable master of the ship in which he returned.[55] The diary of the contemporary Bristol Quaker, Sarah Fox, noted many of the comings and goings of the local abolition movement, including her acquaintance with Thomas Clarkson. Not least, Fox recorded that on 3 January 1789 her family had been visited by 'a gentleman of the name of Wadstrom, a Swede'. That evening, 'Two of the company so much opposed Clarkson on the subject of the Abolition, that the conversation became irksome to most of the company.'[56] With them was Harry Gandy, a Quaker ex-slaving captain with Swedenborgian sympathies whose correspondence on Sierra Leone Wadström published in *The New Jerusalem Magazine*.[57] The likely route for Wadström to have learned about Panah was through Gandy, particularly as Fox had described how in the 1770s they had adopted 'a little tawny or black boy of which they seemed very fond'.[58] Wadström's reference to a 'Capt. Fraser' of 'an English slave-vessel' as having been involved in Panah's capture increases the likelihood that the ship bearing him to Britain can now be identified as the *Emelia*. This was the second slaving vessel of that name mastered by Fraser (on the first ship, Alexander Falconbridge had been surgeon). Fraser's *Emelia* of 278 tons, armed with three guns, travelled the triangular route from Bristol in May 1787, took on 450 slaves in the Bight of Biafra, sold them in St Thomas, went on to St Kitts and arrived back in Bristol in March or April 1788, the month Wadström negotiated Panah's release.[59] Gandy's role in the rescue of Panah must have been substantial and it is not difficult to imagine how brutalized must have been his and Wadström's shipboard negotiations with Fraser to secure Panah's release and for Fraser to avoid the Mansfield ruling. However, not only had Gandy helped escaped slaves before, he was also crucial in promoting a spiritualized perception of Africa.[60] One evening in Bristol in November 1788, in the company of Sarah Fox and Clarkson, they 'set Harry Gandy talking about the interior of Africa, a beautiful description of which he gave us'.[61] Drawing on what one might surmise about Blake's residual knowledge of his mother's religious beliefs, he would probably have been aware of the several Moravian missions to the Caribbean (about which Harry Gandy had experience), as well as their work with the native North Americans imminently threatened by Barrell and Servanté.[62] Although Panah was in his late teens by the time Blake wrote 'The Little Black Boy', his connection with the East Cheap Swedenborgians helps materialize this African slave as part of a range of pieties and spiritualities associated with the group the Blakes encountered in the spring of 1789.

If only on account of its punctuality, William and Catherine Blake's encounters with the individuals described above, however fleeting and fragmentary, considerably enlarges our knowledge of the couple's personal interaction with London's multiple layers of contemporary metropolitan spirituality on the eve of the French Revolution. With their tantalizing links to popular prophecy, variant notions of Africa, America and the problem of slavery, Blake's meetings with this fascinating group of individuals undoubtedly provided the starting point for a number of the larger issues discussed in the illuminated books of the 1790s.

Notes

1. Robert Hindmarsh, *Rise and Progress of the New Jerusalem Church in England and America* (London: 1861), p. 107.
2. There may have originally been two nineteenth-century copies: see Thomas Robinson, *A Remembrancer and Recorder of Facts and Documents Illustrative of the Genius of the New Jerusalem Dispensation* (Manchester and Boston: 1864), pp. 95–6.
3. *BR*, pp. 50–3.
4. Minute Book, Swedenborg Society, Bloomsbury Square, London, folio 69.
5. Fol. 65. See Richard Hindmarsh, *Rise and Progress*, p. 107. Hindmarsh does not mention the Blakes.
6. Dorothy Gott, *The Midnight Cry, 'Behold, the Bridegroom Comes!'; or, an Order from God to Get Your Lamps Lighted [...] This is My Experience* (London: 1788), p. 17.
7. Jon Mee, *Dangerous Enthusiasm: William Blake and the Culture of Radicalism in the 1790s* (Oxford: Clarendon Press, 1992), pp. 20–74.
8. Gott, pp. 22, 24, 66. Murray's was obviously an adaptation of an earlier device: see John Cluff, *A Description of the Solar; or, Camera Obscura Microscope* (London: *c*.1744).
9. Gott, p. 82.
10. Gustavus Katterfelto, *At No. 24, Piccadilly, This Present Day, and Every Day This Week, From 9 in the Morning till 6 in the Afternoon* (1785); Douglas McKie, 'Priestley's Laboratory and Library and Other of His Effects', *Notes and Records of the Royal Society of London*, 12 (1956), 114–36.
11. George Adams, *An Essay on Vision, Briefly Explaining the Fabric of the Eye* (London: 1789), p. 2. The first quotation comes from an additional page inserted into the BL copy.
12. *A Catalogue Of The Printed And Unprinted Works Of The Hon. Emanuel Swedenborg: To Which Are Added, Some Observations Recommending The Perusal Of His Theological Writings* (London: 1785), p. 20.
13. William Hewson, 'On the Figure and Composition of the Red Particles of the Blood, Commonly Called the Red Globules', *Philsophical Transactions of the Royal Society* 63 (London: 1773), 303–23.
14. Argand's innovations of a glass chimney and circular wick vastly improved the brightness of oil lamps: see John J. Wolfe, *Brandy, Balloons, and Lamps: Ami Argand, 1750–1803* (Carbondale and Edwardsville: Southern Illinois University Press, 1999). For Adam's knowledge of Argand's lamps, see his *Essays on the Microscope* (London: 1787), pp. 23, 78, and his *Plates for the Essays on the Microscope* (London: 1787), Plate III.
15. David Worrall, 'Thel in Africa: William Blake and the Post-Colonial, Post-Swedenborgian Female Subject', in *Blake, Nation and Empire*, ed. by Steve Clark and David Worrall (Palgrave Macmillan, 2006), pp. 40–63, and

The Reception of Blake in the Orient (London and New York: Continuum, 2006), ed. by Steve Clark and Masashi Suzuki, pp. 17–28.

16. National Archives, Kew, Board of Trade 6/10, 378–89, 553–62.

17. Wadström, *Observations on the Slave Trade, and a Description Of Some Part of the Coast of Guinea, During a Voyage Made in 1787, and 1788* (London: 1789).

18. Deirdre Coleman, *Romantic Colonization and British Anti-slavery* (Cambridge: Cambridge University Press, 2005), pp. 66, 73; Marsha Keith Schuchard, 'The Secret Masonic History of Blake's Swedenborg Society', *BIQ* 26 (1992), 40–51. However, Wadström does refer to 'the abundance of gold [...] found in the inland parts' of western Africa (*Observations*, p. 45).

19. C. B. Wadström, *An Essay on Colonization Particularly Applied to the Western Coast of Africa with some Free Thoughts on Cultivation and Commerce* (1794), Part ii, pp. 40, 236–7.

20. Wadström, *Essay*, Part ii, p. 236.

21. Susan Matthews, 'Africa and Utopia: Refusing a "local habitation"', in *The Reception of Blake in the Orient*, pp. 104–20.

22. Matthews, pp. 109–11.

23. Joseph Priestley, *Dr Priestley's Letter to the Inhabitants of Birmingham: Mr Keri's Vindication of the Revolution Dinner* (1791).

24. Folio 61; Carl Theophilius Odhner, *Robert Hindmarsh: A Biography* (Philadelphia: Academy Bookroom, 1895), pp. 10–11. Peter Provo's *Wisdom's Dictates; or a Collection of Maxims and Observations Concerning Divine, and Spiritual Truths; and that Process of Regeneration, or Renewal of Life, From the Lord, Which is Truly Saving* (London: 1789), contains the strikingly Blakean maxim that 'The Action of Life is Desire' (p. 54).

25. William Spence, *Essays in Divinity and Physic, Proving the Divinity of the Person of Jesus Christ, and the Spiritual Sense of Scripture: In Refutation of Dr J. Priestley, and the Socinian System* (London: 1792), p. 19.

26. William Spence, *Essays in Divinity and Physic*, pp. 20–1.

27. *Difference of Sentiment No Objection to the Exercise of Mutual Love: A Sermon, Preached at the Annual Meeting of Ministers, in Dudley, May 16, 1780* (Birmingham: 1780), p. iii.

28. Benjamin Carpenter, *A Letter to the Rev. R. Foley, M. A. Rector of Oldswinsford: In Answer to the Charges Brought Against the Dissenters In Stourbridge* (Stourbridge: *c*.1792), pp. 14n.–15n., 35–42; Joseph Priestley, *An Appeal to the Public, on the Subject of the Riots in Birmingham, Part II: To Which is Added, a Letter from W. Russell, Esq. to the Author* (1792), Appendix XIX.

29. Benjamin Carpenter, p. 36.

30. See Andrew Lincoln's notes in William Blake, *Songs of Innocence and of Experience: The Illuminated Books*, ed. by Lincoln (London and Princeton, NJ: William Blake Trust and Princeton University Press, 1991), p. 160.

31. Thomas Scott, *The Force Of Truth: An Authentic Narrative*, rev. edn (London: 1789), p. 62.

32. Scott, *The Force Of Truth*, p. 118.

33. *DNB*.

34. Thomas Scott, *Thoughts On the Fatal Consequences of Female Prostitution; Together With the Outlines of a Plan Proposed to Check Those Enormous Evils* (London: 1787), pp. 5, 15.

35. Thomas Scott, *An Estimate of the Religious Character and State of Great Britain, Being the Substance of a Sermon, Preached on Friday, April 19th, 1793* [...] *at thr* [sic] *Lock Chapel, and St Mildred's Church, Bread-Street* (London: 1793), pp. 20, 23–4, 28, 38.

36. See Wadström, *Plan*, p. 51.

37. On p. viii.

38. For Servanté's occupation, see *The London Calendar, or Court and City Register for England, Scotland, Ireland, and America, for the Year 1787* (1787), p. 152. His signature can be found in *Minutes*, p. 42.

39. *The American Kalendar; or, United States Register, for ... 1796* (London: 1796), p. 10.

40. *Barrell and Servanté, No. 6, Ingram-Court, Fenchurch-Street, London, Agents for the Purchase and Sale of American Lands, Stocks, &c* (London: 1796), pp. 1–2.

41. Colborn Barrell and Henry Servanté, *Observations on the North-American Land-Company, Lately Instituted in Philadelphia* (London: 1796).

42. Martin P. Schipper, *Slavery in Ante-Bellum Southern Industries* (Black Studies Research Resources), Series C: Selections from the Virginia Historical Society Part 2: Railroad and Canal Construction Industries and Other Trades and Industries (Bethesda, MD: University Publications of America 1997) microfilm, Reel 1, Section 36.

43. Imlay wrote that 'the Indians continued to increase their depredations, under a belief, that if once the Whites were suffered to establish themselves on their side of the Ohio, there would be no end to their incroachments until they became extirpated' (*A Topographical Description*, p. 32).

44. Barrell and Servanté, *Observations*, p. xvii.

45. Francois Hippolyte Barthélemon, *The AFRICAN'S pity on the WHITE MAN: Humbly Dedicated to Madame Vilars de Malortie, Composed, with an Accompaniment for the Harp or Piano Forte* (London: *c*.1798).

46. Albert W. Cooper, *Benjamin Banks, 1727–1795, the Salisbury Violin Maker: a Detailed Survey of his Work, Life, and Environment* (Haslemere: Ashford Publications, 1989).

47. Pamela McGairl, 'The Vauxhall Jubilee, 1786,' *The Musical Times* 127 (1986), 611–15; Josephine R. B. Wright, 'George Polgreen Bridgetower: An African Prodigy in England 1789–99', *The Musical Quarterly* 66 (1980), 65–82.

48. Francois Hippolyte Barthélemon, *Oithóna: A Dramatic Poem, Taken From the Prose Translation of the Celebrated Ossian: As Performed at the Theatre Royal in the Hay Market* (London: 1768), pp. 5–6.

49. Carl Theophilius Odhner, *Robert Hindmarsh*, p. 98.

50. Peter Linebaugh and Marcus Rediker, *The Many-Headed Hydra: Sailors, Slaves, Commoners, and the Hidden History of the Revolutionary Atlantic* (London: Verso, 2000), pp. 258ff.

51. James Ball, 6 December 1797, *The Proceedings of the Old Bailey*, Ref: t17971206–18.

52. The spelling discrepancy between the 'Aspinshaw' of the Swedenborg records and the 'Ashpinshaw' of Equiano's subscriber's list appears to be a vagary of eighteenth-century non-standard spelling. 'Aspinshaw' was known to be a 'smith' living at 60 Leather Lane, and probably the same as the 'Mr Aspinshaw' residing at an unspecified Leather Lane address whose

trade was probably goldsmith at the Mint and who is recorded in the Old Bailey proceedings. However, this identity should also be collated with what appears to be another relative, Thomas Ashpinshaw, of 61 Leather Lane, who is listed in trade directories between 1785 and 1805 as a printers' smith, pressmaker and composing stick-maker (the tray used by compositors to hold type). The Aspinshaws or Ashpinshaws were clearly of the same family, worked in cognate trades and lived in close proximity to one another. See Ian Maxted, *The London Book Trades 1775–1800: A Preliminary Checklist of Members* (Folkestone: Dawson, 1977) and http://www.devon.gov.uk/library/locstudy/bookhist/.

53. See Vincent Carretta, *Equiano The African: Biography of a Self Made Man* (Athens, GA, and London: University of Georgia Press, 2005), pp. 270–5.

54. S. E. Ogude, 'Swedenborg and Blake's "Little Black Boy"', *Asemka* (Ghana) 4 (1976), 85–96.

55. National Archives, Kew, Colonial Office 267/9. C. B. Wadström writes, 'In the month of April, 1788, I was accidentally informed, that a young African was going to be conveyed on board a vessel bound for *Sierra Leona*' (10 October 1790, 45 Upper Mary-le-Bone Street).

56. *The Diary of Sarah Fox née Champion, Bristol 1745–1802, Extracted in 1872 by John Frank*, ed. by Madge Dresser, Bristol Record Society's Publications, Vol. 55 (Bristol: Bristol Record Society, 2003), p. 111.

57. Worrall, 'Thel in Africa'.

58. *The Diary of Sarah Fox*, p. 52.

59. *Bristol, Africa and the Eighteenth-Century Slave Trade to America, Vol. 4 The Final Years, 1770–1807*, ed. by David Richardson, Bristol Record Society's Publications, Vol. 47 (Bristol: Bristol Record Society, 1996), pp. 28, 111, 122.

60. *The Diary of Sarah Fox*, p. 262, n. 88.

61. *The Diary of Sarah Fox*, pp. 109–10.

62. Frank Wesley Pitman, 'Fetishism, Witchcraft, and Christianity Among the Slaves', *The Journal of Negro History*, 11 (1926), 650–68; Jane T. Merritt, 'Dreaming of the Savior's Blood: Moravians and the Indian Great Awakening in Pennsylvania', *The William and Mary Quarterly*, 54 (1997), 723–46; S. Scott Rohrer, 'Evangelism and Acculturation in the Blackcountry: The Case of Wachovia, North Carolina, 1753–1830', *Journal of the Early Republic*, 21 (2001), 199–229.

4
Impurity of Diction: The 'Harlots Curse' and Dirty Words

Susan Matthews

It was only at the last stage of redrafting that Blake hit on the word 'charter'd' for the opening of 'London'. In the early drafts, the poem began:

> I wander thro each dirty street
> Near where the dirty Thames does flow.[1]

As E. P. Thompson showed brilliantly in 1978, 'charter'd' draws on a rich set of meanings within the politicized discourses of the time.[2] But the flatly unpoetic 'dirty' was there for a reason. Dirt is not only a literal feature of Blake's Lambeth but also an image of the corruption of childhood and of marriage, of the intimate relations of sexuality through poverty and disease that the final stanza describes:

> But most thro' midnight streets I hear
> How the youthful Harlots curse
> Blasts the new-born Infants tear
> And smites with plagues the Marriage hearse.
> ('London', *Experience*, ll. 13–16, E27)

These lines, which analyze the corruption of sexuality, have been seen in an acute recent commentary as evidence that Blake's own writing cannot escape from the contaminated world that it describes: for Susan

Wolfson, the image of the 'harlots curse' shows that 'Blake's female figures shape general questions [...] in terms that convey processes and prejudices that fall into drastic differentials of gender, no less then than now.'[3] And Wolfson is right insofar as the 'harlots curse' as a reference to venereal disease is both coy and malignant; it is a phrase that turns the prostitute (but not her client) into an agent of death. Anne Mellor has attacked the tendency of Blake's readers to see him 'as he might have liked to be seen: as an artist deeply at odds with his culture and times'. Instead she insists that Blake is 'complicit in the racist and sexist ideologies of his culture'.[4] Surveying recent critical accounts, Robert Essick concludes that Blake was 'deeply ambivalent about female sexuality', and that in his 'later works [...] the evidence for misogyny increases'.[5]

These worries (anachronistic though they may be) are worth considering on the grounds that Blake is part of our contemporary culture, still a figure of veneration and belief for many. But they also raise a wider question: Blake's claims for 'art' can be seen as part of the Romantic ideology which stands for the power of art to work a kind of magic by which old meanings are transformed and cleansed. For critics who have recently argued for the presence of racist, sexist and Orientalist ideology in Blake's writing, redemptive readings of Blake naively accept claims that poetry can 'repeal | Large codes of fraud and woe'.[6] Despite this, I am going to argue for the transformative power of Blake's writing, resting my (possibly tendentious) claims not on the ability of poetry to cleanse but to bring to the surface and to refigure meanings.

The figure of the harlot that Blake uses in 'London' draws on a century's conflicted feelings about the role of prostitution in the formation of the new polite order. The harlot is everywhere in the culture of Blake's period, a figure that is endlessly circulated.[7] The power of the image lies in the way it came over the course of the eighteenth century to delimit new structures of marriage, of commerce and of national identity. The harlot is the anti-type of what the century might see as its great achievement: the creation of a new form of domestic happiness. *Paradise Lost* defines 'wedded love' (which Milton, oddly, places before the fall) in opposition to 'the bought smile | Of harlots, loveless, joyless, unendeared'.[8] What Milton does in *Paradise Lost* is to link marriage with the unfallen state of Adam and Eve in Eden. Dustin Griffin points out that the *Tatler* papers 'invariably' quoted Milton in praise of married love and that Thomson called Milton's lines from *Paradise Lost* Book iv the 'divine Hymn on Marriage'.[9] This construction may have been in

Blake's mind as he wrote the *Songs of Experience*. Michael Phillips shows that the Notebook drafts of the *Songs of Experience* express in part Blake's response to *Paradise Lost*, coinciding with sketches probably intended for Fuseli's Milton Gallery project.[10] The General Title Page to the combined *Songs* shows a despairing Adam whose body shelters a cowering Eve from the flames of experience. In his 1732 edition of *Paradise Lost*, Richard Bentley suggested replacing the bleak last lines of the poem with a more optimistic vision of the world of experience as a place of safe sociability. Instead of Milton's lines, 'They hand in hand with wand'ring steps and slow, | Through Eden took their solitary way', Bentley proposed: 'Then hand in hand with social steps their way | Through Eden took; with heav'nly comfort cheer'd'. In a copy of Bentley's edition with annotations by 'W B' these lines are simply crossed out: this deletion (which Phillips believes to be the work of Blake) rejects the claim that it is the 'social' quality of domesticity that reinstates the comfort of Eden.[11] Linking the harlot and marriage in 'London', Blake threatens a constitutive element of the national self-image: the claim that society can incorporate and make safe sexual pleasure.

It is standard, now, to read the contrast between the 'spiritual' and the 'corporeal' in Blake's later writing as a sign of his hostility to sexuality (and to women insofar as they are associated with embodiment and the material), an ambivalence (at the very least) which might be read as latent in the figure of the harlot in 'London'.[12] But the location of sexuality within the category of the 'corporeal' was not universally assumed in the long eighteenth century. For many mainstream writers, Protestant culture allows an understanding of the spirituality of sexual love, of what Oothoon in *Visions of the Daughters of Albion* calls 'lovely copulation' (7: 26, E50). A positive account of sexuality has recently been associated with such marginal religious groups as the Swedenborgians and Moravians, but equally positive accounts appear in works by members of the established church, underpinning even so idiosyncratic a scheme as that offered in the 1780 *Thelyphthora* by Cowper's cousin, Martin Madan.[13] Madan's proposal that legalized polygamy would solve the problem of prostitution derives from a conviction of the sacredness of intercourse and locates the logical flaw in Milton's account: Madan argues that because there was no marriage ceremony in Eden, '*the union of the man* and *woman* in *personal knowledge of each other*' is 'the only *marriage-ordinance* which we find revealed in the sacred scriptures'.[14] Intercourse, therefore, *is* marriage. Madan's solution was a serious reconsideration of what remained a lingering alternative direction for the institution of marriage, one that Richardson regularly invoked and rejected in his novels.[15]

Madan's learned work was widely read and debated. It was owned by Hayley and is a probable source for his account of the role of virginity in the early church in the *Essay on Old Maids*.[16] Madan claims to represent a true Protestant understanding of sexuality and presents the Christian cult of virginity as a form of enthusiasm – or superstition, to maintain Hume's distinction – which characterizes Catholic cultures. It is this charge that is acted out in Matthew Lewis's gothic novel *The Monk* in its portrait of the convent as the place of deformed sexual relations. According to Madan, the Reformation acceptance of a married priesthood is a sign of a healthy Protestant sexual culture which defines not only sexual but gender identities by discouraging sodomy; he quotes 'the excellent *authors* of *the History* of *Popery*' in their claim that 'a certain *unnatural vice* in *England*' was unheard of until '*priests* were forbidden marriage'. 'Popish celibacy' is dangerous because it attempts to damn the natural force of sexuality: 'When we endeavour to stop the course of a river by laying a dam across the stream, the effect must be, that it will either make its way, bearing down all before it, or it will make a passage over its banks, and overflow and destroy the country.' Britain's Protestant identity is rooted in a version of marriage that values sexuality and enables domestic happiness by providing a 'natural course' for 'those desires which the Creator hath implanted in us'.[17] Sexual desire, according to Madan, is God given.

Sexuality is frequently imaged in terms of the flow of water in the eighteenth century. Even in *Sir Charles Grandison*, Harriet Byron uses the image of channelled water to describe the regulation of desire, confirming her belief that she is 'in the less danger of falling in love with any man, as [she] can be civil and courteous to all' with the analogy of 'a stream' for if 'sluiced off into several channels, there is the less fear that it will overflow its banks'.[18] Like Madan, Mary Hays' Emma Courtney describes the destructive power of blocked sexuality in images of the blocked flow of water: 'I regret these natural sensations and affections, their forcible suppression injures the mind – it converts the mild current of gentle, and genial sympathies, into a destructive torrent.' In similar terms, she imagines Catholic culture as a contaminated water supply: 'From monastic institutions and principles have flowed, as from a polluted source, streams, that have at once spread through society a mingled contagion of dissoluteness and hypocrisy.'[19] These terms appear as well in medical writing where venereal disease contaminates the circulation of sympathy, the agent that binds society together. John Hunter opens his 1786 *Treatise on the Venereal Disease* with an account of sympathy as the mechanism central to the operation of all disease. Fever is a sign that the whole body is reacting to the distress of a single part: it is 'an universal sympathy with a local disease'. But this sympathetic mechanism 'takes place oftener and in a greater degree in the *lues venerea* than in any other form of the disease'.[20] The functioning of this circulatory process is therefore seen as critical both to the health of the individual body and to the health of the nation.

From early in the century, the visible presence of prostitution on the streets of London threatened the social order supposedly established by the Glorious Revolution. In the 1720s, the Societies for the Reformation of Manners determined to clean up the streets of the metropolis by targeting prostitution, though the result may have been to increase violence against street prostitutes.[21] If sexuality in a Protestant nation could be a positive force, the engine of population increase and cement of domestic happiness, it clearly needed to be managed. Yet in the 1724 *A Modest Defence of Publick Stews* Mandeville sees the attempt to suppress prostitution as dangerous:

> What else could we hope for, from Your persecuting of poor strolling Damsels? From Your stopping up those *Drains* and *Sluices* we had to let out Lewdness? From Your demolishing those *Horn-works* and *Breast-works* of Modesty? Those *Ramparts* and *Ditches* within which the Virtue of our Wives and Daughters lay so conveniently intrench'd?[22]

Mandeville imagines the regulation of sexuality in terms of flood defences: prostitution provides a safety valve ('*Drains* and *Sluices*') in the system that protects the virtue of 'our Wives and Daughters', and so defines the identity of 'our' class. It is also a barrier ('*Horn-works* and *Breast-works*') which protects the virtue of the middle-class woman. The prostitute defines (as limit and as opposite) the virtue of woman and of society, but also marks the point at which the identity of woman and the social breaks down (insofar as the prostitute is both female and the provider of a social service). But in any case, attempts at suppression were seen to fail; a pamphlet of 1734 describes the *Pretty Doings in a Protestant Nation* from the viewpoint of a French Catholic visitor. The voice of 'Father Poussin', like Mandeville's ten years earlier, is more salacious than condemnatory. 'Father Poussin' sees prostitutes proliferating unstoppably, like shoals of fishes: '*Where the Devil do all these B—ches, come from?* being a common *Fleet-street* Phrase...when each revolving Evening sends them up from *White-Chapel* to *Charing-Cross*, as plenty as Mackrel after Thunder in hot Seasons.'[23] Prostitution allows the influx of sexuality from the common east of London (Whitechapel) to the polite west (Charing Cross).[24] Imagining prostitutes as 'Mackrel after Thunder', Father Poussin sees them swimming down the still open Fleet river. London offers the 'deplorable Sight' of 'Numbers of little Creatures pil'd up in Heaps upon one another, sleeping in the publick Streets, in the most rigorous Seasons, and some of them whose Heads will hardly reach above the Waistband of a Man's Breeches.'[25] The last open section of the Fleet River from Holborn to Fleet Street, which had long defined the western boundary of the city, was finally covered in 1765 and by Blake's time ran underground. As a 1761 writer describes: 'Fleet Ditch now extends no higher than Fleet Bridge, all above being arched, covered over, and converted into a market; and the building of a fine bridge at Black Friars, will soon occasion all that is left of this ditch to be filled up.'[26] But as the boundary between east and west moves westward towards Charing Cross and the waters of the Fleet are covered over, the problem of prostitution only seems to spread.

Many reform plans covertly acknowledge the functional necessity of the prostitute. In 1758 the philanthropic reformer Jonas Hanway admitted that 'It has been often debated how far it is adviseable, supposing it were practicable, *totally* to suppress prostitutes.' Yet he seems unable to spell out the implications of his statement – that prostitution is not just ineradicable but necessary: 'The subject is *delicate*', he says, 'and will hardly admit of a strict examination.' What is important is to remove the visible signs: 'Let it suffice that it is, or should be, in the power of the civil magistrate, to drive common prostitutes, from the public streets.'[27] Prostitution, like the dirty waters of the Fleet, needs to go underground or indoors. With the setting up of the Foundling Hospital for abandoned children in 1739, the Lock Hospital for the treatment of prostitutes infected with venereal disease at Hyde Park in 1746 and (Hanway's own project) the Magdalen House for repentant prostitutes in 1758, London sought to demonstrate its commitment to the regulation of sexuality.[28] The failure of this charitable endeavour was evident to De Quincey in 1821 when he writes of the street prostitute Ann:

> Her's was a case of ordinary occurrence [...] and one in which, if London beneficence had better adapted its arrangements to meet it, the power of the law might oftener be interposed to protect, and to

avenge. But the stream of London charity flows in a channel which, though deep and mighty, is yet noiseless and underground; not obvious or readily accessible to poor houseless wanderers.[29]

In De Quincey's sentimental model it is the water of charity that is channelled while prostitution is still above ground on London's streets.

The figure of the harlot is inextricable from the image of the nation as well as the city for, as Susan Sontag claimed, there is a 'link between imagining disease and imagining foreignness'.[30] Writing in the century dominated by military conflict with France, Mandeville sees the 'French Disease' as the only one in which the body does not ultimately cure itself: it is 'such a busy restless Enemy, that unless resisted, he is never at a Stand, but gathers Strength every day, to the utter Disquiet of the Patient'.[31] It testifies to the foreignness of the sexual drive, an uncontrollable force which divides the self. In the culture of guilt provoked by the loss of America in 1776 the fact of prostitution is used to reveal the falsity of the nation's claims. Martin Madan, in 1780, can see that London's prostitution orientalizes the nation, revealing the fallacy in its claim to moral superiority, which rests, by this time, specifically on its ability to foster and protect women.[32] As power and virtue shift west to America, Britain is the new Orient. According to Madan, the Mahomedans 'shame us' with the respect they afford to women.[33] Madan develops a theme already present when Hanway in 1758 described England as a 'Christian country where vast numbers of the common people have worn off all sense of their religion, and adopted notions and customs which *Mohammed* would have been ashamed of'.[34] The 'common people' are not part of the Christian nation, but foreigners in our midst. Madan sees 'public brothels' as 'our *Seraglios in England*', institutions that uncover the Orient deep in the heart of London, more horrible, more disgraceful, than 'the *Grand Seignior's* SERAGLIO, or the HARAM of a *Turkish Bassa*'. Manning the boundary between west and east, the harlot once again lets the foreigner in. But Madan knows that the fantasy of the Orient is a displacement of Britain's shame:

The doors of these *houses* of *infamy* are open to every *comer*, the women the temporary property of every visitor [...] – these *houses* are accommodated to men of all ranks and degrees, from the highest to the lowest; and, lest the plan of lewdness should suffer by being narrowed within the boundaries of walls, every public street, after a

certain time of night, exhibits a kind of *itinerant Seraglio*, where men
are saved the trouble of going out of their way.[35]

It's a curious comparison given that the seraglio is surely not 'open to
every comer'. But the brothel undoes the categories which make sense
of the world: public/private, indoors/outdoors, polite/impolite, British
liberty/Eastern tyranny. These categories can neither be held in the
brain nor 'narrowed within the boundaries of walls'. It is no accident
that the virtue of Richardson's Clarissa is defined by her difference from
the prostitutes amongst whom she is lodged. With some irony, she
describes herself to Lovelace as 'a creature whom thou hast levelled with
the dirt of the Street, and classed with the vilest of her Sex'.[36] The crucial distinction between the domestic interior and the street breaks
down here; as Laura Rosenthal explains, prostitution was unsettling
because it undermined 'the separation of the public and private spheres
at the moment of their inception' by putting 'in the marketplace the
very thing [...] understood to define the private sphere'.[37] The intensity
of Madan's reaction derives not only from the depth of his investment
in a sacramental view of sexuality but also from the destruction of the
categories that define his world.

Prostitution was also seen as a problem of language and of sound, a
threat to verbal propriety, remedied in Handel's association with the
Foundling Hospital by the creation of harmony out of the dissonance of
illegitimate sexuality.[38] The word 'harlot' may itself represent an attempt
to cleanse the language of the Bible from contamination by illegitimate
sexuality: according to the *Oxford English Dictionary*, the currency of the
word derives from the search by sixteenth-century Bible translators for
a less offensive alternative to Wyclif's 'hoore'. It is particularly through
its use in the Bible that 'harlot' comes to mean prostitute rather than
simply 'vagabond, beggar, rogue, rascal, villain, low fellow, knave'. In its
new sexual and gendered meaning, the word reveals the process of com-
partmentalization, the separation of sexual from non-sexual meanings,
on which the new polite order rests. The word 'sex', in the eighteenth
century, refers to division: appropriately so if the end of eighteenth century is the period, as Thomas Laqueur argues, which sees the creation of
new assumptions about gendered behaviour:

The commonplace of much contemporary psychology – that men
want sex while women want relationships – is the precise inversion
of pre-Enlightenment notions that, extending back to antiquity,
equated friendship with men and fleshliness with women. Women,

whose desires knew no bounds in the old scheme of things, and whose reason offered so little resistance to passion became in some accounts creatures whose whole reproductive life might be spent anesthetized to the pleasures of the flesh.[39]

To writers in tune with the new order, prostitution undermines assumptions about the nature of woman. Jonas Hanway insists that: 'There is a certain delicacy of manners essential to good order: and the distinctions which the sexes show to each other is one great means of supporting that *order*.' The harlot's curse particularly distresses him: 'We frequently hear those tongues, which God of nature designed should soften the distresses of human life, and give a relish to its joys, uttering the highest indecencies, and the most dreadful imprecations!'[40] The redemption that Hanway hoped to achieve in his plans for the Magdalen House in 1758 was marked by the adoption of refined language: he insists that the inmates are not to be embarrassed by 'too frequent mention of the word *Prostitute*'.[41] For Madan, the brothel is the place where 'filthiness and obscenity defile [...] conversation'.[42] 'Criminal conversation' was the standard legal term for adultery in divorce trials, but conversation, a key category for the period, is equally dirtied in the brothel.

Prostitution presents an intransigent problem: the harlot is necessary to the stability of the social order but destructive to population increase and to domestic happiness. It is possible to read the harlot in 'London' as simply reproducing this construction: Zachary Leader sees the speaker as somehow 'deadened', revealing symptoms of an 'anaesthetized matter-of-factness'.[43] But Blake's poem brings to the surface a construction that the period would rather forget. 'London' insists on the visibility of the prostitute, reversing the struggle to cleanse commerce of contamination by the amorality of prostitution. Reading the 'harlots curse' as a reference to disease leads E. P. Thompson to stress that ' "London" is a literal poem'. He writes: 'the blood of the soldier is for real, as well as apocalyptic, and so is the venereal disease that blinds the new born infant'.[44] But if the reference is literal, the language is not. Sontag insisted that 'illness is *not* a metaphor' but as Susan Wolfson realizes so clearly the 'harlots curse' is no more a literal reference to disease than 'The Sick Rose' is about gardening.[45] The phrase could plausibly belong to the rhetoric of purity and contamination of Hannah More's *Cheap Repository Tracts* from the 1790s. In the 1796 'Story of Sinful Sally Told by Herself', the seduced-country-girl-turned-city-prostitute destroys the bloom of others: 'how many youths so blooming | By my wanton looks I've won'.[46] She is a spider who casts her web of death:

> Thus the cruel spider stretches
> > Wide his web for every fly;
> Then each victim that he catches
> > Strait he poisons till he die.[47]

Destroyed in the end by her own disease ('See how all my flesh is rotted, | Stop, O Stranger, see me die!'), 'Sal' – for she no longer deserves the dignity of the name Sally – is saved by her belated recognition that she is 'the vilest Harlot'.[48] Whereas the more liberal Hanway avoids the word 'prostitute', the harsh name here is redemptive. A new emphasis on the guilt of the prostitute – and her distance from the polite – enters the rhetoric of later evangelical reformers.

Whilst Anne Mellor has portrayed Blake as led astray by his desires, identifying the 'free love' celebrated in *Visions* as 'a male fantasy that serves the interests only of the male libertine', she has celebrated Hannah More as a critic of sexual ideology.[49] But it is the *Cheap Repository* poem that reveals a sexual imagination in love with pain, offering the interchange of pain as the operation of redemption: 'Savior, whom I pierc'd so often, | Deeper still my guilt imprint!' Sal's story may be *'told by herself'* but her voice is contaminated by the corrosive guilt of the evangelical cure which depends on the belief Enitharmon tries to promote in *Europe* that 'Womans love is Sin' (5: 5, E62).[50] Blake's *Book of Ahania* analyzes the process by which the female is identified as 'Sin' through the splitting of Urizen:

> Dire shriek'd his invisible Lust
> Deep groan'd Urizen! stretching his awful hand
> Ahania (so name his parted soul)
> He siez'd on his mountains of jealousy.
> He groand anguishd & called her Sin.
> > > (2: 30–4, E84)

In this noisy scene the 'invisible' is made explicit. If Blake is consistent in rejecting the language of sin, then it would seem unlikely that he invokes this language in the figure of the harlot in 'London'. The poem, I suggest, critiques rather than belongs with the evangelical account of prostitution; it is Hannah More, rather than Blake who presents the more disturbing account of prostitution.

Or is it? In lines from Blake's Notebook, the whore is again set in contrast to the wife: inverting Milton's opposition between 'wedded love' and 'the bought smile | Of harlots', it is the whore who offers the 'lineaments of Gratified desire':

> In a wife I would desire
> What in whores is always found
> The lineaments of Gratified desire.
>   (E474)

The apparent meaning is that whores unlike wives reliably provide male sexual pleasure. Another jotting offers to answer the question of what women want that would later stump Freud:

> What is it men in women do require
> The lineaments of Gratified Desire
> What is it women do in men require
> The lineaments of Gratified Desire.
>   (E474–5)

Men and women desire the same thing: the sight of their partner's pleasure (their own pleasure would be more easily detected by feeling than by sight). If this is the correct reading, then what is desired 'in a wife' is not so much male sexual gratification as the woman who consistently experiences pleasure. But in this case, the Notebook seems to reveal an even stranger assumption about the 'whore'. With a voice like Bromion's (we should not make the mistake of reading the Notebook as private confession or as providing access to a 'true' Blake), these lines conjure up not the harlot as sentimental victim but the earlier eighteenth-century figure of the 'woman of pleasure', the libertine whore whom Katherine Norberg assumes is 'utterly fictional, an image which has more to do with male fantasy than with social reality'.[51] It is also worth considering, however, Lynn Hunt's argument that '[e]arly modern pornographers [...] at least until the 1790s, often valorized female sexual activity and determination much more than did the prevailing medical texts'.[52] The figure of the libertine whore derives from a world in which female sexuality is no different from male: the gendered split described by Laqueur between a mechanical and an affective model has not yet occurred. The libertine emphasis on female sexual pleasure can take on a political meaning in Blake's poetry, standing for the possibility of transforming change. The nation or the earth is often rendered as merely responding to a male agent, but in the *Song of Los* what Helen Bruder describes as the 'wildly orgasmic female grave' is an image of revolutionary change: [53]

> The Grave shrieks with delight, & shakes
> Her hollow womb, & clasps the solid stem:
> Her bosom swells with wild desire:
> And milk & blood & glandous wine
> In rivers rush & shout & dance,
> On mountain, dale and plain.
>
> (7: 35–40, E69–70)

Read as a metaphor of political change, revolution is done *by* not *to* the nation.

When Donald Davie used the term 'purity of diction' to describe the language of eighteenth-century poets including Wesley and Cowper, his own terms, derived from Goldsmith, drew explicitly on sexual categories: 'chastity in writing is the best safeguard against frigidity; and frigidity is "a deviation from propriety owing to the erroneous judgment of the writer, who, endeavouring to captivate the admiration with novelty, very often shocks the understanding with extravagance"'.[54] In Davie's terms, Blake's diction is strikingly impure: words are shifted in meaning and metaphor flourishes impertinently. Davie follows Samuel Johnson in his claim that pure diction is language which is close to educated conversation: purity is achieved by handling, but handling only by the educated. Davie's judgements sound like those of Thomas Butts who worried about 'certain opinions' of Blake, which are 'imbibed from reading, nourish'd by indulgence, and rivetted by a confined Conversation'.[55] For these writers, metaphor needs to be regulated by use; it needs to be part of a shared educated language.

Blake's technique in 'London' – as elsewhere – is to give form to error, and it is through the restating and metaphorical shifting of categories that new meanings are created. 'London' is a poem that refuses to provide synonyms, overworking to the point of exhaustion a few words: 'mark', 'marks', 'every', 'cry'. It is also a poem that destroys familiar categories: you cannot hear 'manacles' or see 'sighs', nor do curses normally 'blast'. In the context of Blake's 'London', the figure of the harlot takes on new meanings. Madan worried that the currents of conversation were defiled in the brothel, but, rejecting the model of linguistic purity, Blake gives new meanings to the harlot's curse. Blake imagines the harlot not as speaking but as cursing (in 'London') or crying (in *Auguries of Innocence*). Words are replaced by inarticulate sounds, sounds that blur the boundaries of words. Although the 'Harlots curse' is often presumed to signify venereal disease, the absence of the apostrophe, especially taken together with the pause created visually by the line ending, allows a second meaning to emerge:

> But most thro' midnight streets I hear
> How the youthful Harlots curse [...]

If the curse is verb rather than noun, then it can turn into the anger of the harlots at the exploitation that has enslaved them. It would be hard to *hear* the curse of venereal disease, but the rude language of the harlots is audible on the street.

In 'London', social circulation is 'charter'd' in streets and in the Thames, but these forms of regulation do not keep the domestic privacy of marriage apart from the suffering of the young prostitute. The boundaries that the philanthropists (of all varieties) would set up are ineffective, and are so not because there are not enough hospitals but because (as the *Song of Liberty* reveals), the fall of one eternal brings the whole edifice of eternity crashing down. The virtuous cannot redeem the fallen because the marks appear in 'every face'. As he revised the poem, Blake changed 'midnight harlots curse' to 'youthful Harlots curse', but in both versions the adjective reminds us of the existence of a person and makes the phrase unstable, slipping from person to disease as the eye moves from 'youthful Harlot' to 'Harlots curse'.[56] Hannah More draws on an idea of linguistic purity when she claims that the Bible is marked by its lack of figuration: 'There is perhaps no book', she insists in 1799, 'in which adjectives are so sparingly used.' Establishing clear definitions guards social morality. She attacks women who rush into print as 'these trope and figure ladies', and believes that learning to distinguish meanings will protect their virtue: 'By these means they would go forth armed against many of the false opinions which through the abuse or ambiguous meaning of words pass so current in the world.'[57] The work of Blake's tropes and figures is to create ambiguity: the adjective 'youthful' alters the force of the phrase 'harlots curse' almost in the way that Blake's Miltonic phrase the 'human form divine' creates an unstable alternation between god and man, poised on the rocker of 'form'.

The harlot is a frequent presence in the clotted and difficult language of the late epics where we meet 'Mystery the Virgin Harlot Mother of War,

| Babylon the Great, the Abomination of Desolation!' (*Milton*, 22: 48–9, E117). According to E. P. Thompson, the shifted meanings that Blake gives to the 'harlot' in the late epics belong to the language of radical Dissent in which 'the whore of Babylon was not only the "scarlet woman" of Rome, but [...] all compromise between things spiritual and the temporal powers of the State, and hence, very specifically [...] the Church of England'.[58] Thompson conceptualizes 'State Religion' as a form of impurity, the inadmissible mixture of the spiritual and temporal. But the problem, for Blake, may lie as much in the demand of religion for purity as in the mixing of categories. The whore of Babylon, ironically, is Hannah More and the conservative project of evangelical morality, which now proposes a view of sexuality which is much more hostile than Madan's. As Thompson reminds us, the best gloss is provided by Blake's annotation to Watson: 'The laws of the Jews were (both ceremonial & real) the basest & most oppressive of human codes. & being like all other codes given under pretence of divine command were what Christ pronouncd them The Abomination that maketh desolate. i.e. State Religion which is the Source of all Cruelty' (E618). In this new reading of Revelations, the Whore of Babylon becomes a 'State Religion' obsessed with sexual sin.

The oddity of the epic poems derives in part from these new networks of meaning: surprising things happen to the language of sexual typology when the language of the book of Revelations is taken over by a radical discourse. One of Blake's targets is the culture of female sexual purity within which Jerusalem, the sexual woman, is labelled 'as a Harlot'. The standard categories of female sexual status, 'Virgin', 'Harlot', 'Mother', cancel each other out, becoming negatively associated with 'War' and 'Mystery'. In Blake's use, Rahab is a harlot associated with empire and with purity, with the use of notions of moral virtue to justify political aggression. As G. A. Rosso demonstrates, Blake's figure of Rahab is a recoding and reinterpretation of a figure 'revered to this day in both Jewish and Christian traditions'.[59] Blake's Rahab is negative not because she is sexual but because she uses her sexuality to enable the destruction of the people of Jericho by Israel. It is because Blake uses terms and categories whose meanings he has changed that his words are often misread.

In *Jerusalem* the harlot's cry is one of the sounds heard by 'Los raging round his Anvil | Of death'. The cries are part of the cacophonous pain of the city:

> loud the Corn fields thunder along
> The Soldiers fife; the Harlots shriek; the Virgins dismal groan

The Parents fear: the Brothers jealousy: the Sisters curse
Beneath the Storms of Theotormon & the thundring Bellows
Heaves in the hand of Palamabron who in Londons darkness
Before the Anvil, watches the bellowing flames.

(16: 5–10, E159)

The Thames is 'the black trough of his Forge; Londons River' where Rintrah quenches his burning hammer (16: 14, E160). The harlot's curse of 'London' is replaced by 'the Harlots shriek' which mingles with the 'Virgins dismal groan' as one of the myriad sounds of suffering. Rather than developing the element of misogyny in the 'Harlots curse' the new image is simply one of the sounds of the suffering city. Writing within a one-sex model, Blake can assume in 'London' that the harlot's cry is included in 'every cry of every Man'; in *Jerusalem*, the soldier, the harlot, the virgin, parents, brothers and sisters are all categories that will be changed in Los's 'bellowing flames' into forms of the human. The figure of the Harlot brings together a tangled web of discourses: luxury and commerce (as in Hogarth's harlot); sin (as in Sinful Sally); the victim of sensibility; the penitent whore as a demonstration of national benevolence; the libertine whore of pornography; the Whore of Babylon; the agent of disease and of death. Blake draws on all of these discourses; yet we need to remember Thompson's warning to the allusion spotter in us all ('if so, *what does Blake do with it?*') for none of these discourses emerges unchanged.⁶⁰ Blake's early critical account of the regulation of sexuality is not replaced in the late epics by hostility to women and to sexuality expressed within the language of religious misogyny. When Blake includes the 'Harlots cry' again it is in the *Auguries of Innocence*: the harlot's cry will 'weave Old Englands winding Sheet' not just because prostitution threatens fertility but also because it unravels the structures of the nation's complacent self-image (ll. 115–16, E492). Although the chartering of the Thames fixes its course, in Blake's writing meanings are always capable of redefinition.

In 'Holy Thursday' of *Songs of Innocence*, the children are imagined as water: 'they like Thames waters flow' (19: 4, E13). The Thames, like the Fleet, is unlikely to be pure but these children are still innocent for innocence is not the same as purity. The image of free-flowing water returns in *Jerusalem* to describe the reconciliation of the unfaithful Mary with Joseph. In opposition to the evangelical campaign against the adulterous woman, these lines show sexual categories as transient.

Here the flood that Mandeville wanted to contain is transformed into a positive force:

> Then Mary burst forth into a Song! she flowed like a River of
> Many Streams in the arms of Joseph & gave forth her tears of joy
> Like many waters, and Emanating into gardens & palaces upon
> Euphrates & to forests & floods & animals wild & tame from
> Gihon to Hiddekel, & to corn fields & villages & inhabitants
> Upon Pison & Arnon & Jordan.
>
> (61: 28–33, E212)

Emanation is a form of metamorphosis that flows from the relatively predictable process of simile ('like a River of Many Streams') to a dispersal of identity into 'gardens & palaces', 'forests & floods & animals', 'corn fields & villages & inhabitants'. The process is one which is not confined to female characters: giving 'forth her tears of joy' Mary is also like Albion who in the inscription on *Albion Rose* 'Giving himself for the Nations [...] danc'd the dance of Eternal Death' (E671). This is not the controlled identification offered by the workings of sympathy nor does it sound like a missionary project that prints the British system onto the world. Drawing instead on the eroticized language of the Song of Songs, this passage describes transformation in sexual terms.

Whereas Susan Fox saw the inherently metaphorical status of the female in Blake's writing as undermining its capacity to bear a positive meaning, I have argued that identities, insofar as they are open to transformation, are inherently metaphorical.[61] Metaphor is not necessarily, as Sontag argues, a failure to confront the reality of disease. The impurity of the harlot is also the positive impurity of poetry whose layered meanings are the traces left by successive readers. It is this impurity that makes it impossible to circumscribe the meanings and the contexts of words. Kristeva's 1982 *Powers of Horror* describes impurity as central to poetry: 'To Platonic *death*, which owned [...] the state of purity, Aristotle opposed the act of *poetic purification* – in itself an impure process that protects from the abject only by dint of being immersed in it.'[62] Kristeva welcomes impurity because her linguistic model derives from Bakhtin who values the ability of language to reveal the 'socially heteroglot multiplicity of its names, definitions and value judgements'.[63] For Bakhtin the 'poetic image narrowly conceived' preserves its ' "virginal," still "unuttered" nature'. But Blake's poetry is not 'virginal'; the words he uses bring with them the dirt and the noise of the city. Thompson's 1978 essay is still notable for its insistence that writing poetry allows

Blake to change the meanings of the words he uses. Blake's attack on the categorization of moral discourse operates through an impure language: in this sense, at least, the harlot's curse is in the end a blessing.

Notes

1. See Michael Phillips, *William Blake: The Creation of the Songs, from Manuscript to Illuminated Printing* (London: British Library, 2000), pp. 64–6.
2. E. P. Thompson, 'London', in *Interpreting Blake: Essays Selected and Edited by Michael Phillips* (Cambridge: Cambridge University Press, 1978), pp. 5–31 (p. 23).
3. See Susan Wolfson, 'The Strange Difference of Female "Experience"', in *Women Reading William Blake,* ed. by H. Bruder (Basingstoke: Palgrave Macmillan, 2007), pp. 261–9 (p. 267).
4. Anne K. Mellor, 'Blake, Gender and Imperial Ideology: A Response', in *Blake, Politics, and History*, ed. by Jackie DiSalvo, G. A. Rosso, and Christopher Z. Hobson (New York: Garland, 1998), pp. 350–3 (pp. 350, 351).
5. Robert Essick, 'William Blake's "Female Will" and its Biographical Context', *Studies in English Literature, 1500–1900*, 31 (1991), pp. 615–30 (p. 617).
6. Percy Bysshe Shelley, 'Mont Blanc', in *The Major Works*, ed. by Zachary Leader and Michael O'Neill (Oxford: Oxford University Press, 2003), ll. 80–1, p. 122.
7. On the harlot in eighteenth-century culture, see Laura Rosenthal, *Infamous Commerce: Prostitution in Eighteenth-Century British Literature and Culture* (Ithaca, NY: Cornell University Press, 2006). For a historical account of prostitution, see Tony Henderson, *Disorderly Women in Eighteenth-Century London: Prostitution and Control in the Metropolis 1730–1830* (Harlow: Pearson Education, 1999).
8. John Milton, *Paradise Lost*, ed. by Alastair Fowler (London: Longman, 1968; repr. 1971), iv. 750, 765–76.
9. Dustin Griffin, *Regaining Paradise: Milton and the Eighteenth Century* (Cambridge: Cambridge University Press, 1986), pp. 126, 125.
10. Phillips, p. 33.
11. *Ibid.*, pp. 55–7.
12. See, for example, Leopold Damrosch, Jr, *Symbol and Truth in Blake's Myth* (Princeton, NJ: Princeton University Press, 1980).
13. For the association of Blake's mother with a Moravian band, see Keri Davies, 'William Blake's Mother: A New Identification', *Blake: An Illustrated Quarterly*, 33 (1999), 36–50. On Moravian sexual cultures, see Craig D. Atwood, 'Sleeping in the Arms of Jesus: Sanctifying Sexuality in the Eighteenth-Century Moravian Church', *Journal of the History of Sexuality*, 8 (1997), 25–51.
14. [Martin Madan], *Thelyphthora; or, a Treatise on Female Ruin, in its Causes, Effects, Consequences, Prevention*, 3 vols, 2nd edn (London: 1781), i, 13. This statement is also included in the two-volume first edition of the previous year.
15. See Felicity A. Nussbaum, 'Polygamy, Pamela, and the Prerogative of Empire', in *The Consumption of Culture, 1600–1800: Image, Object, Text*, ed. by Ann Bermingham and John Brewer (London: Routledge, 1995), pp. 217–36 (p. 226).

16. Susan Matthews, 'Blake, Hayley and the History of Sexuality', in *Blake, Nation and Empire*, ed. by Steve Clark and David Worrall (Basingstoke: Palgrave Macmillan, 2006), pp. 83–101.
17. Madan, i, 171 and fn, 172.
18. Samuel Richardson, *Sir Charles Grandison*, ed. by Jocelyn Harris (Oxford: Oxford University Press, 1986), p. 67.
19. Mary Hays, *Memoirs of Emma Courtney* (Oxford: Oxford University Press, 1996), p. 129.
20. John Hunter, *A Treatise on the Venereal Disease* (London: 1786), p. 1.
21. Rosenthal describes how the 'SRMs [Societies for the Reformation of Manners] launched an unprecented and violent vigilante campaign against prostitution in the late seventeenth and early eighteenth centuries' (*Infamous Commerce*, p. 44). See also her discussion of the motivation of the SRMs on pp. 45–52.
22. [Anon], *A Modest Defence of Publick Stews; or, an Essay upon Whoring, as it is Now Practis'd in these Kingdoms: Written by a Layman* (London: 1724), p. i.
23. Father Poussin, *Pretty Doings in a Protestant Nation, being A View of the Present State of Fornication, Whorecraft, and Adultery, in Great-Britain, and the Territories and Dependencies Thereunto Belonging* (London: 1734), p. 1.
24. John Barrell suggests that Charing Cross was on the cusp of East and West in the 1790s – the boundary had been further east at Temple Bar a few decades before. See his chapter 'Charing Cross and the City', in *The Spirit of Despotism: Invasions of Privacy in the 1790s* (Oxford: Oxford University Press, 2006), pp. 16–74 (p. 25).
25. Father Poussin, p. 2.
26. *London and Its Environs Described*, 6 vols (London: 1761), ii, p. 308.
27. Jonas Hanway, *A Plan for Establishing a Charity-House, or Charity-Houses, for the Reception of Repenting Prostitutes* (London: 1758), p. x.
28. See Donna T. Andrew, *Philanthropy and Police: London Charity in the Eighteenth Century* (Princeton, NJ: Princeton University Press, 1989).
29. Thomas De Quincey, *Confessions of an English Opium-Eater and Other Writings*, ed. by Grevel Lindop (Oxford: Oxford University Press, 1985), p. 21.
30. Cited by Alan Bewell, *Romanticism and Colonial Disease* (Baltimore, MD: Johns Hopkins University Press), p. 6.
31. [Anon], *A Modest Defence of Publick Stews*, p. 19.
32. See Harriet Guest, *Small Change: Women, Learning, Patriotism, 1750–1810* (Chicago, IL: University of Chicago Press, 2000), p. 50.
33. Madan, ii, 85.
34. Hanway, p. viii.
35. Madan, ii, 86–7.
36. Samuel Richardson, *Clarissa; or, the History of a Young Lady*, 6th edn, 8 vols (London: 1768), v, 345.
37. Rosenthal, p. 2.
38. Handel conducted benefit concerts of the *Messiah* at the Foundling Hospital from 1750–4, and the concerts became an annual event. See Roy Porter, ' "Every Human Want": The World of Eighteenth-Century Charity', in *Enlightened Self-Interest: The Foundling Hospital and Hogarth*, ed. by Rhian Harris and Robin Simon (London: Draig Publications, 1997), pp. 12–15 (p. 14).

39. Thomas Laqueur, *Making Sex: Body and Gender from the Greeks to Freud* (Cambridge, MA: Harvard University Press, 1992), pp. 3–4.
40. Hanway, p. xv.
41. *Ibid.*, p. 3.
42. Madan, ii, 86.
43. Zachary Leader, *Reading Blake's Songs* (Boston, MA: Kegan Paul, 1981), p. 196.
44. Thompson, 'London', p. 18.
45. Susan Sontag, *Illness as Metaphor* (Harmondsworth: Penguin, 1977), p. 7.
46. Hannah More, 'Story of Sinful Sally Told by Herself', in *Tales for the People and Other Cheap Repository Tracts*, ed. by Clare Macdonald Shaw (Nottingham: Trent Editions, 2002), pp. 130–6 (ll. 109–10) (p. 134). This poem is not included in More's collected works.
47. More, 'Story of Sinful Sally', ll. 113–16, p. 134.
48. More, 'Story of Sinful Sally', ll. 147–8, p. 135; l. 157, p. 136.
49. Anne K. Mellor, *Mothers of the Nation: Women's Political Writing in England, 1780–1830* (Bloomington and Indianapolis: Indiana University Press, 2000), pp. 19–21; Mellor, 'Blake, Gender and Imperial Ideology', p. 353
50. More, 'Story of Sinful Sally', ll. 161–2, p. 136; p. 131.
51. Katherine Norberg, 'The Libertine Whore: Prostitution in French Pornography from Margot to Juliette', in *The Invention of Pornography: Obscenity and the Origins of Modernity, 1500–1800*, ed. by Lynn Hunt (New York: Zone Books, 1993), pp. 225–52 (p. 226).
52. Hunt, 'Introduction: Obscenity and the Origins of Modernity, 1500–1800', in *The Invention of Pornography*, pp. 9–45, (p. 44).
53. Helen Bruder, *William Blake and the Daughters of Albion* (Basingstoke: Macmillan, 1997), p. 177.
54. Donald Davie, *Purity of Diction in English Verse and Articulate Energy* (Manchester: Carcanet, 1992; repr. 2006), p. 16.
55. *The Letters of William Blake with Related Documents*, ed. by Geoffrey Keynes (Oxford: Clarendon Press, 1980), p. 26.
56. See Phillips, p. 65. The earlier version 'midnight harlots curse' seems to me to achieve this effect to a lesser extent.
57. Hannah More, *Strictures on the Modern System of Female Education*, 2 vols (London: 1799), i, 203; 201, 200.
58. Thompson, 'London', p. 23.
59. G. A. Rosso, 'The Religion of Empire: Blake's Rahab in Its Biblical Contexts', in *Prophetic Character: Essays on William Blake in Honor of John E. Grant*, ed. by Alexander S. Gourlay (West Cornwall, CT: Locust Hill Press, 2002), pp. 287–326 (p. 299).
60. Thompson, 'London', p. 11.
61. Susan Fox, 'The Female as Metaphor in William Blake's Poetry', *Critical Inquiry*, 3 (1977), 507–19.
62. Julia Kristeva, *Powers of Horror: An Essay on Abjection*, trans. by L. S. Roudiez (New York: Columbia University Press, 1982), p. 28.
63. M. M. Bakhtin, *The Dialogic Imagination: Four Essays*, trans. by Caryl Emerson and Michael Holquist (Austin, TX: University of Texas Press, 1981), p. 278.

5
'She Cuts his Heart Out at his Side': Blake, Christianity and Political Virtue

David Fallon

In a letter to Alexander Gilchrist, dated 23 August 1855, Samuel Palmer recalled the political inflection of Blake's religion: 'The Bible, he said, was the book of liberty and Christianity the sole regenerator of nations.'[1] Blake's Christianity tended to sound a political note, while his distinctive version of liberty was made up of many strains. His notion of freedom, as I hope to show in this essay, also carried a debt to the ideas and language that constituted traditional republican discourse. Central to Blake's pursuit of political liberty was an attempt to marry a rejection of the ineffectual 'Yea Nay Creeping Jesus' with a rhetoric of classical, republican masculinism, albeit with increasing qualification of the latter in his later work. His texts recurrently stage a complex conflict between this republican discourse and Christian principles. These tensions are present throughout Blake's *oeuvre*, but here I will focus on *Europe, The [First] Book of Urizen*, and *Jerusalem*, in which clashes and overlaps between republican and Christian values also have implications for Blake's treatment of gender. I wish to trace in Blake's texts a developing transformation of gendered republican rhetoric, including his attempts to open positive, active spaces for women, in which stereotypically 'feminine' characteristics come to assume public significance and the vigour traditionally claimed as the preserve of the male. Blake's complex representations of gender do not simply reflect an essentialist antipathy towards women, but more often an encounter with – and struggle against – the limits of republican discourse.[2]

I can only briefly define the complex republican terms 'civic humanism' and 'civic virtue' here. These labels have been retrospectively applied by historians of ideas to the rediscovery of the classical

republican tradition from the early Renaissance onwards, often thought
to mark a decisive shift towards modern notions of liberty.[3] J. G. A.
Pocock and Quentin Skinner have examined the genesis and permutations of the modern language of civic humanism from the Italian
Renaissance and Machiavelli through to American independence. The
term civic humanism comprehends a number of beliefs, which I will
attempt to summarize here.[4] Most significantly, the exercise of civic
virtue is believed to be possible only in a republic of autonomous, active
citizens. Such political association represents the highest freedom to
which men can aspire. Virtue comprehends both relations between
citizens and the health of the individual citizen. Vigorous and selfless
commitment to the public good and opposition to tyranny and corruption are essential to maintain the republic. Civic virtue is traditionally
articulated in a language of 'manliness', with femininity and the female
associated either with domestic rather than public life or, more malignly,
with the corruption of the state. The citizen should be independent
from influence and economic obligations, bear arms and be committed
to defending the nation, preventing dependence on a standing army.
Vigilance against lures of tyranny, private interests, passivity and,
especially in commercial eighteenth-century Britain, luxury was vital.

Skinner has observed in Machiavelli, and some of his contemporaries,
a decisive break with the religious affiliations of the majority of previous
advocates of these values.[5] Machiavelli was a major proponent of a
secular civic humanism that was highly cynical about Christianity's
political value. In his *Discourses on the First Ten Books of Titus Livius*
(1531), he suggested that the problems faced by his contemporary
republican city states, especially in maintaining their independence,
originated because Christianity, 'having taught us the truth and the
true way of life, leads us to ascribe less esteem to worldly honour'. This
contrasts with the classical pagans' ardour for liberty:

> The old religion did not beatify men unless they were replete with
> worldly glory: army commanders for instance, and rulers of republics.
> Our religion has glorified humble and contemplative men, rather
> than men of action. [...] [I]f our religion demands that in you there
> be strength, what it asks for is strength to suffer rather than strength
> to do bold things.[6]

Perhaps in anticipation of his critics, however, Machiavelli suggested
that Christianity did not necessarily lead to this state of 'effeminacy',
which was 'due rather to the pusillanimity of those who have interpreted

our religion in terms of *laissez faire* [*l'ozio*], not in terms of *virtù*'. Religion could foster zeal for the nation and the will 'to train ourselves to be such that we may defend it'.[7] Despite this, it is clear that traditional Christian virtues – forgiveness, charity, sincerity, humility and so on – had no place for Machiavelli in the maintenance and defence of the republic. The seeds of this argument were to bear fruit in the civic humanism of Enlightenment sceptics, notably Voltaire, Hume and Gibbon, against whom Blake famously railed.

By contrast, writers in the English 'Commonwealthman' tradition found the values of classical republicanism compatible with a Protestant and often Dissenting affiliation. Caroline Robbins's *The Eighteenth-Century Commonwealthman* (1959) links English authors in this line of political thought, including Milton, James Harrington and Andrew Marvell, and later Richard Price and Joseph Priestley, as well as leaders and supporters of the American Revolution.[8] Blake's political beliefs have been likened to the republican positions (and often radicalism) articulated by writers associated with this tradition. In his biography, Alexander Gilchrist related Blake's political sympathies via a fictitious 'friend', who suggests his affinity with earlier English Commonwealthmen.

> He loved liberty, and had no affection for statecraft or standing armies, yet no man less resembled the vulgar radical. His sympathies were with Milton, Harrington, and Marvel – not with Milton as to his Puritanism, but his love of a grand ideal scheme of republicanism.[9]

Gilchrist links Blake with Commonwealthmen distinguished for upholding manly, independent political values, favouring religious toleration for Dissenters, calling for reform of the franchise, and resisting expansionist war. Although they tended to emphasize aristocratic and constitutional approaches to liberty, their masculine idiom and attacks on corruption appealed to radicals of all ranks, especially during the 1790s, as evidenced by the presence of excerpts from Milton, Harrington and Sydney in popular radical works such as Thomas Spence's *Pig's Meat* (1793–5).

Blake's ballad 'The Mental Traveller', from which the quotation in my title is drawn, strikingly dramatizes these gendered tropes found in republican writings. It features among the poems in the so-called Pickering Manuscript, the composition of which G. E. Bentley, Jr, has placed between 1800 and 1804, in suggestive proximity to Blake's work on his epics *The Four Zoas*, *Milton* and *Jerusalem*.[10] The ballad describes mysterious male and female figures locked in recurrent cycles of conflict, during which each dominates and drains the energy of their antagonist, before the situation is reversed. At the outset of the poem, the male child 'born in joy' and the 'Woman Old' are described in lines charged with symbolic power (E483, 484), guiding the reader beyond the opposition of the sexes into suggestive discursive domains:

> And if the Babe is born a Boy
> He's given to a Woman Old
> Who nails him down upon a rock
> Catches his Shrieks in Cups of gold
>
> She binds iron thorns around his head
> She pierces both his hands & feet
> She cuts his heart out at his side
> To make it feel both cold & heat
>
> Her fingers number every Nerve
> Just as a Miser counts his gold
> She lives upon his shrieks & cries
> And She grows young as he grows old.
>
> (E484)

The boy's crown clearly alludes to Jesus's Passion, while the woman's 'Cups of gold' suggest the Whore of Babylon and her cup of fornications in Revelation 17: 4. The latter figure has traditionally been used by Protestants to personify state religion and mystery, in the guise of Rome for the orthodox, or the Establishment of Church and State for Dissenters and radical polemicists. Although Blake did not explicitly identify the boy 'born in joy' as Christ here, for those familiar with these traditions, Blake's lines would evoke arguments that institutional religion had corrupted and enervated an original, active Christianity. The stanzas indicate that his antipathy towards the doctrine of Christ's atonement was not only a recurrent theme in his works, but also intimately bound up with notions of power expressed in conventionally gendered terms of active independence and passive subservience. Blake's use of such discourse makes most sense in relation to tensions between Christianity and the republican tradition.

The image of the excised heart recalls Paine's complaint in *Rights of Man*, Part One, that the Parisian crowd's cruel revenges in the French Revolution reflected their internalization of brutal *ancien régime* justice, exemplified by its public punishments: 'In England the punishment in certain cases is by *hanging*, *drawing* and *quartering*; the heart of the

sufferer is cut out and held up to the view of the populace.' Such puni-
tive spectacles 'destroy tenderness, or excite revenge', sundering benev-
olent social bonds.[11] Whereas Paine referred to literal and obviously
public punishment, Blake troped it into a more ambiguous process, by
which power operates insidiously. Merging the images of the miser, the
numbering of the boy's nerves and the removal of his heart with the
parasitic symbiosis between the sexes, Blake aligned the historical
narrative of his ballad with ideas common in Enlightenment historiography. He allied commerce with forces that sap the masculine vigour
associated with republican conceptions of citizenship and the body
politic. For Blake, who asserted that 'Duty to [*my*] [...] country is the
first consideration & safety the last' (E611), the patriot's crucial task is
to defend the body politic against enervating and corrupting forces.

Despite its importance to the illuminated books, Blake's sense of
republican duty has not received the attention it merits, although it
has been discussed in relation to other areas of his output. In *The
Political Theory of Painting* (1986), John Barrell emphasized the civic
humanist discourse in Blake's writings on art. Placing Blake's civic
humanist rhetoric in the context of that of Joshua Reynolds and James
Barry, Barrell noted his commitment to republican art aimed at
fostering an enlivened and democratic body politic.[12] In addition,
Andrew Lincoln has persuasively argued that Blake, to a surprising
degree, absorbed into his own works elements of Enlightenment
historiography and social theory more often associated with sceptics
including Hume and Gibbon.[13] For such writers, history showed that
great republics of liberty, exemplified by Rome, fell after the onset of
corruption, luxury and passivity in their citizens and body politic led
to despotism and selfish commercialism.

After 1688, politicians readily applied civic humanist language to the
liberties purportedly guaranteed by the mixed British constitutional
monarchy, especially in contrast to the perceived despotism of absolutist
regimes in continental Europe, especially France.[14] Political factions wishing to display devotion to British liberty claimed allegiance to the values
encoded in this rhetoric, regardless of political affiliation. Both parties in
the revolution controversy in England of the 1790s, for example, adopted
this discourse. In the October Days section of *Reflections on the Revolution
in France* (1790) Edmund Burke's rhetoric appeals to civic humanist values
of independence and virtue. He famously bemoaned the waning of the
age of disinterested and manly chivalry and noble ideals, which was now
succeeded by self-interested and commercial 'sophisters, oeconomists,
and calculators'. Instead 'the unbought grace of life, the cheap defence of

nations, the nurse of manly sentiment and heroic enterprize is gone!' Although radical rejoinders often mocked his effusive praise of the culture of chivalry as an artificial and effeminized debasement of republican values, for Burke this ideal represented a blend of traditional, classical masculine citizenship with a nascent form of the affective virtues and sensibility of modern commercial society. This amalgam nevertheless barred female political agency; Burke's portrait of Marie Antoinette suggests that chivalry also prescribed female characteristics of passivity, emotionalism and domesticity. The Parisiennes who marched to remove the French royal family from Versailles appear as 'furies of hell, in the abused shape of the vilest of women'.[15] Burke suggests that their assumption of political agency is grotesquely unnatural, a usurpation of a normally male role. His use of the discourse of manners thus places value upon softening masculine virtues rather than modifying 'natural' female character.

Mary Wollstonecraft was one of a number of writers radically to inflect this republican vocabulary, as she did in *Vindication of the Rights of Men* (1790) and *Vindication of the Rights of Woman* (1792). For a time she was associated with Richard Price's Dissenting circle at Newington Green. She was also a member of the liberal group surrounding the publisher Joseph Johnson, which included Price and Priestley among its number. Wollstonecraft was thus in contact with two late eighteenth-century inheritors of the Commonwealthman tradition. In *Vindication*, she cast Burke in an invidious role as the defender of luxury, sensualism and effeminacy rather than manly virtue. She charged that his 'politics and morals, when simplified, would undermine religion and virtue to set up a spurious, sensual beauty, that has long debauched your imagination, under the specious form of natural feelings'.[16] For her, Burke's dramatic rhetoric embodied luxurious corruption. As G. J. Barker-Benfield has noted, in the *Vindication of the Rights of Woman* her emphasis on the cultivation of female virtue and rational independence as opposed to a state of feeble lassitude, dependence and luxury also displays features of Commonwealthman rhetoric.[17] Although in a polemic on the status and education of the sexes, particularly one which attacks 'natural' notions of gender, Wollstonecraft's adoption of this traditionally male-biased republican discourse is not without its problems, the very fact that a female writer could claim these positions as her own indicates the extent to which civic humanist language saturated political discourse in England and was available for appropriation and adaptation by writers from a range of backgrounds.

The ubiquitous presence of this rhetoric during the 1790s should encourage us to consider its role in Blake's political poetry. Even late in his career, he pointedly identified his aesthetic with republicanism, complaining to George Cumberland in a letter dated 12 April 1827:

> I know too well that a great majority of Englishmen are fond of The Indefinite which they Measure by Newtons Doctrine of the Fluxions of an Atom. A Thing that does not Exist. These are Politicians & think that Republican Art is Inimical to their Atom. (E783)

Blake evidently had a keen interest in political theory. In the *Public Address*, he attributed the denigration of the arts in England and Europe to the 'Wretched State of Political Science which is the Science of Sciences' (E580). Angry annotations to an edition of Francis Bacon's *Essays* include a snipe at Elizabethan 'Machiavels' and contain lively comments on constitutional issues. Despite the negative reference to Machiavelli, much of this marginalia shares concerns with civic humanist and Commonwealthman ideology. Blake asserted that 'A Tyrant is the Worst disease & the Cause of all others' (E625), figuring despotism as the infection of the body politic's lifeblood. Additionally he mocked Bacon's self-interest and dependence upon the monarch, asserting that 'Bacon has no notion of anything but Mammon' and 'King James was Bacons Primum Mobile' (E632). Blake's distaste for Bacon's 'atheism' is politically inflected: 'If what Bacon says is True what Christ says Is False If Caesar is Right Christ is Wrong both in Politics & Religion since they will divide them in Two' (E620). Characteristically, he asserted the unity of politics and religion and opposed a citizen Jesus against a dictator credited with turning the Roman republic into an Empire.

Blake was thus to some extent familiar with theoretical republican ideas. Notably, the sceptical Enlightenment thinkers against whom he railed included several who pointedly dissociated Christianity and civic virtue. Blake regarded true Christian and political values as indivisible – thus in *Jerusalem*, 'the Great Voice of the Atlantic' questions 'Are not Religion & Politics the Same Thing? Brotherhood is Religion' (57: 10, E206). His Enlightenment bugbears saw things very differently. David Hume, Voltaire and Edward Gibbon were attracted to classical traditions of civic virtue and often described Christianity in terms antithetical to true citizenship. In *The Natural History of Religion* (1757), Hume mockingly contrasted Christian and classical virtue:

> The place of HERCULES, THESEUS, HECTOR, ROMULUS, is now supplied by DOMINIC, FRANCIS, ANTHONY, and BENEDICT.

Instead of the destruction of monsters, the subduing of tyrants, the defence of our native country; whippings and fastings, cowardice and humility, abject submission and slavish obedience are become the means of obtaining celestial honours among mankind. [...] This gave rise to the observation of MACHIAVEL, that the doctrines of the CHRISTIAN religion (meaning the catholic; for he knew no other) which recommend only passive courage and suffering, had subdued the spirit of mankind, and had fitted them for slavery and subjection.[18]

Hume's zeal for the active feats of heroes means that even the politic exclusion of Protestantism from his polemic rings rather hollow. Here he polarizes the masculine and public virtues of classical champions against the passive, private and implicitly feminine virtues of monks. Voltaire and Gibbon both made this critique, especially in relation to the fall of Rome. In chapters 15 and 16 of the first volume of *The History of the Decline and Fall of the Roman Empire* (1776), Gibbon notoriously attacked primitive Christianity for contributing to the decline of the empire. He sniped that while Christians 'cheerfully submitted' to the public benefits of the pagan magistracy, political institutions and military, they 'inculcated the maxims of passive obedience, they refused to take any active part in the civil administration or the military defence of the empire', and thus sapped Rome's civic vigour.[19] Voltaire, discussing monasticism in his *Essay on the Manners and Spirits of Nations* (1756), quipped that 'Christianity opened the gates of heaven, but it occasioned the loss of the empire'.[20] Rousseau, another Blakean nemesis in *Milton* and *Jerusalem*, favoured Spartan and primitive cultures over modern, 'effeminate' society.[21] In the chapter on 'Civil Religion' in *The Social Contract* (1762), he criticized Christianity as an otherworldly and private affair which detached the allegiance of the citizen from the political and social bonds of the state. His judgement would have grated with Blake: 'But I am deceiving myself in talking about a Christian republic; these terms are mutually exclusive. Christianity preaches only servitude and dependence.' Rousseau preferred the profession of allegiance to a secular, civic religion, separate from private faith, which would prove useful to the state, especially in times of war.[22]

Blake's verbal sallies against these thinkers are usually taken as evidence of his objection to natural religion – which is undoubtedly important – but he also targeted their common investment in classical notions of civic virtue at the expense of the affective Christian virtues. In *Milton*, the witnesses Rintrah and Palamabron abhor developments in European religious life. They complain to Los that:

> Rahab created Voltaire; Tirzah created Rousseau;
> Asserting the Self-righteousness against the Universal Saviour,
> Mocking the Confessors & Martyrs, claiming Self-righteousness;
> With cruel Virtue: making War upon the Lambs Redeemed;
> To perpetuate War & Glory. to perpetuate the Laws of Sin.
>
> (22: 41–5, E117)

With their opposition of 'cruel Virtue' and 'War' to 'the Lambs Redeemed', these lines allude to the problematic status of the milder virtues of Christianity from the militarized perspectives of classical and Machiavellian republicanism.[23] Blake seems to have been one of a number of republican writers who were seeking other ways in which civic virtue could be conceived and exercised.[24]

With the outbreak of war between Britain and the French Republic in 1793, not only did liberals and democrats find the language of civic humanism powerfully invoked by loyalists, but many radicals also found the rhetoric of active citizenship increasingly at odds with Christianity. The state clergy were instrumental to the government-led discouragement of political disputation, especially among radicals. Anglican ministers repeatedly preached against Christians meddling in public affairs. For example, on the occasion of the public fast for 19 April 1793, William Gilbank, Rector of St Ethelburga in Bishopsgate, addressed 1 Thessalonians 4. 11, 'And that ye study to be quiet, and to do your own business'. He advised the congregation to be 'content' with the perfections of the English constitution and government, recommending this over radicalism which is 'the issue of a restless and perturbed Spirit'.[25] It is easy to see how such injunctions jarred with the republican ideal of the active life. Clerical and governmental proscriptions of political dispute riled critics of the state and its church. The self-publishing linen-draper Thomas Bentley issued a pamphlet in May 1794 arguing that 'it is impossible for a man faithfully to search the Scriptures, but he must see the duty and danger of the *governors*, as well as of the *governed*'.[26] He argued that the precedents of the prophets and Jesus legitimated a Christian's active involvement in politics. If believers considered the issue properly:

> instead of forbidding remonstrances to rulers, they would say, *wou'd God that all the Lord's people were prophets or preachers to them, and that*

He wou'd pour out His Spirit upon them for that purpose. – We know that Kings, Counsellors, and Parliaments are *only* men. – always fallible, – often mistaken, – sometimes very foolish and wicked.[27]

In a pamphlet defending the right to free political debate, the quotation from Numbers 11: 29 also echoes Milton's use of the phrase in *Areopagitica*.[28] For both Milton and Bentley, a vigorous engagement with the political sphere characterized a masculine Christianity. Both writers were suggesting that the public and assertive Christian corresponded to the inspired prophet, with his divine vocation to rebuke and arouse the nation to reject its corruptions. The defensive tone of Bentley's pamphlet indicates the extent to which loyalists and the state clergy were successfully dividing religious from political values. The former, with their connection to man's eternal rather than temporal life, would surely prevail.

Blake's *Europe* echoes similar concerns to those voiced by Bentley. From the outset of the prophecy, the reader is plunged into a murky world in which masculine agency and feminized passivity are at odds. The reappearance of Urizen and the advent of Enitharmon's night both occur when the active male Urthona is subdued. Los addresses his sons:

> Again the night is come
> That strong Urthona takes his rest,
> And Urizen unloos'd from chains
> Glows like a meteor in the distant north
> Stretch forth your hands and strike the elemental strings!
> Awake the thunders of the deep.
>
> (3: 9–14, E61)[29]

The vigorous, independent and sublime voice of prophecy for which Los appeals is instead usurped by a culture of dependent relations and luxury, as represented in the response of the Sons of Urizen:

> Sieze all the spirits of life and bind
> Their warbling joys to our loud strings
> Bind all the nourishing sweets of earth
> To give us bliss, that we may drink the sparkling wine of Los
> And let us laugh at war,
> Despising toil and care,
> Because the days and nights of joy, in lucky hours renew.
>
> (4: 3–9, E62)

The illumination surrounding these lines shows a fire-headed youth, either Christ or Orc, covered with a dark drape by a female figure, probably Enitharmon. Above her head, several languorous bodies loll on clouds. Among a page of Blake's sketches, a female closely resembling the reclined figure directly above Enitharmon's head is labelled with the word 'Luxury'.[30] Judging from the lazy, sensual demands of the Sons of Urizen, Enitharmon's night seems to usher in this condition. Her 'Eighteen hundred years' long 'female dream' of Christian history has the result that 'Man was a Dream' (9: 1–5, E63), a phrase suggestive not only of emasculation but also of conditions in which the collective body of mankind is thoroughly subdued. In contrast to the Sons of Urizen, who spurn and denigrate the duty of mental warfare as they 'laugh at war' and 'despise toil and care', when Los is roused by the advent of Orc in France the language is visceral, martial, and a masculine rejoinder to the passivity of Enitharmon's night:

> Then Los arose his head he reard in snaky thunders clad:
> And with a cry that shook all nature to the utmost pole,
> Call'd all his sons to the strife of blood.
>
> (15: 9–11, E66)

Blake was reasserting the role of the prophet in galvanizing collective energies. Though often glossed as a reflection of Blake's disillusionment with republican violence, here it seems that in the red dawn Los returns to the palpable mental 'strife' and the pulsating circulation of the social body which had ceased with the advent of the 'secret child'.[31] There are of course overtones of martial aggression, but it is difficult to find the critical judgement against France that critics like John Beer and Harold Bloom have believed Blake was making. Even the conventionally negative adjective 'snaky' seems emptied of its moral baggage in favour of revivification; whereas prior serpentine images in the poem have connotations of constriction or repression, here the 'snaky thunders' indicate energy unleashed. If *Europe* was composed during 1793, Blake may have been celebrating the success of the French republican army against the invading Austrians, Prussians and *émigrés*. If so, Los's belligerent cry summons his fellow citizens from a state of lassitude to exercise an apparently martial commitment to the defence of the republic against external aggressors.

Blake's embodiment in Enitharmon of a negative vision of femininity perhaps indicates that he was courting an audience of radical republicans by adopting the traditionally gendered terms of republican rhetoric. But it seems that, like many radicals, he was anxious to develop such language in order to emphasize that this negative 'femininity' was metaphorical rather than an essential characteristic of women. By the time of *The [First] Book of Urizen*, Blake came both to use and to adapt the traditional gendering of republican rhetoric. Los again appears as the active prophet-citizen, selflessly acting on the behalf of the wider community of the Eternals, of which he is a part (5: 38–6: 1, E73). In a move typical of radical Protestant writing infused with civic humanist rhetoric, the figure of Los as the independent and devoted citizen is opposed to the authoritarian prelate Urizen. Just as in *Europe* the languid Sons of Urizen usurp the prophetic function of Los's sons, here the primeval priest Urizen is a secondary product of the prophet-citizen Los:

9. Los wept howling around the dark Demon:
And cursing his lot; for in anguish,
Urizen was rent from his side;
And a fathomless void for his feet;
And intense fires for his dwelling.

10. But Urizen laid in a stony sleep
Unorganiz'd, rent from Eternity.
(6: 2–8, E73–4)

Blake represents Urizen as an Eve figure, a passive entity born from the side of a more active, independent and implicitly male citizen, Los. The allusion to Genesis invites the reader to associate the male primeval priest with a more stereotypically feminine passivity. As if to emphasize the metaphorical nature of this gendered discourse, when Enitharmon is born from Los, Blake suggests a much more visceral and active relationship. The emanation issues from a globe of lifeblood dividing from 'His bosom' which 'earthquak'd with sighs'. The birth is characterized by 'pangs' and 'trembling', terms characteristic of existence and activity, albeit under oppressive conditions (13: 49–59, E77). The growth of the globule suggests organic life, characterized by the active verbs 'branching' and 'writhing' (18: 2–3, E78). In the illumination on plate 11 (copy A) this globe issues not from the side of what appears to be the male, but from his chest, head, back and thighs. There is a much more intimate and animated relationship between the sexes than between the poet-citizen and feminized priest. Even though the dynamic between Los and Enitharmon is antagonistic, Los, in contrast to the astonished Eternals, seeks to embrace rather than to reject his separated feminine affections. Of course, critics such as Mellor are correct to note that Blake accorded historical primacy to the male in this pairing and in the passage above the birth of the female is hardly celebratory. Nevertheless, the fact that Blake distinguishes between the births of the inert Urizen and energetic Enitharmon clearly indicates an interest in disambiguating positive and negative modes of 'femininity'. Most importantly, it affirms a crucial connection between vitally human characteristics associated with the female Enitharmon and the work of the male citizen Los.

By the time of *Jerusalem*, Blake had begun to reshape the traditionally gendered terms of republican discourse so that true citizenship was identified with Christian values, and distinguished from its classical martial variety. Los is the friend of the nation, Albion, and even in tormented isolation selflessly continues to oppose its corruption. In this work, Blake characterized Los as the founder of a city, Golgonooza, which he heroically continues to renew against the threat of decline. At the beginning of Chapter Three, Los's civic labour is described:

> Here on the banks of the Thames, Los builded Golgonooza,
> Outside of the Gates of the Human Heart, beneath Beulah
> In the midst of the rocks of the Altars of Albion. In fears
> He builded it, in rage & in fury. It is the Spiritual Fourfold
> London: continually building & continually decaying desolate!
> (53: 15–19, E203)

Los builds the city 'for the protection of the Twelve Emanations of Albions Sons' (53: 23). 'Outside' suggests a walled city which preserves the beating heart of a human community within from the cruelty and sacrifices associated with the druidic 'Altars of Albion' without. The emphasis Blake places upon Los's continuous attempts to preserve the city and its community reflects the importance accorded in civic humanist writings to the citizen's constant vigilance against seductions of luxury, corruption and tyranny. Blake elaborates further upon this in the illumination to plate 72, where two weeping angels flank a map of the world, within which spiral the words 'Continually Building. Continually Decaying because of Love & Jealousy' (E227). Love, a key term in Christianity and the New Testament, is valorized as the basis of a mutual community. By contrast 'Jealousy' is associated with the entropy of the city. For Blake the term had connotations of tyranny; the imprisoned protagonist of 'Earth's Answer' in *Songs of Experience* complains that 'Starry Jealousy does keep my den | Cold and hoar' (31: 7–8, E18). If we accept Lincoln's compelling reading of *The Four Zoas* as a spiritual history which transforms models of Enlightenment historiography, its final subtitle 'The torments of Love & Jealousy in The Death and Judgement of Albion the Ancient Man' would correlate with civic humanist historical narratives which describe the virtuous rise of free states and their corrupt and tyrannous fall (E300). Especially in *Jerusalem*, Los's capacity continually to maintain the process of civic renewal preserves Jerusalem, the holy city, in the teeth of tyranny, collapse and corruption. This commitment to renewal provides the conditions for the reappearance of the New Jerusalem at the conclusion of the poem. Los is finally celebrated as the apogee of republican citizenship, when Albion calls the Zoas to their roles in the apocalypse:

> Urthona he beheld mighty labouring at
> His Anvil, in the Great Spectre Los unwearied labouring &
>   weeping
> Therefore the Sons of Eden praise Urthonas Spectre in songs
> Because he kept the Divine Vision in time of trouble.
>   (95: 17–20, E255)

Los achieves the distinction of 'glory' or 'honour' bestowed on him by his fellow-citizens, the chief accolade towards which the republican citizen was expected to aspire.

Despite these evident affiliations with civic humanism, Blake made distinctive alterations to produce the type of citizenship he valorized in *Jerusalem*. Los's weeping, a behaviour more readily associated with the culture of Sensibility than with austere classical republicanism, strikes an unusual note, but one which exemplifies Blake's reclamation of public virtues for a society formed on a Christian basis. Throughout *Jerusalem*, Los's weeping perhaps alludes to Jesus, who wept over the corpse of Lazarus before resurrecting him (John 11: 35). Recurrently, republican discourse is given a Christian inflection. Where traditional civic humanism was concerned with ultimate allegiance of the citizen to the good of the state, Blake conceived of a much wider commonwealth. Jesus, the Saviour, and the Divine Vision recurrently appear as stimuli to Los and Jerusalem to remain active and not despair, offering a vision of a wider human community within and beyond the confines of despotic Albion. By contrast, in response to Jesus's appeal to a universal, common and fraternal humanity, 'the perturbed Man', Albion, 'away turns down the valleys dark' (4: 22, E146). He is given to petulant expressions of selfishness, backed up by martially enforced nationalism:

> My mountains are my own, and I will keep them to myself!
> The Malvern and the Cheviot, the Wolds Plinlimmon &
>   Snowdon
> Are mine. here will I build my Laws of Moral Virtue!
> Humanity shall be no more: but war & princedom & victory!
>   (4: 29–32, E147)

Albion's rejection of Universal Humanity is the source of his corruption, which leads him to sicken, make war on his own friends and emanations, and sleep passively on his death couch. He becomes subject to the illusory dominance of his daughters, and their 'Female Will', which Blake placed in opposition to the emanations Jerusalem and her daughters. The latter enable communication and the circulation of energies in the collective social body, although Blake privileged the male citizen's role in stimulating this process. Hence Los admonishes the uncooperative Enitharmon, telling her 'Man cannot Unite with Man but by their Emanations' (88: 10, E246). Critics generally concede that, although they 'stand both Male & Female at the Gates of each Humanity' (88: 11), Blake's emanations are predominantly female. But whereas Mellor has taken this as further evidence of Blakean misogyny, seeing this role as mediatory and subordinate, it seems equally plausible that the emanations in fact constitute the social body and are its major source of existence.[32]

Unlike the emanations associated with Jerusalem, Vala and the Daughters of Albion deploy their cruel virtue to contract, afflict and sever the fibres of Albion's bodily politic: plate 25 shows three females torturing the kneeling Albion. In Chapter 3 the Daughters carry out druid sacrifices on their male victim, using 'Knives of flint' to 'cut asunder his inner garments: searching with | Their cruel fingers for his heart' in order to remove it (66: 26–8, E218). Their only creation is a dark covering, like dead flesh, which renders the body of Albion sluggish and opaque to external influence. Blake's language gestures towards the republican anxiety over effeminacy and corruption, most starkly when Vala taunts that Man is 'Female, a Male: a breeder of Seed'

(64: 13, E215). But even at this point, Blake subverted classical ideals of citizenship. In the preceding lines, Vala appears as a war goddess:

> Her Hand is a Court of Justice, her Feet: two Armies in Battle
> Storms & Pestilence: in her Locks: & in her Loins Earthquake.
> And Fire. & the Ruin of Cities & Nations & Families & Tongues.
>
> (64: 9–11, E215)

Whereas Machiavelli regarded militarism as a valuable means of invigorating the republic, Blake portrayed martial virtue enfeebling and destroying the body politic. In contrast to Albion's wasting addiction to nationalistic war, at the conclusion of the poem he is inspired by the Jesus, the Divine Humanity, and recognizes his errors. His subsequent action is a corrective to his prior behaviour; he throws himself 'into the Furnaces of affliction' (96: 35, E256) – described on the engraving of *Albion Rose* as Albion 'Giving himself for the Nations' in his 'dance of Eternal Death' (E671). His actions result in the extraordinary expansion and flourishing of the resurrected body and the manifestation of Jerusalem. The conclusion of the poem exalts a selfless and generous act as true citizenship, which produces a sublime renewal of the body politic.

Nevertheless, Blake adapted rather than totally dismissed the civic humanist emphasis on the citizen's martial commitment to the defence of the polis. He again championed Christianity as active prophetic resistance, personified by Los as a true citizen associated with independent, assertive and masculine virtues, fighting to preserve the nation from enemies within and without. But aside from Blake's commonly identified commitment to 'Mental' rather than 'Corporeal' war, the martial component of Los's Christian citizenship has as its ultimate aim the preservation of the female constituents of the body politic:

> Los with his mace of iron
> Walks round: loud his threats, loud his blows fall
> On the rocky Spectres, as the Potter breaks the potsherds;
> Dashing in pieces Self-righteousness: driving them from Albions
> Cliffs: dividing them into Male & Female forms in his Furnaces
> And on his Anvils: lest they destroy the Feminine Affections
> They are broken.
>
> (78: 3–9, E233)

Whereas Los's masculine belligerence concludes *Europe*, in *Jerusalem* he protects Jerusalem and tries to reunite Albion with his feminine and affective emanation of liberty.

By reemphasizing the significance of feminine characteristics, Blake was attempting to rehabilitate what were traditionally regarded as private Christian virtues by rendering them in active language. In the proem to Chapter Three of *Jerusalem*, he defended the supposedly passive Grey Monk against emperors and the representatives of the modern Inquisition, Gibbon 'with a lash of steel' and 'Voltaire with a wracking wheel' (52: 5–6, E202). The Monk's Christian acts become metaphorically martial virtues:

Titus! Constantine! Charlemagne!
O Voltaire! Rousseau! Gibbon! Vain
Your Grecian Mocks & Roman Sword
Against this image of his Lord!

For a Tear is an Intellectual thing;
And a Sigh is the Sword of an Angel King
And the bitter groan of a Martyrs woe
Is an Arrow from the Almighties Bow!
(52: 21–8)

Similarly, Blake's depictions of Christ merge a musculature suggestive of masculine power with his performance of affective, conventionally feminine roles. When Jesus intervenes to encourage Los, he communicates vigour: 'the Divine hand was upon him, strengthening him mightily' (42: 56, E190). Blake's attempt to energize stereotypically 'feminine' characteristics recurs when he represents the Daughters of Los. In Chapter Three, they work at the looms, 'Endless their labour, with bitter food. void of sleep' (59: 30, E209), their selflessness a counterpart to Los's friendship to Albion:

Yet the intoxicating delight that they take in their work
Obliterates every other evil; none pities their tears
Yet they regard not pity & they expect no one to pity
For they labour for life & love, regardless of any one
But the poor Spectres that they work for.
(59: 34–8, E209)

With Los's daughters fulfilling this selfless duty to the life of the individual and political body and the emanations facilitating circulation,

Blake signals that male-oriented classical civic virtue is seriously flawed, serving to weaken rather than strengthen the citizen and the nation. Though his descriptions of the 'Female Will' in *Jerusalem* have received the most attention from critics, Blake made women essential to a liberatory renewal of the social body. In one instance, they are accorded a priority that subverts even the pre-eminence of Los and Jesus as agents of this process. Los tells Albion that Jesus creates woman at the Limit of Contraction (42: 29–6, E189). Not only does woman allow Jesus, the Universal Humanity, to be born, but she also enables the human body to begin to expand once more. Like the emanations' ability to offer exchange and circulation, the sublime vigour of the universal body politic is as feminine as it is masculine. While this significant role accorded to women is conceived as primarily biological, the paradox of Jesus creating woman in order that he may exist destabilizes the sort of priority which critics like Mellor consider Blake to be attributing to the male.

Blake tells us that 'Jerusalem is called Liberty among the Children of Albion' (54: 5, E203), and his epic is the story of liberty lost and recovered. He represents a complex conflict between Christian, universal and altruistic liberty, and pagan, nationalistic liberty, sustained by military aggression. *Jerusalem* describes the crisis when the former is occluded by the latter. Though speeches on the 'Female Will' voice the misogynistic side of republican discourse, Blake also attempted to undermine traditionally binary gender oppositions in civic humanist rhetoric. By making the prophet Los the heroic friend of Albion and Jerusalem, Blake was asserting that the masculine values of republicanism can be compatible with the Christian affections.

But as I suggested when discussing Chapter Three of *Jerusalem*, Los's citizenship suggests another important distinction between Blake and civic humanists. The latter, following Aristotle's *Politics*, have tended to regard the exercise of civic virtue as the self-fulfilling object of the citizen *tout court*. By contrast, Blake appears to have more in common with modern proponents of what is termed 'civic republicanism', who have argued that the activities associated with republican civic virtue are not constitutive of liberty itself, but rather of instrumental value in establishing and preserving it. The flourishing life of citizens in such a free society need not be focused on the demands of the state but produced in a context of security against oppression, achieved through the exercise of civic virtue.[33] At the conclusion of *Jerusalem*, although Los/Urthona continues to labour at his anvil, the focus switches to the redeemed Albion's manifestation and an expansive vision of the humanising universe, produced by the free converse of the Zoas. In these conditions of an unrestricted body politic, Jerusalem, liberty, is ultimately manifested.

Jerusalem suggests that Blake wished to challenge some traditional republican assumptions, particularly the classical emphasis on literal soldiership and masculinity, substituting more metaphorical warfare and more fluid and integrated notions of gender. If it is the cruelty of the Daughters of Albion that excises man's heart, it is the emanations who return its beat to the body politic. It is the voice of 'England who is Brittannia' that finally pierces 'Albions clay cold ear' and wakes him from his slumber (94: 20, 95: 1, E254).

Notes

1. The letter was reproduced in Alexander Gilchrist, *Life of William Blake, 'Pictor Ignotus'*, 2 vols (London: Macmillan, 1863), i, 303. Quoted in *BR*, p. 57.
2. Ann Mellor's account of 'Blake's consistently sexist portrayal of women' has been challenged by critics including Helen Bruder who, without simply offering apologia, have situated Blake's contradictory treatment of gender within wider contexts. See Mellor, 'Blake's Portrayal of Women', *Blake: An Illustrated Quarterly*, 16 (1982–3), 148–55 (p. 148), and Helen Bruder, *William Blake and the Daughters of Albion* (Basingstoke: Macmillan, 1997), as well as her survey essay 'Blake and Gender Studies', in *Palgrave Advances in William Blake Studies*, ed. by Nicholas M. Williams (Basingstoke: Palgrave, 2006), pp. 132–66.
3. The historian Hans Baron coined the phrase 'civic humanism' as early as 1925. Much subsequent work on the concept has been concerned with challenging and developing his argument, from J. G. A. Pocock's *The Machiavellian Moment: Florentine Political Thought and the Atlantic Republican Tradition* (Princeton, NJ: Princeton University Press, 1975) onwards.
4. For more comprehensive expositions, see: Pocock, *Machiavellian Moment*, pp. 49–80; Quentin Skinner, *The Foundations of Modern Political Thought: The Renaissance* (Cambridge: Cambridge University Press, 1978), pp. 41–8, 69–112; and John Barrell, *The Political Theory of Painting from Reynolds to Hazlitt: 'The Body of the Public'* (New Haven and London: Yale University Press, 1986), pp. 3–13.
5. Skinner, *Foundations*, pp. 131–8.
6. Niccolò Machiavelli, *The Discourses*, ed. by Bernard Crick, trans. by Leslie J. Walker (Society of Jesus) (Harmondsworth: Penguin, 1970), pp. 277–8.
7. *Ibid.*, pp. 278–9.
8. Caroline Robbins, *The Eighteenth-Century Commonwealthman* (Cambridge, MA: Harvard University Press, 1959).
9. Gilchrist, i, 329–31, quoted in *BR*, p. 58.
10. See G. E. Bentley, Jr, *Blake Books: Annotated Catalogues of William Blake's Writings* (Oxford: Clarendon Press, 1977), pp. 341–2.

11. Thomas Paine, *Rights of Man*, in *The Thomas Paine Reader*, ed. by Michael Foot and Isaac Kramnick (Harmondsworth: Penguin, 1987), p. 213.
12. Barrell, especially pp. 222–57.
13. Andrew Lincoln, 'Blake and the "Reasoning Historian"', in *Historicizing Blake*, ed. by Steve Clark and David Worrall (Basingstoke: Macmillan, 1994), pp. 73–85, and *Spiritual History: A Reading of William Blake's* Vala, *or* The Four Zoas (Oxford: Clarendon Press, 1995), especially pp. 161–85.
14. See Robbins, p. 5.
15. Edmund Burke, *Reflections on the Revolution in France* (Harmondsworth: Penguin, 1986), pp. 170, 136, 165.
16. Mary Wollstonecraft, *A Vindication of the Rights of Men* (1790), in *Political Writings* ed. by Janet Todd (Oxford: Oxford University Press, 1994), pp. 48–9.
17. G. J. Barker-Benfield, 'Mary Wollstonecraft: Eighteenth-Century Commonwealthwoman', *Journal of the History of Ideas*, 50 (1989), 95–115.
18. David Hume, *The Natural History of Religion*, in *Essays and Treatises on Several Subjects*, 2 vols (London: 1777), ii, 440–1.
19. Edward Gibbon, *The History of the Decline and Fall of the Roman Empire*, 6 vols (London: 1776–88), i (1776), 486.
20. Voltaire, *An Essay on the Manners and Spirit of Nations*, in *The Works of M. de Voltaire*, trans. by William Campbell, J. Johnson and others, 5 vols (London: 1779), i, 113.
21. For example Jean-Jacques Rousseau, *Discourse on the Sciences and the Arts* (1750), in *The Basic Political Writings*, ed. by Peter Gay, trans. by Donald A. Cress (Indianapolis: Hackett, 1987), pp. 1–21.
22. Rousseau, *The Social Contract*, in *Basic Political Writings*, pp. 223–6.
23. For this doctrine in Renaissance civic humanism, especially Machiavelli's formulation, see Pocock, *Machiavellian Moment*, pp. 183–218, and Skinner, *Renaissance*, pp. 74–6. A similar impulse animates Rousseau's celebration of Sparta in the *Discourse on the Arts and Sciences*, p. 7.
24. Blake shares affinities with those American republicans who sought to construct a modern republicanism in which the softened manners associated with commerce could fulfil a positive social role. See Paul A. Rahe, *Republics Ancient and Modern: Classical Republicanism and the American Revolution* (Chapel Hill, NC: University of North Carolina Press, 1992), pp. 249–59.
25. William Gilbank, *The Duties of Man, a Sermon Preached on the Occasion of the Public Fast, April 19, 1793* (London: 1793), pp. 12–13, 19.
26. Thomas Bentley, *An Appeal to Scripture and Reason, For the Lawfulness of a Christian's Intermeddling with Politics*, 3rd edn (London: 1794), p. 1.
27. *Ibid.*, p. 12.
28. Writing in 1644, Milton believed that 'the time seems come [...] when not only our sev'nty Elders, but all the Lords people are become Prophets'. See *The Riverside Milton*, ed. by Roy Flanagan (Boston and New York: Houghton Mifflin, 1998), p. 1019.
29. The lines from 3: 9–4: 14 lack clear attribution. For a summary of different approaches to this textual issue, see *The Continental Prophecies*, ed. by Detlef W. Dörrbecker, William Blake's Illuminated Books, 4 (London: Tate Gallery/William Blake Trust, 1995), pp. 145, 268–9. I agree with Erdman's

attribution of 3: 9–14 to Los, 4: 1–2 to a description of the effect of his call, 4: 3–9 to the sons of Urizen and 10–14 to Enitharmon. See *Blake, Prophet Against Empire*, 3rd edn (Princeton: Princeton University Press, 1977), p. 266.

30. Martin Butlin, *The Paintings and Drawings of William Blake*, 2 vols (New Haven and London: Yale University Press, 1981), II, plate no. 247.

31. For the former, see John Beer, *Blake's Humanism* (Manchester: Manchester University Press, 1968), p. 132, and Harold Bloom, *Blake's Apocalypse: A Study in Poetic Argument* (New York: Doubleday, 1963), pp. 160–1. Jon Mee has recently discussed Blakean metaphors of blood and circulation in his essay 'Bloody Blake: Nation and Circulation', in *Blake, Nation and Empire*, ed. by Steve Clark and David Worrall (Basingstoke: Palgrave, 2006), pp. 63–82.

32. Mellor, p. 151.

33. Writings questioning the extent to which republicanism constitutes 'the good life' in itself include Quentin Skinner, 'The Paradoxes of Political Liberty', in *Liberty*, ed. by David Miller (Oxford: Oxford University Press, 1991), pp. 183–205, and Philip Pettit, *Republicanism* (Oxford: Oxford University Press, 1999), especially pp. 171–205.

6
From Donation to Demand? Almsgiving and the 'Annotations to Thornton'

Sarah Haggarty

> When law offers to prescribe rules for the exercise of beneficence, or to lay its compulsory hand on a virtue, [...] it not only extinguishes the virtue; but it puts an end to all those responses of glad and grateful emotion, which its presence and its smile and the generosity of its free-will offerings awaken in society. [...] And what is worse, it is substituting in their place, the hoarse and jarring discords of the challenge and the conflict and the angry litigation.
>
> Thomas Chalmers

> The poor are by no means inclined to be visionary. Their distresses are always real, though they are not attributed to the real causes.
>
> Thomas Malthus[1]

Blake's annotations to the 1827 edition of Robert John Thornton's *The Lord's Prayer, Newly Translated* are characteristically disputatious. A comment on the title-page frames Blake's marginalia as a counterattack against the assault 'upon the Kingdom of Jesus By the Classical Learned thro the Instrumentality of Dr Thornton' (E667). This counterattack has in its sights not only an individual translator or translation, but also a 'Warlike' culture that 'will Rob & Plunder & accumulate into one place, [...] & Buy & Sell' – a description, this essay will suggest, of currents in the political economy, natural religion and evangelicalism of Blake's Britain, as much as a description of classical 'Rome & Greece' (*On Virgil*, E270). The ground contested here is the Pater Noster, which

Figure 6.1 William Blake, *Illustrations of the Book of Job*, pl. 5/obj. 7, 'Satan Going Forth from the Presence of the Lord and Job's Charity' (1826). Reproduced with kind permission from *The William Blake Archive*, ed. Morris Eaves, Robert N. Essick and Joseph Viscomi, 24 September 2007 (http://www. blakearchive.org/).

is cast, in Blake's annotated copy of Thornton, in several forms: Thornton's translation from the Greek, with explanatory notes; Blake's parodic retranslation of the 'subtext' of Thornton's petition; and Blake's 'own' version of the prayer.[2] The instability of Blake's written and overwritten parody, however, seems even to destabilize its ground, the Lord's Prayer, construed as the 'authoritative paradigm' of 'what God regards to be the "real needs" of humanity'.[3] This essay explores the vexed relationship between all four of these statements of the Lord's Prayer in the context of late eighteenth- and early nineteenth-century writings about charity. It suggests how the sixty-nine-year-old Blake's notion of the charitable gift of bread as 'due & Right' might sustain the political radicalism of his early prophetic epics, even as Blake prioritizes treasures in heaven over treasures upon earth.

Blake had a poor opinion of charity. Plate 5 of his designs to the Book of Job (see Figure 6.1) presents us with Job's gift of a loaf of bread to a beggar, bent over in thanks. Job is at this point still labouring under his misapprehension of the nature of divinity. He may be capable of charity, but he is also mindful of his own interests: holding another loaf back, on his lap, he gives on the condition that he and his wife are adequately provided for. Framed as it is by the inscription, 'Did I not weep for him who was in trouble? Was not my Soul afflicted for the Poor', his act would also seem to be motivated not by genuine compassion, but by a self-conscious wish to be *seen* to give charitably.

Matthew 6: 1–4, counsels against such display. 'Take heed that ye do not your alms before men, to be seen of them,' says Christ. 'Verily', the 'hypocrites' who do so shall 'have their reward'. Rather, Christ teaches, 'when thou doest alms':

> let not thy left hand know what thy right hand doeth: That thine alms may be in secret: and thy father which seeth in secret himself shall reward thee openly.

The right hand gives autonomously, hidden from the eyes of other men. It gives out of duty to God alone, regardless of terrestrial economy, the hypocrites' reward. Yet its charities will not pass unnoticed: just as, in verses 19 to 20 of the same chapter of Matthew, 'treasures in heaven' supersede 'treasures upon earth', so here the finite reward of the hypocrite is superseded by the infinite reward of God.

By one exegetical tradition, most scrupulously refined by Jacques Derrida in *The Gift of Death*, 'the dissociation between right and left [...] breaks up the pair, the parity or pairing, the symmetry between, or homogeneity of two economies'.[4] It is not enough, for Derrida, that one gives alms inconspicuously, rather than ostentatiously. Rather, one should give, he writes, 'without even having it known to oneself'. Derrida's gift is a free gift, a gift given without the slightest hint of calculation, and having nothing to do with 'reciprocity, return, exchange, countergift, or debt'. The offering of Matthew's almsgiver may therefore appear 'too calculating still', 'one that would exceed an economy of retribution and exchange [...] only to capitalize on it by gaining a profit or surplus value that was infinite, heavenly, incalculable, interior, and secret'.[5]

Those who upheld the freedom of almsgiving in Blake's lifetime were less scrupulous: discriminating between the relative merits of the recipients of charity, and allowing that virtuous actions could be accomplished unconsciously (a concession disallowed by Derrida).[6] So stinted are the kindnesses of these gifts, and so susceptible are they, still, to self-interest, that one might ask whether they are gifts at all. Here Blake, like Derrida, might be sceptical. But where Derrida wants to isolate a gift yet more free, Blake, I think, prompts us to question why we would want the gift to be free in the first place. Blake is sceptical not only when the terms of worldly calculation infiltrate spiritual discourse, but also when spiritual discourse denies the necessities of the world – a trait, perhaps, of Derrida's 'impossible' utopianism.[7] For what is the left hand up to whilst the right gives alms?

Blake's *Laocöon* has no truck with worldly economy, at least not in a certain sense. 'The True Christian Charity', it reads, is 'not dependent on Money' (E275). In *Jerusalem*, likewise, Jehovah's Angel tells Joseph: 'Jehovah's Salvation | Is without Money & without Price' (61: 17–26, E212). The fifth plate of Blake's *Job* unmasks a benevolence fully aware that it is more blessed to give than to receive. Job's gift, face-to-face and hand-to-hand to a beggar, means not only that the beggar gets bread, but also that Job lays up treasures in heaven. That you can get by giving, though, is not, it seems to me, the focus of plate 5's irony; rather, it is ironic that Job's charity is itself complicit in the beggar's poverty. Charity, even the direct, voluntary charity so lauded in the late eighteenth and early nineteenth centuries, was in many respects designed to reconcile 'the poor' to the inequality of their status – a reconciliation of especial importance during periods of special crisis.[8] Charity might even create that inequality: like the *Songs of Experience*'s 'Pity', it might 'be no more, | If we did not *make* somebody Poor' ('The Human Abstract', *Experience*, ll. 1–2, E27; emphasis added).

The trend during Blake's lifetime 'was in favour of "voluntary" rather than "legal" charity – and, within "voluntary" charity, in favour of less institutionalized, more individualized forms of giving'. Although a 'mixed economy of welfare' persisted in actuality, 'it came to be supposed that any charitable enterprise, voluntary or public, with anything approaching guaranteed funding was likely to fall into one or another form of abuse.'[9] This scepticism informed Edmund Burke's 1800 *Thoughts and Details on Scarcity*, which deferred charitable giving to 'private discretion'. Only when 'a man can claim nothing according to the rules of commerce, and the principles of justice', ruled Burke, did he come 'within the jurisdiction of mercy'. 'Charity to the poor' may be 'a direct and obligatory duty upon all Christians', but it is unequivocally 'next in order', he says, to 'the payment of debts'.[10] Burke thus separates the gift from exchange, and allows for an almsgiver whose moral right hand supposedly does not know what his economistic left hand is doing.[11]

The infamous second edition in 1803 of Thomas Malthus's *Essay on the Principle of Population* leavened a like suspicion of organized charity with a belief in the poor's natural indolence and prognostications of scarcity. Five loaves and two fishes, it seems, would no longer stretch far enough. In what Godwin was to call 'the most dreadful passage that ever poor printer for his sins was condemned to compose', albeit one omitted from subsequent editions of the *Essay*, Malthus wrote: 'A man who is born into a world already possessed, if he cannot get subsistence from his parents on whom he has a just demand, and if the society do not want his labour, has no claim of *right* to the smallest portion of food.'[12] He might only be saved from the extremities of hunger, continued the Reverend, by 'the pity of some kind benefactor'. Malthus celebrates charity pre-eminently for what he calls its 'purify[ing] and exalting effect on the mind of the donor', even to the exclusion of any positive effect on the recipient:

> Supposing it to be allowed, that the exercise of our benevolence in acts of charity is not, upon the whole, really beneficial to the poor, yet we could never sanction any endeavour to extinguish an impulse, the proper gratification of which has so evident a tendency to purify and exalt the human mind.[13]

For such a donor, the content of the gift, and so the needs of the recipient, become negligible. He could 'Boast of high Things with Humble tone | And give with Charity a Stone' (*Everlasting Gospel*, E518). Malthus doesn't, however, quite go to this extreme. Although, like so many of those he influenced, he raises up the affections of the donor, he also maintains that (voluntary) charity 'blesseth him that takes'.[14]

And in nurturing social unity, voluntary charity would also reinscribe social hierarchy. It is by 'the exercise of kindness and benevolence by the one class, and of dependence and gratitude by the other', writes James Stevens, in 1831, that 'the necessary union between the two grand divisions of the community is formed and cemented'.[15] Like social gift-giving in general, charity 'work[s] at once to mark social distinctions and to maintain social solidarity'.[16] Charity, moreover, is virtually always a gift given downwards.[17] A social differential has already been announced, of course, in Malthus's designation of 'taker' rather than 'receiver'[18]: even, it seems, when the poor expect nothing, living day to day, the notion that they might need support renders them robbers, even as this need sustains what Stevens calls 'the divinely-appointed basis of mutual voluntary compact'.[19]

These views, as they are refracted through *The Four Zoas*, appear peculiarly Urizenic, and as such inimical to Blake's own project. 'If you would make the poor live with temper', says Urizen:

> With pomp give every crust of bread you give with gracious cunning
> Magnify small gifts reduce the man to want a gift & then give with pomp. (80: 15–16, E355)

Urizen's naturalizing intent is contradicted by the revisions within his circular rhetoric, which imply that want is not natural, but produced. A man tellingly described, a few lines earlier, as 'pale | With labour & abstinence', should surely himself be able to afford (or else by rights be afforded) the bread that by Urizen's scheme is in the gift of the employer. Urizen's disregard for the man's children – 'let them die', he says, 'there are enough | Born even too many & our Earth will be overrun' – again recalls Malthus's *Essay*. An illegitimate infant, says Malthus, is, 'comparatively speaking, of no value to society, as others will immediately supply its place'.[20] Thomas Paine, whose views Malthus sought, explicitly, to counter, thought that poverty was not the inevitable product of natural laws, but created, through an exercise of what he called 'extraordinary violence' upon the common holdings of men in their natural state.[21] If this is the violence of political tyranny, it is important to recognize that it is the violence, too, of the Urizenic gift. *The Four Zoas*'s passage from pomp to pomp lays bare the calculation and coercion of Urizen's 'small gift', whose cunning, 'gentle violence', to use Pierre Bourdieu's terms, is shown to mask the 'overt violence' of infanticide. 'There are only two ways of getting and keeping a lasting hold over someone', writes Bourdieu, in *The Logic of Practice*: 'the overtly economic obligations imposed by the usurer, or the moral obligations [...] created and maintained by the generous gift, in short, overt violence or symbolic violence', that is, 'censored, euphemized [...] violence'. It is only ' "the way of giving" ', Bourdieu thinks, that separates one from the other. To give with pomp, then, would be 'to make [...] the external forms of the action a practical denial of the content of the action and of the potential violence it can conceal'. The 'clear connection between these two forms of violence' reiterates the connection between symbolic and material economies. For the clear-eyed social scientist, suspicious of 'the mysteries of subjectivity', this means that not only the charitable gift, but also all gifts, are ultimately reducible to an economic logic.[22] Even treasures in heaven, by this analysis, will perish.

Blake's annotations to Thornton sustain *The Four Zoas*'s nuanced critique of the gift as well as its antipathy to charity. 'Incensed at the idea of begging one's daily bread from any god', as Erdman notes in *Prophet against Empire*, '[Blake's] own prayer – or', qualifies Erdman, his 'demand', was: 'Give us the Bread that is our due & Right by taking away Money or a Price or Tax upon what is Common to all in thy Kingdom' (E668).[23] The politics of this statement could be perceived to be wilfully anachronistic,[24] and they were certainly out of step with much of the political economic and evangelical thought of Blake's contemporaries. For Malthus, and several influential writers after him, the Poor Laws were pernicious in leading men to expect charity as a right. Indeed, by discouraging self-sufficiency, and stimulating population growth, the Laws might provoke poverty.[25] Want, poverty and – according to the second edition of Malthus's *Essay* – even death from starvation, were not only natural, but also providentially ordained.[26] The 'human enactment' of laws to relieve poverty interfered with 'the laws of nature', which were 'the laws of God'.[27] The poor's 'importunate demands' for relief were drowned out by the naturalized current of 'demand' in the international marketplace.[28] Any expectation of bounty from one's superiors could lead to 'seditio[n]' and 'mob' violence.[29] It certainly extinguished kindly affections, and fractured social bonds. 'Deference cannot be expected, in men, to whom the goodwill of their superiors is a matter of indifference', wrote Sumner in 1831:

> gratitude cannot be expected where bounty is not given, but extorted; dependence cannot be expected, where the poor have been led to consider themselves as having an absolute claim, a kind of inherent and unalienable right to a portion of the property of the higher ranks.[30]

Even when it was conceded, by Malthus, in the appendix to the third edition of his *Essay* (1806), and by Edward Copleston, in *A Second Letter to the Rt Hon. Robert Peel* (1819), that those most in need might be granted relief, this relief was conceived to be conditional, rather than compulsory. The poor still had 'no claim of *right* to support'.[31] As Copleston maintained, focusing on charitable donation, 'An action to be virtuous must be voluntary.'[32] Having said this, the distinction between voluntary and legal charity remained, in practice, provisional. As Joanna Innes reminds us, voluntary relief encompassed 'bequests, charitable subscriptions, alms, and even contributions to self-help schemes', practices 'so diverse as to place a question-mark over the utility of this simple dichotomy'.[33]

Burke's distinction between 'charity to the poor' and 'the payment of debts' was to be more scrupulously refined in evangelical writings of the late 1810s, 1820s and 1830s. The Poor Laws, thought Copleston, had confused 'moral duty with the task of legislation'. There will always be poverty and distress in society, but 'that this poverty and distress, when unable to relieve itself, ought to be relieved by others, is also a Christian maxim'. Charity, when it is provided, pre-eminently by 'the clergy', must be from moral obligation only – 'that is a debt, "still paying, still to owe," for the liquidation of which no sinking-fund can ever be provided'. Man cannot be charitable '*by proxy*', for 'to throw off the care of want, and disease, and misery upon the magistrate, is to convert humanity into police, and religion into a statute-book'.[34] Copleston announces a Christian charity separate from, but necessarily supplementary to, economic and juridical action. How far his invocation of Milton's Satan supports this distinction, though, is open to question (for the Satan of *Paradise Lost*, gratitude to his Creator is a 'debt immense', 'So burdensome still paying, still to owe'). Satan's species of moral obligation is marked by political ambition and petty account-keeping, and is superseded, as he is well aware, by a properly Christian gratefulness, which 'By owing owes not, but still pays'.[35] Copleston's final appeal is to a generous voluntarism, untroubled even by Miltonic 'payment': the 'public benefit' derived from voluntary charity, he says, 'cannot be exhibited in the balance of an account'. 'Moral amelioration', he concludes, '*must* be promoted' – although in the realm of "what is", to which Copleston's purified rhetoric leaves us, public benefit, 'from its being incapable of reduction to any mechanical standard, will of course be always questioned, and often overlooked'.[36] Divorced from economy, charity may be morally desirable, but it is so attenuated as to be susceptible to extinction.

The writings of Thomas Chalmers further drew out and enlarged some of the implications of Copleston's separation between moral and Christian, and economic and juridical, obligation – that is, in Chalmers's words, between 'spiritual' and 'temporal' necessities, or between charitable 'giving' and 'political economy'.[37] Copleston and Sumner had been able, by 1820, to accommodate political economy to Christian orthodoxy, but a decade later, the new science, hijacked by the Philosophic Radicals to 'their avowedly atheistic program of reform', reared its head as a new enemy.[38] Chalmers writes, in *On the Adaptation*:

> It is altogether a vain and hopeless undertaking to legislate on the duties of beneficence; for the very nature of this virtue, is to do good freely and willingly with its own. [...] The force of law and the freeness of love cannot amalgamate the one with the other. Like water and oil they are immiscible. We cannot translate beneficence into the statute-book of law, without expunging it from the statute-book of the heart; and to whatever extent we make it the object of compulsion, to that extent we must destroy it.

In his emphasis on the freedom of almsgiving, Chalmers surely endeavours to distinguish it from what he calls in a later work, *On the Sufficiency*, the calculation and the 'heartlessness' of 'political economy'.[39] And yet political economy too advocates the free gift: charity, writes Richard Whately – then Principal and Select Preacher at St Alban's Hall, Oxford, and soon to be Drummond Professor of Political Economy – is 'fre[e] relief', the 'fre[e] bestow[al]' of 'a bountiful gift'.[40] It nonetheless remains impossible for Chalmers to conceive of a free gift apart from the motivations of self-interest. Law and love may be immiscible, but both are regulated by a 'statute-book'. To impel charity, in such a world, one must appeal pragmatically to men's spiritual self-interest, rather than their benevolence. *On the Sufficiency* proffers 'a rich harvest of gratification' for those who 'sacrifice a very few hours' in the 'precious walk of home charity'. Such, Chalmers advises the rich man, in complex tone, will purchase him 'the greatest enjoyment for the least money'.[41] The category of the free gift thus seems 'an empty set' – set apart from economics and law, and yet unimaginable in any other terms. 'The official motive' for such a separation, as Simon Jarvis maintains, may be 'to avoid contaminating the gift with the world; but we may wonder whether its real motive was not to rid the world of the gift, and so to make it possible for us to enjoy the misery of fallen life as though it were a providential harmony of interests'.[42] This is not to say that writers like Copleston, Chalmers and Whately were not in practice philanthropic: they were; but we might, now as much as then, measure how grateful we can be for the individual example that cuts across societal and legislative neglect.[43]

Blake's 'own prayer – or demand' for bread has a more obvious affinity with the writings of a previous era.[44] In 1785, William Paley's *Principles of Moral and Political Philosophy* had urged not 'voluntary bounty', but *'being charitable upon a plan'*. Paley cites 1 Corinthians 16: 2 as a precedent: 'Upon the first *day* of the week let every one of you lay by him in store, as *God* hath prospered him'. With startling historical revisionism, he then proceeds to attack the system of private property, calling, like Blake, on Acts 4: 32, and 'what is Common to all in thy Kingdom' (E668). 'All things were originally common', says Paley: 'no one being able to produce a charter from Heaven had any better title to a particular possession, than his next neighbour'.[45] A decade later, Paine's *Agrarian Justice* asked (in fact, it paradoxically 'pleaded') for the redistribution of resources as 'not charity but a right, not bounty but justice'. Individual efforts at charity were 'magnificent', but 'it is only by organizing civilization upon such principles as to act like a system of pulleys, that the whole weight of misery can be removed'. Paine's scheme nonetheless profits from the motivating and, he seeks to persuade us, the uncoercive spur of voluntarism. Relieving a man of his property upon his death in order to return it to the common fund, Paine claims, would be 'the same as if every individual were *voluntarily* to make his will and dispose of his property in the manner here proposed'. Furthermore, such justice will 'gro[w] spontaneously out of the principles of the revolution'.[46] Paine may be responding to what he sees as the 'extraordinary violence' of a prior expropriation, but he cannot disguise the coerciveness of his own designs. William Godwin's *Enquiry Concerning Political Justice*, published in 1793, which likewise cancelled charity with right, introduced problems of its own. Godwin inveighs against those 'professors [of religious morality]' who 'treat the practice of justice, not as a debt, which it ought to be considered, but as an affair of spontaneous generosity'.[47] Representing charity as the payment of debt, however, might render the gift as 'due & Right' little different from the 'debts & Taxes' of Caesarian economics (E668, 669).

Such redefinitions of charity as right, and appeals to narratives of originary commonality, were, however, not confined to the later eighteenth century. The natural rights agrarianism of Paine and especially Thomas Spence continued to exert its influence in the first few decades of the nineteenth century, and in 1817 William Hone's *Political Catechism* gave voice to the poor's demand for 'Wages – not *Alms*; Work – not *Charity*'.[48] 1817 also saw the publication of Hone's *The Late John Wilkes's Catechism* (as well as the pamphlet's subsequent, unsuccessful prosecution for blasphemous libel). Hone here rehearses the so-called 'Minister's Memorial', a parody of the Pater Noster. 'Our Lord who art in the Treasury,' it reads:

> whatsoever be thy name, thy power be prolongued, thy will be done throughout the empire, as it is in each session. Give us our usual sops, and forgive us our occasional absences on divisions; as we promise not to forgive them that divide against thee. Turn us not out of our Places; but keep us in the House of Commons, the land of Pensions and Plenty; and deliver us from the People. Amen.

The 'Minister's Memorial', writes Marcus Wood, 'takes the reciprocal generosity of the prayer formula, and transforms it to express the hypocritical interdependency central to the relationship of the briber and the bribed.' The left hand is well aware here of what the right hand is doing, indeed, one hand washes the other: these ministers are 'in charity with those only who have something to give'. Punning on the word *sop* – conjuring 'a piece of bread dipped or steeped in water or wine', 'an idiot' and 'a bribe' – and perverting mutual forgiveness into self-interested bargain, Hone's parody transforms gift relationship into corrupt contract.[49]

Blake's retranslation of Thornton's prayer likewise deploys parody to measure the extent of Thornton's corruptions of Christianity. The parody saves particular vitriol for what would seem to be Thornton's pecuniarism. As Blake retranslates Thornton's fourth petition: 'Give us day by day our Real Taxed <Substantial Money brought> Bread'. Humanity cannot be divinized as long as God's kingdom, patterned after Roman despotism, 'come[s] upon Earth first & thence in Heaven' (E669). Assuming that Thornton's classical learning is the principal target of Blake's parody, Morton D. Paley has remarked that the object of Blake's ire is 'the interconnectedness', in Thornton's writings, 'of Church and State'. 'For Blake at the end of his life', suggests Paley, 'the spiritual and earthly kingdoms were distinct, though linked, and projects like Thornton's were an attempt to blur the distinction.'[50] Where Thornton upheld Samuel Johnson's learned commentary on the Bible, and commended a classical education in *The Pastorals of Virgil* (as well as commissioning, but expressing his dissatisfaction with, Blake's woodcuts for the third edition in 1821), Blake maintained that 'The Beauty of the Bible is that the most Ignorant & Simple Minds Understand it Best' (E667). It's possible, though, that Blake's discomfort with Thornton's *Lord's Prayer* might have been sparked by its separation of spiritual and earthly, and consequent subordination of the former to the latter, rather than their blurring.

That Thornton endeavoured to separate spirit and earth is evident in the very absence from his prayer of the pecuniarism that Blake parodically attributes to him. Where Blake's parody has '<Money bought> Bread', Thornton suggests: 'Grant unto *me*, and *the whole world*, *day* by *day*, an abundant supply of *spiritual* and *corporeal* food'. To be sure, this pairing, and the valorization of the corporeal, makes little positive sense in a Blakean idiom, and may have prompted Blake to reduce Thornton's 'food' to 'Substan[ce]', and hence to the realm of the money-bought. Inasmuch as Thornton presumably seeks to express the human need for a sustenance that is at once divine and determinately actual, however, and inasmuch as bread is an 'incarnation' of 'both God's graciousness and humanity's acceptance of and utilization of th[at] graciousness',[51] Blake's parody appears heavy-handed, or, perhaps, motivated by something else besides Thornton's '*spiritual* and *corporeal* food'. Thornton, after all, makes clear in his commentary the necessity of excising the pecuniary language of debt from what should be a purely spiritual idiom. Christ's words at Matthew 6: 12 – 'forgive us our debts, as we forgive our debtors' – were rehearsed in the English version of the Lord's Prayer from Wycliffe's bible in 1390 to the Geneva bible of 1557,[52] and were incorporated, with but few qualms, into commentaries on the Lord's Prayer contemporaneous with Thornton's.[53] The Anglican *Book of Common Prayer* (1662), however, renders the line as 'forgive us our trespasses, as we forgive them that trespass against us'. Thornton's gloss is yet more diffuse: 'forgive us our transgressions against thee,' he writes, 'as we *extend* our *kindness* and *forgiveness to all*.' 'The word *debt*', he comments, would be unsuitable in a theological context, making as it does our prayer 'a *money account*'.[54]

Thornton's measured use of the word *forgive* further marks a distinction between prayer and pecuniarism, spirit and earth. Christ's language in Matthew chapter 6 is reciprocal: God forgives as we forgive. The repetition of the term *forgive*, even as there is a qualitative difference between God's forgiveness and our forgiveness, shows at once the continuity of earth and heaven, and the special alchemy by which God can render the finite, infinite. This may be said of the double use of *reward* and *treasures* also. Thornton's formulation is less certainly reciprocal: God forgives; humankind extends a more dilute 'kindness and forgiveness to all'. The breach between humankind and divinity opens yet wider when Thornton invokes God's '*uncontrolably* powerful [WILL]', which 'must prevail one way or another: either with our *will*, or against it'. This breach – which seems more the result of the projection of an essentially human despotism onto the deity, than of an essential dissimilitude between God and man – serves to reinscribe the relation of indebtedness Thornton works so hard to remove from the word of the Pater Noster.

The relationship between God and man – whether structured by the overt violence of the 'Tyrant', in Blake's retranslation (E669), or the concealed violence of the 'best friend' who, Thornton implies, nonetheless prescribes your gratitude[55] – emerges from Thornton's commentary as one of overwhelming asymmetry. God gives gratuitously and his grace is inexhaustible – 'What must be the overflowings of that good-will,' marvels Thornton, 'which prompted our creator to adapt existence to beings, in whom it was not necessary?' So humble a supplicant is man, however, that for him this gift is unthinkable. He cannot ask for a gift, even as he petitions. For 'When we deliver a Petition,' explains Thornton, 'we ought to use the word *Grant*; the word *give* is objectionable as being too familiar, and ill adapted to a *supplicant*, thus no beggar would say "give me a halfpenny" '.[56]

Thornton's determined separation of the gift from pecuniarism works by this reading to refine the gift out of existence. But in spite of this, Thornton preaches '*contentment of mind*': this prayer, he writes, teaches us 'in whatsoever state or condition of life we are placed, therewith to be *content*, for we are *Pilgrims* here, travelling to another country, our true home'.[57] His petitioner, disallowed from asking for relief even when he is in want, is abandoned, rather as he is by the voluntaristic almsgiver of a Malthus or a Copleston, to what the latter calls 'that state of discipline and trial which his present existence is clearly designed to be'.[58] Thornton's drive to rid the gift of terrestrial account-keeping is thus complicit with the very pecuniarism it seeks, ostensibly, to counter. This is because, like the exchange of commodities, the gift that cannot be exchanged – the voluntary, unilateral gift, that is – denies relation: relation between donee and donor, buyer and seller, and, decisively, economy and morality.[59] In this way, Thornton's antipathy to revealed debt, as much as his promulgation of concealed indebtedness, capitulates to the economism it denies.

Blake's own version of the Lord's Prayer, like Thornton's, resists making our prayer a money account. It asks not for the forgiveness of debt, but for the taking away of 'Money or Debt or Tax' (E669). Demanding bread as a 'due & Right', it seems too to resist the purification of the gift, or at least of charitable giving, which remains firmly within the realm of politics. To grant the orant not just the capacity to petition but to *dare divinity* allows for a gift-relationship, rather than an unanswerable, unilateral gesture. Blake's annotations still scarcely yield any coherent gloss. His "straight" version of the prayer, in particular, is poised uneasily between its variants:

> Give [*me*] <us> This Eternal Day [*my*] <our> [*Ghostly*] <own right> Bread & take away Money or Debt or Tax <a Value or Price> as we have all things common among us Every Thing has as much right to Eternal Life as God who is the Servant of Man. (E669)[60]

Hovering in '[*Ghostly*] <own right> Bread' is an ambivalence to legislation. Blake's first choice of adjective, 'ghostly', recalls an earlier parody, which insinuated that the priorities of 'Law' relegated spirit to fantasy ('The Holy Ghost [...] is Unlawful [...] Spirits are Lawful but not Ghosts especially Royal Gin is Lawful Spirit' [E668]). The revised demand for bread as 'right' seems thus dogged by the secular. Calling God 'the Servant of Man' likewise jars in the context of a sacred petition. Responding to the violence of a prior expropriation, which conceives of bread as not right but charity, seems destructively and vengefully to reiterate an impulse to domination (they make us servants, so we make them servants). Furthermore, despite Blake's circumspect framing of the self-interest of Job's benevolence, in his 'own' prayer he moves troublingly between an expression of individual need, and the needs of a community ('[*me*] <us> [...] [*my*] <our>').

Blake's prayer critiques the stinted kindness and tyrannical violence of men, and the God their petitions project. Its formal ambivalences and its ironies also trouble their ground, particularly as the Lord's Prayer can be perceived to subordinate humankind to an authoritarian patriarch (Our Father makes us servants, so we subjugate him). But the assumption that our addresses to God do not admit of demand – or what Jon Mee, in the essay to come, might call 'severe contentions of friendship' – relies on an attenuated understanding of prayer (*Jerusalem*, 91: 17, E251). The anthropologist Marcel Mauss, from whose relational notion of the gift Derrida peremptorily breaks, proposes an enlarged, 'infinitely supple' notion of prayer: 'here it is a brusque demand, there an order, elsewhere a contract, an act of faith, a confession, a supplication, an act of praise, a hosanna'.[61] Hans Dieter Betz remarks on the presence

Figure 6.2 William Blake, *Illustrations of the Book of Job*, pl. 19/obj. 21, 'Every Man also Gave Him a Piece of Money' (1826). Reproduced with kind permission from *The William Blake Archive*, ed. Morris Eaves, Robert N. Essick and Joseph Viscomi, 24 September 2007 (http://www.blakearchive.org/).

even in Matthew chapter 6 of a variety of genres: of satire, in the hypocrites' sounding of trumpets, and of comedy, in the left hand's ignorance of what the right hand is doing. There was, moreover, 'never only *one original written* Lord's Prayer'.[62] As Hone demonstrated so brilliantly in his three trials, a carnivalesque tradition of parodying has long persisted alongside sacred writ.[63] Indeed, parody seems positively encouraged by the multiplicity of genres and registers which thrive in the 'poetic tales' of the Bible itself (*Marriage*, pl. 11, E38).

And yet the petition that is also a demand seems scarcely to accommodate its own imperative, *give*. This is because demand unsettles the rules of gift-relationships, politely (and narrowly) conceived. Assured of its rights, and anticipating a return, demand might be overtly exchangist. Alternatively, in its uncompromising indignation, demand might preclude the possibility of relationship altogether. Perhaps this giving-way of giving is the point: the bread necessary to human life is not in the gift of (voluntary) charity at all. Nor, at the same time, is it something owed to us: for Blake, unlike Godwin, does not refigure spontaneous generosity as the payment of a debt. In Blake's prayer, the opposition between gift and debt remains intact, even as the gift is demanded. This demand may put gift-relationship in hazard. But without 'tension and risk', the divine gift 'would be nothing'.[64] What Blake's works suggest, I think, is that to demand a gift is not always already to have legislated for it.

I began this essay by invoking plate 5 of Blake's *Job* designs. Plate 19 (see Figure 6.2) represents an act of giving complementary to but still qualitatively different from that on the previous plate. In the later plate, what is given is not bread, but 'a piece of Money', most distinctly, 'an earring of gold', held out in the donor's left hand.[65] The line of her forearm leads our gaze on to the seated Job's right hand, laid, for the moment, on his knee. In this plate, Job's friends are the donors, and Job himself is the recipient. Their relationship is not without its dissonances: Job and his wife sit near what may be the ruins of their house, while the gift-givers stand over them. Job is nonetheless on more of an equal footing with his givers than the beggar was with him in the preceding plate. Inclining their heads, in a concave posture delineated too by the fruitful fig tree beside and above them, Job and his wife – by implication, but by implication only – open themselves to a grateful receipt.

Rather as the donor's left hand holds, but does not cement, the possibility of connecting with the right hand of the potential recipient, so, perhaps, do Blake's annotations to Thornton finally refuse to discriminate donation, one the one hand, from demand, on the other.

Notes

1. Thomas Chalmers, *On the Adaptation of External Nature to the Moral and Intellectual Constitution of Man*, 2 vols, The Bridgewater Treatises On the Power Wisdom and Goodness of God as Manifested in the Creation, Treatise 1 (London: 1833), ii, 25; T[homas] R[obert] Malthus, *An Essay on the Principle of Population [...]*, rev. edn (London: 1803), Bk iv, Ch. 6, p. 532.
2. See Morton D. Paley, *The Traveller in the Evening: The Last Works of William Blake* (Oxford: OUP, 2003), pp. 284, 295.
3. Hans Dieter Betz, *The Sermon on the Mount: A Commentary on the Sermon on the Mount, Including the Sermon on the Plain (Matthew 5:3–7:27 and Luke 6:20–49)*, ed. by Adela Yarbro Collins (Minneapolis, MN: Fortress Press, 1995), p. 369.
4. On the tradition of thinking about the gift to which Derrida might belong, see Simon Jarvis, 'The Gift in Theory', *Dionysius*, 17 (1999), 201–22 (p. 211).
5. Jacques Derrida, *The Gift of Death*, trans. by David Wills (Chicago, IL: University of Chicago Press, 1995), pp. 107, 109; *Given Time: I. Counterfeit Money*, trans. by Peggy Kamuf (Chicago, IL: University of Chicago Press, 1992), p. 12.
6. See for example Thomas Chalmers, *On the Sufficiency of the Parochial System, Without a Poor Rate, For the Right Management of the Poor* (Glasgow, 1841), p. 36, commending the secrecy of almsgiving in Matthew 6. 1–4, and p. 59, on the almsgiver's good moral example; see also Chalmers's *On the Adaptation*, p. 17, on unconscious virtue, and Derrida, *Given Time*, pp. 13, 16, on 'absolute forgetting'.
7. Derrida's impossible gift can re-enter the economy, but only after first having broken with it. It is with the necessity of initially denouncing reciprocity that I take issue, as I hold to Mauss's conception of a gift both free and obligatory; I would also take issue with Derrida's favouring of a Nietzschean genealogy of giving (see *The Gift of Death*, pp. 109, 114–15).
8. Margot C. Finn, *The Character of Credit: Personal Debt in English Culture, 1740–1914* (Cambridge: Cambridge University Press, 2003), pp. 84, 127; Joanna Innes, 'The "mixed economy of welfare" in Early Modern England: Assessments of the Options from Hale to Malthus (*c.* 1683–1803)', in *Charity, Self-Interest and Welfare in the English Past*, ed. by Martin Daunton, The Neale Colloquium in British History (London: UCL Press, 1996), pp. 139–80 (p. 146); and Michael J. D. Roberts, 'Head versus Heart? Voluntary Associations and Charity Organization in England *c.* 1700–1850', in *Charity, Philanthropy and Reform from the 1690s to 1850*, ed. by Hugh Cunningham and Joanna Innes (Basingstoke: Macmillan Press; New York: St Martin's Press, 1998), pp. 66–86 (pp. 73, 78).
9. Innes, 'The "mixed economy of welfare"', pp. 169, 140, 163.
10. Edmund Burke, *Thoughts and Details on Scarcity* (London: 1800), p. 18.
11. I take this point from Jarvis, 'The Gift in Theory', p. 210.
12. William Godwin, *Of Population: An Enquiry Concerning the Power of Increase in the Numbers of Mankind, Being an Answer to Mr Malthus's Essay on That Subject* (London: 1820), p. 554, in *The Making of the Modern World*, available at: <http://galenet.galegroup.com/servlet/MOME?af=RN&ae=U3606975807&srchtp=a&ste=14> (accessed 24 September 2007).

13. Malthus, *Essay* (1803), Bk iv, Ch. 6, p. 531; Bk iv, Ch. 7, p. 540; Bk iv, Ch. 9, p. 560.

14. Malthus, *Essay* (1803), Bk iv, Ch. 9, p. 563. In his attack on the Poor Laws, Sumner wrote in 1824 that, 'The effect upon the giver is certainly no better than that upon the receiver of these legal alms; and thus the most valuable part of real charity is thrown away'. See [?John Bird Sumner], 'Poor-laws', in *Supplement to the Fourth, Fifth and Sixth Editions of the Encyclopaedia Brittanica [...]* (Edinburgh: 1824), pp. 293–306 (p. 301), in *The Making of the Modern World*, available at: <http://galenet.galegroup.com/servlet/MOME?af=RN&a e=U3604534980&srchtp=a&ste=14> (accessed 24 September 2007). Boyd Hilton suggests that this entry is written by Sumner: see Boyd Hilton, *The Age of Atonement: The Influence of Evangelicalism on Social and Economic Thought, 1785–1865* (Oxford: Clarendon Press, 1988; repr. 1991), p. 102.

15. James Stevens, *The Poor Laws an Interference with the Divine Laws [...]* (London: 1831), p. 24. Chalmers's *On the Adaptation* likewise discriminates 'the free interchanges of good-will on the side of the dispenser, and of gratitude on the side of the recipient' (pp. 13–14).

16. Finn, p. 81.

17. Edward Copleston thought that, 'A poor man should not be expected to save for another – it is quite enough, and it is quite as much as we can ever expect to do, to make him save for himself.' Copleston refers his readers to Davison's *Considerations on the Poor Laws* (1817), which suggests that 'pecuniary charity' is 'out of [the poor's] province. Their own real wants forbid it; and they have not the feeling which such a sacrifice requires.' Writing in 1841, Thomas Chalmers, by contrast (and somewhat surprisingly), recognizes the 'little unseen gifts and liberalities' that 'pass and repass between next-door neighbours by an internal process of charity among themselves'. See Copleston, *A Second Letter to the Rt Hon. Robert Peel [...] On the Causes of the Increase of Pauperism, and On the Poor Laws [...]* (Oxford: 1819), p. 103, in *The Making of the Modern World*, available at: <http://galenet.galegroup.com/servlet/MOME?af=RN&ae=U3603537940&s rchtp=a&ste=14> (accessed 24 September 2007); John Davison, *Considerations on the Poor Laws* (Oxford: 1817), p. 18, in *The Making of the Modern World*, available at: <http://galenet.galegroup.com/servlet/MOME?a f=RN&ae=U3603381836&srchtp=a&ste=14> (accessed 24 September 2007); Chalmers, *On the Sufficiency*, p. 53.

18. See also Chalmers, *On the Sufficiency*, p. 64, which announces that almsgiving 'is an operation twice blest – blessing him who gives and him who takes'.

19. Stevens, p. 30.

20. Malthus, *Essay* (1803), Bk iv, Ch. 7, p. 540.

21. Thomas Paine, *Agrarian Justice* [1797], in *Political Writings*, ed. by Bruce Kuklick, Cambridge Texts in the History of Political Thought, rev. edn (Cambridge: CUP, 2000), pp. 319–38 (pp. 333, 325).

22. Pierre Bourdieu, *The Logic of Practice*, trans. by Richard Nice (Cambridge: Polity Press, 1990; repr. 1992), pp. 127, 126, and Bourdieu, *Outline of a Theory of Practice*, trans. by Richard Nice, Cambridge Studies in Social Anthropology, 16 (Cambridge: Cambridge University Press, 1977), p. 4.

23. David V. Erdman, *Blake: Prophet Against Empire*, 3rd edn (New York: Dover Publications, 1977; repr. 1991), p. 492.

24. Erdman is not quite an ally here, referring us back to a handbill of 1797 (p. 492n.).
25. See Malthus, *Essay* (1803), Bk iv, Ch. 7, p. 536, Bk iv, Ch. 9, p. 561, and passim; see also [?Sumner], 'Poor-laws', p. 294.
26. See Malthus, *Essay* (1803), Bk iv, Ch. 7, p. 539; Bk iv, Ch. 12, p. 602.
27. Stevens, p. 2; Malthus, *Essay* (1803), Bk iv, Ch. 7, p. 540.
28. See Malthus, *Essay* (1803), Bk iv, Ch. 9, p. 562; and cf. Bk iv, Ch. 11, p. 596, on the effect of supply and demand on the price of provisions. See also Sumner, on the 'demands' *of* the labourer (pp. 304, 301), and the 'demand' *for* labour ('Poor-laws', pp. 295, 304).
29. Copleston, p. 26; [?Sumner], 'Poor-laws', p. 304; Malthus, *Essay* (1803), Bk iv, Ch. 6, p. 525.
30. [?Sumner], 'Poor-laws', p. 26.
31. Malthus, *Reply to the Chief Objections Which Have Been Urged Against the Essay on the Principle of Population [...]* (London: 1806), cited approvingly by [?Sumner], 'Poor-laws', p. 300. See also Copleston, p. 97: 'The absurd notion also of a *right* to a full supply of wheaten bread must be steadily denied or disregarded.'
32. Copleston, p. 18.
33. Innes, 'The "mixed economy of welfare"', p. 168.
34. Copleston, pp. 16, 40, 102, 19.
35. John Milton, *Paradise Lost*, ed. by Alastair Fowler (London: Longman, 1968; repr. 1971), Bk iv, ll. 52 –3, 56, pp. 193–4.
36. Copleston, p. 103.
37. Chalmers, *On the Sufficiency*, pp. 43, 35.
38. See Waterman, 'The Sudden Separation of Political Economy', p. 119.
39. Chalmers, *On the Adaptation*, p. 24; *On the Sufficiency*, pp. 34, 35.
40. Richard Whately, *Essays on Some of the Peculiarities of the Christian Religion* (Oxford: 1825), pp. 77, 78. Boyd Hilton makes a more general point: 'Many [...] Christian, and especially evangelical, writers developed their views in conscious opposition to utilitarian or classical economics. With hindsight, however, it can be seen how similar the two philosophies were, besides leading to identical policy recommendations' (pp. 6–7).
41. Chalmers, *On the Sufficiency*, p. 63.
42. Simon Jarvis, 'The Gift in Theory', p. 212; and 'Problems in the Phenomenology of the Gift', *Angelaki*, 6.2 (August 2001), 67–77 (p. 75).
43. 'When he became a bishop [in 1827],' writes Waterman, 'Copleston spent every penny of his income from the episcopate upon charities within his diocese.' Sumner and Chalmers, writes Hilton, 'certainly believed in the obligation of the rich to give to the poor privately, even though they inveighed against official relief. Whately gave away about £8,000 during 1846–9, even while he was denouncing outdoor relief and the extension of the Poor Laws to famine-smitten Ireland.' See A. M. C. Waterman, *Revolution, Economics and Religion: Christian Political Economy, 1798–1833* (Cambridge: Cambridge University Press, 1991), p. 193, and Hilton, p. 101.
44. Here I focus on the affinity of Blake's writings with radical prose, to the neglect of other Romantic-period writings. For excellent studies of Romanticism (though not Blake) and political economy, see: Philip Connell, *Romanticism, Economics, and the Question of Culture* (Oxford: Oxford

University Press, 2001), and Catherine Gallagher, *The Body Economic: Life, Death, and Sensation in Political Economy and the Victorian Novel* (Princeton, NJ: Princeton University Press, 2006), pp. 1–61.

45. William Paley, *The Principles of Moral and Political Philosophy* (London: 1785), pp. 203–5. It's worth recalling here that in Early Christian practice, 'almsgiving include[d] financial contributions to funds for the poor' (Betz, p. 355).

46. Paine, p. 331; see also pp. 327, 332, 328.

47. William Godwin, *An Enquiry Concerning Political Justice, and its Influence on General Virtue and Happiness*, 2 vols (London: 1793), ii, bk. 8, p. 797.

48. See Malcolm Chase, *'The People's Farm': English Radical Agrarianism 1775–1840* (Oxford: Clarendon Press, 1988); [William Hone], *A Political Catechism [...]* (n.p.: 1817), p. 7.

49. [William Hone], *The Late John Wilkes's Catechism of a Ministerial Member* (London: 1817), pp. 6, 8; Marcus Wood, 'Popular Satire in Early Nineteenth-Century Radicalism, with Special Reference to Hone and Cruikshank' (unpublished D. Phil. thesis, Oxford University, 1989), pp. 265–6.

50. Paley, *Traveller*, p. 299.

51. Michael Joseph Brown, ' "Panem Nostrum": The Problem of Petition and the Lord's Prayer', *The Journal of Religion*, 80 (Oct 2000), 595–614 (p. 604).

52. See Finn, p. 29.

53. See for example Luke Booker, *Lectures on the Lord's Prayer: With Two Discourses on Interesting and Important Subjects* (London: 1824), for which Luke's sins, Mark's trespasses and Matthew's debts are interchangeable (p. 95). William Barker Daniel, *Plain Thoughts, of Former Years, Upon The Lord's Prayer: With Deference, Addressed to Christians, At the Present Period* (London: 1822), thought the word *debt* 'not [Improper]' to describe 'Injuries both to God and Man' (p. 164). Samuel Saunders, *Discourses on The Lord's Prayer, In a Series of Lectures* (London: 1825), needed to explain that in the context of this petition, *debt* 'alludes chiefly [...] to personal injuries, rather than to pecuniary obligations'. Spirit and world again converge, though, as Saunders adds that even pecuniary debt ought not to be treated unfeelingly or vindictively (pp. 219–20).

54. Robert John Thornton, *The Lord's Prayer, Newly Translated from the Original Greek, with Critical and Explanatory Notes* (London: 1827) (repr. as *Doctor Thornton's Pamphlet on The Lord's Prayer Annotated by William Blake*, rotographs made at the H. E. Huntington Library, California, USA ([n. pub.]: 1925)), pp. 1, 8.

55. God, writes Thornton, 'in all his dealings with us purely doth aim at our good, never charging any duty of us, or dispensing any event to us, so much with intent to exercise his power over us, as to express his goodness towards us [...] [D]oth not such a WILL deserve regard, doth it not demand compliance from us? to neglect or infringe it, what is it; is it not palpable Folly, is it not detestable Ingratitude?' (p. 6).

56. Thornton, p. 7.

57. *Ibid.*

58. Copleston, p. 16.

59. See Jarvis, 'Problems', p. 73.

60. By Erdman's typography, italics within square brackets indicate words deleted or erased or written over, or replaced even though uncancelled; angle brackets enclose words written to replace deletions, or as additions (see E788).

61. *Marcel Mauss on Prayer*, ed. and introd. by W. S. F. Pickering, trans. by Susan Leslie (New York, Durkheim Press; Oxford: Berghahn Books, 2003), p. 21.

62. Betz, pp. 356, 360, 370. Written versions of the prayer are nonetheless preceded and regulated, for Betz, by the authoritative words of the historical Jesus (see p. 349).

63. See [William Hone] *The First Trial of William Hone, On An Ex-Officio Information [...] For Publishing The Late John Wilkes's Catechism of a Ministerial Member*, 10th edn (London: 1817), p. 18 and passim; see also Mikhail Bakhtin on the sacred parodies of the Middle Ages in, 'From the Prehistory of Novelistic Discourse', in *The Dialogic Imagination: Four Essays*, ed. by Michael Holquist, trans. by Caryl Emerson and Michael Holquist, University of Texas Slavic Series 1 (Austin: University of Texas Press, 1981), pp. 41–83 (pp. 69, 74). This connection is also made by Marcus Wood, *Radical Satire and Print Culture 1790–1822* (Oxford: Clarendon Press, 1994), p. 12.

64. Bob Plant, 'Christ's Autonomous Hand: Simulations on the Madness of Giving', *Modern Theology*, 20 (2004), 547–66 (p. 559).

65. See Job 42: 11.

7

'A Little Less Conversation, A Little More Action': Mutuality, Converse and Mental Fight

Jon Mee

> A single expression, boldly conceived and uttered, will sometimes put a whole company into their proper feelings; and whole nations are acted upon in the same manner.
>
> Thomas Paine, *Rights of Man*[1]

> That God does & always did converse with honest Men Paine never denies.
>
> William Blake, 'Anns to Watson' (E615)

Those who follow Elvis Presley in calling for a little less conversation and a little more action invoke an opposition that we might have expected to find in Thomas Paine. Yet Paine himself suggests a spur to action might erupt spontaneously within a conversation, and even act upon a whole nation. Elvis's position has been reiterated of late by David Simpson, suspicious of a new lauding of conversation in transatlantic political culture. For Simpson the valorization of conversation – found in academia, but also in the various 'big conversations' on offer in the liberal democracies since the mid-1990s – is at best a species of utopianism that privileges discourse over issues of redistribution and access.[2] At worst, from Simpson's point of view, conversation is simply a form of control that wants to muffle righteous indignation with the codes of politeness. I am largely in sympathy with Simpson; not least in tracing the outlines of today's double think of 'conversation' back to the eighteenth-century culture of politeness. Where I differ from him is in thinking the history of the idea of conversation (and, I might add, its present and future) as exhausted by politeness.

For one thing, by the time Blake came to produce his illuminated books, there was an intensifying emphasis on sentiment and sincerity in the conversible world, exerting its own torque on earlier eighteenth-century ideas of politeness. For Mary Hays, writing in 1793, 'general converse' now depended upon being 'unaffected, open, ingenuous'.[3] The idea of politeness was not abolished by the emphasis on sincerity of feeling, but, as Jenny Davidson has shown, it did become more vulnerable to charges of hypocrisy.[4] William Godwin, a member of the same conversational circles as Hays for much of the 1790s, was one of those sceptical about the muffling of candour by politeness, although he came to recalibrate their relative merits in his two-part essay on 'Politeness' in *The Enquirer* (1797).[5] In terms of his ideas on conversation, Godwin was the scion of a tradition of Dissent apt to think 'collision' and conflict as part of any genuine conversational encounter, although few representatives of this tradition perhaps went as far as Blake in their willingness to risk disjunction or even silence therein. When Blake writes of conversations in visionary forms dramatic at the end of *Jerusalem*, I believe he is quite deliberately invoking eighteenth-century ideas of conversation. This essay attempts to sketch out something of those ideas, and, as far as possible in limited space, Blake's engagement with them across his career.

Jürgen Habermas's influential account of the emergence of the bourgeois public sphere makes conversation the technology that turned the opinions of private men into a new idea of public opinion.[6] The transformation took place not just in the home, but also in the new places of leisure provided by a commercial society: assembly rooms, exhibition spaces and (most famously of all) coffee houses. Supposedly anyone was allowed into such spaces, regardless of class and, once inside, or so it seemed for many foreign visitors to eighteenth-century Britain, rank was less important than what was said. Habermas's version of the eighteenth-century coffee shop may be an idealization, but it was to become crucial to the national imaginary of Britons as 'a polite and commercial people'.[7] Within this culture, conversation became increasingly figured as the key form of social interaction, 'capable' as Stephen Copley has put it, 'of accommodating serious and consequential concerns', but also offering a figure for the larger unity of interests in an emergent commercial society.[8] In Britain prior to the Revolution in France, the idea of conversation was often implicitly contrasted with French despotism dominated by monarchical authority and courtliness. Writing in 1711, Addison looked for 'an unconstrained Carriage, and a certain Openness of Behaviour' as 'the height of Good Breeding'.[9] Writing as late as 1792, Francis Grose claimed that 'provided a man has a clean shirt and three pence in his pocket he may talk as loud in a coffee house as a squire of ten thousand pounds a year'.[10] Of course, a clean shirt and three pence was not the same thing as open access, but we might also note that Grose seems to care less about polish than participation.

If this culture of polite conversation had a founding text, then it was Addison and Sir Richard Steele's *Spectator* project. They represented their essays as originating out of coffee house conversations and feeding back into them. Habermas, for instance, notes that 'the periodical articles were not only made the object of discussion by the public of the coffee houses but were viewed as integral parts of this discussion'.[11] The participatory aspect of this discourse on and in conversation is captured by Steele's opinion that 'Equality is the Life of Conversation; and he is as much out who assumes to himself any Part above another, as he who considers himself below the rest of Society', but this emphasis ought to be balanced against Brian Cowan's more recent account of the ways it was as concerned to regulate sites of economic and social commerce as to celebrate them.[12] Addison believed that 'the Mind never unbends it self so agreeably as in the Conversation of a well chosen Friend [...] Next to such an Intimacy with a particular Person, one would endeavour after a more general Conversation with such as are able to entertain and improve those with whom they converse.'[13] A polite concern for easy familiarity might mean that contention was disallowed. Swift and many others agreed that 'the Itch of Dispute and Contradiction' was inimical to conversation.[14] Here we see one regulatory aspect of polite conversation discussed by Cowan: Steele's emphasis on equality has been transformed into a more narcissistic desire to converse with friends whom one knows well, the possibilities of unpleasant collision and disagreement thereby being reduced.

The janus-faced nature of the *Spectator* essays sketched out for succeeding decades the parameters of what David Hume (contrasting it with the 'learned' world) called 'the conversable world'.[15] For Hume women were 'the sovereigns of the empire of conversation'. This empire he took to be the product of the expansion of commerce – a term often used as synonymous with conversation in eighteenth-century writing – which polished the manners by diversifying 'the fund of conversation'.[16] Conversation was widely regarded as a feminine arena, an assumption important for any analysis of Blake's representation of it. By the second half of the eighteenth century, salons such as Elizabeth Montagu's were widely regarded as a source of national pride.[17] Yet a discourse of femininity and even female presence were not necessarily the same thing as participation for women themselves and could involve restrictive conformity to a range of polite roles. Hannah More's 'Essay on Conversation' suggests that the finest contribution of women might be made through 'obliging attention'.[18] Elsewhere I've suggested that Anna Laetitia Barbauld may have grown sceptical about the restrictions of politeness operating in these circles.[19] Moving to London in the 1780s, Barbauld encountered a vibrant Dissenting culture of conversation, especially associated with the publisher Joseph Johnson, which later involved contentious women such as Mary Wollstonecraft and Mary Hays.[20] Barbauld's niece later explicitly contrasted this world with Montagu's salon:

> At the splendid mansion of her early and constant admirer Mrs Montague [sic], Mrs Barbauld beheld in perfection the imposing union of literature and fashion; – under the humbler roof of her friend and publisher, the late worthy Joseph Johnson of St Paul's Church-yard, she [Barbauld] tasted, perhaps with higher relish, 'the feast of reason and the flow of soul'.[21]

Two different cultures of conversation are identified here: one more polite and consensual, the other capacious enough to include contention and dispute. The candour of the latter was dear to the Dissenting tradition in which Barbauld was educated.[22] Isaac Watts, a key figure in this tradition, saw conversational friction as one of the most important means of human improvement: 'Often has it happened in *free Discourse* that new Thoughts are strangely struck out, and the Seeds of Truth sparkle and blaze through the Company, which in calm and silent Reading would never have been excited.'[23]

Much anthologized, including in Barbauld's own *Female Speaker* anthology, Watts was echoed in William Godwin's *Enquirer* essays (1797).[24] Godwin described his 'passion for colloquial discussion', claiming that 'in the various opportunities that have been afforded him in different scenes of life, the result seemed frequently to be fruitful both of amusement and instruction. There is a vivacity, and, if he may be permitted to say it, a richness, in the hints struck out in conversation, that are with difficulty attained in any other method.' The *Enquirer* essays are presented 'not as *dicta*, but as the materials of thinking'.[25] For Godwin, as for Watts, the clash of different opinions might produce forms of knowledge as yet unknown. It was a principle that had already been set out in *Political Justice* with even more emphasis on conflict: 'Indeed, if there be such a thing as truth, it must infallibly be struck out by the collision of mind with mind.'[26] Yet if Godwin's idea of conversation had room for collision, it was one that ought, he believed, to take place in a controlled environment. He was anxious about large mixed assemblies and political associations, worrying that where 'the sympathy of opinion catches from man to man, especially in numerous meetings, and among persons whose passions have not been used to the curb of judgment, actions may be determined on, which solitary reflection would have rejected'. Keen to distance his rational conversation from the disruptive potential of the passions, Godwin favoured small discussion groups, such as the 'Select Club' he proposed setting up in 1793.[27]

To return from Godwin and Rational Dissent to a bigger picture, the eighteenth-century's longing for conversation can be found in the emergence of genres such as 'Table-Talk'.[28] Conversation poems appeared increasingly too, defined less by a dialogic form than the easy informality of their language with an emphasis on sentiment and sincerity. Aside from Coleridge's conversation poems, perhaps the best-known example of the genre was William Cowper's *The Task*. Cowper also wrote a poem called 'The Conversation'. The opening wrestles with the problem of rules for a speech genre whose attractions lie in its openness and informality:

> Conversation in its better part
> May be esteemed a gift and not an art,
> Yet much depends, as in the tiller's toil,
> On culture, and the sowing of the soil.
> Words learn'd by rote a parrot may rehearse,
> But talking is not always to converse.[29]

In the poem that follows he attempts to define conversation negatively by offering an account of the kinds of mistakes that interrupt and disturb the smooth flow of feeling between friends. Ultimately, by distinguishing one from the other, Cowper uses conversation as a space for policing talk. 'The way of chat', to use Shaftesbury's phrase, may have been perceived in general as the way forward for a society that looked to generate its values from human interactions in an 'open' commercial society (rather than from the dogmatic opinion of churches or courts), but anxieties remained that if the gates of conversation were left open they would be torn from their hinges by a mob deemed unable to abide by its tacit rules.[30] The eighteenth century's plethora of handbooks on conversation were partly a response to this anxiety, despite the contradiction of attempting to define a form whose chief attraction was its easy flow, a point that Swift made into a joke in his satirical *Complete*

Collection of Genteel and Ingenious Conversation (1738).[31] Far from being an advocate of the conversational freedoms of the new commercial society, Swift feared that its coffee shops and clubs – and their unpolished (literally uncourtly) clientele – could not grasp the tacit forms of a genuinely polite society.

Blake, of course, wrote his own satire on the culture of conversation in *An Island in the Moon*, but with a very different object than Swift's. Where Swift derides the commercialized debasement of the classical education of the gentleman, Blake strips away the intelligibility of polite and sentimental circulation. Blake's conversational world reveals stunned silences and indignant disagreement to be an integral feature of open-hearted intercourse.[32] *An Island in the Moon* survives only in a manuscript fair copy written in the 1780s.[33] Its model may be the salon held at the house of Mrs A. S. Mathew that J. T. Smith claimed was 'frequented by most of the literary and talented people of the day'.[34] Michael Phillips suggests that *An Island in the Moon* 'is likely to have been [intended] as a drawing-room "piece" for a few friends who would share in the delight of recognizing in the "Islanders" something of those they knew, or knew of, including themselves'.[35] Even so, the target does not just seem to be individuals, so much as literary types, familiar objects of salon culture, defined, like Etruscan Column the Antiquarian, by their Shandean hobbyhorses. Moreover, the focus seems to be on the kind of talk rather than merely the question of who is doing the talking. The world of *An Island in the Moon* is not the coffee house – continually suspect to writers such as Swift for its failure to live up to standards of genteel politeness – but the informal literary *conversazione* that was a key part of the burgeoning eighteenth-century culture of sociability. This 'improving company' talk (E449), but the talk hardly flows without obstruction. The exchange between Etruscan Column and Inflammable Gass the Wind finder early on in the piece is a case in point. The pair 'fixd their eyes on each other, their tongues went in question & answer, but their thoughts were otherwise employed' (E449). The satire suggests that although polite conversation may take the form of dialogue between participants, the form does not necessarily entail the creative trade that conversation was meant to imply for most eighteenth-century readers.

The question of the role of women at such *conversazione*s is explicitly raised in the course of the satire, when Steelyard the Lawgiver embarks on a lengthy excursus on the subject: 'They call women the weakest vessel but I think they are the strongest A girl has always more tongue than a boy' (E457). The physicality of the image raises a sexual spectre.

While the culture of politeness might see female participation as a regulatory principle, guaranteeing polish and restraint, there was always an anxiety that their presence might work precisely to the contrary and provide a sexual stimulant. Too open-hearted an intercourse with women might translate into 'criminal conversation' (the technical legal term for adultery). Yet in Blake's satire Steelyard's opinion, on whatever level it operates, does not go unchallenged. Scopprell answers: 'I think the Ladies discourses Mr Steelyard are some of them more improving than any book. that is the way I have got some of my knowledge' (E457). 'Improvement' is a complicated word in this kind of context. It could simply mean the getting of knowledge, but it can also imply an Addisonian polish, and so, perhaps, Scopprell's opportunistic superficiality. In terms of the women participants, Mrs Sigtagatist does try and impose a degree of polite improvement by insisting on modesty when talking about matters of religion:

> Dont be prophane said Mrs Sigtagatist. Why said Mrs Nannicantipot I dont think its prophane to say hang Pharoh. ah said Mrs Sinagain, I'm sure you ought to hold your tongue, for you never say any thing about the scriptures, & you hinder your husband from going to church – Ha Ha said Inflammable Gass what dont you like to go to church. no said Mrs Nannicantipot I think a person may be as good at home. If I had not a place of profit that forces me to go to church said Inflammable Gass Id see the parsons all hangd a parcel of lying – O said Mrs Sigtagatist if it was not for churches & chapels I should not have livd so long – there was I up in a Morning at four o clock when I was a Girl. I would run like the dickins till I was all in a heat. I would stand till I was ready to sink into the earth. ah Mr Huffcap would kick the bottom of the Pulpit out, with Passion, would tear off the sleeve of his Gown, & set his wig on fire & throw it at the people   hed cry & stamp & kick & sweat and all for the good of their souls. – Im sure he must be a wicked villain said Mrs Nannicantipot a passionate wretch. If I was a man Id wait at the bottom of the pulpit stairs & knock him down & run away. – You would You Ignorant jade I wish I could see you hit any of the ministers. you deserve to have your ears boxed you do. – Im sure this is not religion answers the other. (E452–3)

Significantly, however, if a woman insists upon the importance of polite restraint in relation to religious matters, so does another, Mrs Nannicantipot, also deny it. Women in the satire are represented neither as simply insisting on polite restraint nor as unusually disputatious. They join in the collisions on different sides of the question with everyone else.

Although usually dated somewhat before Blake's close involvement with Joseph Johnson, it is possible that the manuscript was written later in the 1780s than is usually allowed. Certainly, its version of conversation may even reflect something of the interests and the relatively freer atmosphere found around Johnson's authors. The question of public worship, for instance, raised in the dispute between Mrs Sigtagatist and Mrs Nannicantipot became a hot topic among Johnson authors.[36] Blake need not have attended the evenings mentioned by Barbauld to experience this atmosphere. Johnson's shop, which Blake attended in the way of business, would itself have been a place of sociability and conversation, sufficiently, anyway, to have given him a sense of the nature of intellectual debate there.[37] Not that I am pressing for any exact identification of the conversations in *An Island in the Moon* with what Blake may have experienced in Johnson's shop. The conversations that make up the satire do not anyway take place at a single venue, but reflect the experience of someone used to hearing literary men and women argue about a range of up-to-the-minute topics in different environments. J. T. Smith claimed that soon after Mathew and Flaxman sponsored the *Poetical Sketches* Blake's attendance at the salon dropped off 'in consequence of his unbending deportment, or what his adherents are pleased to call his manly firmness of opinion, which certainly was not at all times considered pleasing by every one'.[38] No doubt Blakean 'Mental Fight' was not conducive to the kind of conversation expected at the Mathew salon (*Milton*, pl. 1, E95). James Chandler sees the dominant rhetorical trope of Blake's treatment of sentiment as chiasmus. Writing from this perspective, Blake was hardly likely ever to represent conversation as a form of smooth circulation or 'flow'.[39] J. T. Smith's gendered emphasis on Blake's 'manly firmness' notwithstanding, the satire does seem to imagine a vigorous site of cultural exchange, often at cross-purposes, whose disputatiousness does not preclude the participation of women. If there is a lot of empty talk, there are also creative collisions out of which several of the poems that will go on to be included in *Songs* take shape. The 'Great confusion & disorder' is productive in this regard at least (E458). Addison assumed that for conversation to progress like must encounter like. In *An Island in the Moon*, Blake represents a much more disputatious conversational scene.

Conflictual engagement rather than the smooth substitutions of sentiment is to be found in many aspects of Blake's illuminated books, from the complicated interactions between Innocence and Experience in the combined *Songs*, many of which, individually, are cast in the form of a dialogue, through to the rousing of the reader's faculties in making sense of the complex relations between verbal and visual in all the illuminated books.[40] There are parallels, if by no means exact ones, between Blake's rousing of his readers by way of mental warfare and Godwin's conversational idea of his texts as material for thinking growing out of the collision of minds. *The Marriage of Heaven and Hell* may be the most obvious example of Blake's continuing interest in the possibilities of conversation: the Memorable Fancies are to a certain extent a series of conversation pieces, estranged from the normal eighteenth-century understanding of the mode only insofar as their participants are angels and devils or biblical figures such as Isaiah and Ezekiel. The narrator breaks off a discussion with his 'friend the Angel', for instance, because, 'we impose on one another, & it is but lost time to converse with you whose works are only Analytics' (pl. 19, E41; pl. 20, E42). The problem here is with the failure to open up to new horizons; instead of a collision between different points of view, each is simply trapped in 'the same dull round' (*There is No Natural Religion*, E3). Earlier we have been told that Swedenborg has written all 'the old falshoods' because 'He conversed with Angels who are all religious, & conversed not with Devils who all hate religion, for he was incapable thro' his conceited notions' (pl. 22, E43). Swedenborg is effectively impugned here for closing himself off from the collision of mind with mind. The attempt to limit Swedenborgian heterodoxy into the institutionalized orthodoxy of the New Jerusalem Church may well have contributed to the disillusionment expressed in *The Marriage of Heaven and Hell*.

Elsewhere in *The Marriage*, however, Blake shows us a form of conversation that seems to reach well beyond even Godwin's conflictual model. Plate 11 describes the familiar after-dinner *conversazione*, but now with Old Testament prophets as participants. Here we do get to listen in to the conversations of famous men, as in the genre of Table Talk, but to pretend to talk to the authors of books of the Bible was likely to provoke the charge of vulgar enthusiasm or profanity or both. Possibly a source for Blake's contrarian imagination, Isaac Watts's discussion of the role of conversation in the development of the human mind had actually bemoaned the fact such a scenario was impossible:

Happy should we be could we but converse with *Moses, Esaiah* and *St. Paul*, and consult the Prophets and Apostles, when we meet with a difficult Text! But that glorious Conversation is reserved for the Ages of future Blessedness.[41]

Blake refuses to wait and insists on imagining the conversation now. For Blake, such radical reimagining of the possibilities of conversation is productive of change: 'This Angel who is now a Devil, is my particular friend: we often read the Bible together in its infernal or diabolical sense which the world we shall have if they behave well' (pl. 24, E44). From being a machine for the reproduction of society in a series of smooth substitutions, conversation here has the transgressive power of sudden inversion, sufficient to convert Angels into Devils. The 'contraries' of conversation produce a 'progression' of sorts, perhaps, but not the synthesis that might be implied either by more consensualist models of politeness or even those codes of 'rational' communicative exchange more open to collision. Cocking a snook at ideas of polite conformity ('if they behave well'), Blake suggests that the infernal conversations he attempts to initiate with his readers may continue on into possibilities as yet unknown.[42]

Both *An Island in the Moon* and *The Marriage of Heaven and Hell* seem to intersect to some extent with the conversational world of London Dissent associated with the Johnson circle. Even as Blake and his graver were marginalized by these circles, he does not seem to have abandoned the utopian possibilities of conversation, and its capacity to facilitate 'contraries' that could be productive of progress. Where does this leave Blake's later writings? Does prophecy allow room for the conversational? Possibly, if we remember the diversity of kinds of conversation and that *Milton*'s 'Mental Fight' seems, superficially at least, akin to Godwin's 'collision of mind with mind'. Where he differs from Godwin, it would seem to me, is in widening further the ambit in which these collisions are imagined taking place. Furthermore, Blake shakes off the Godwinian emphasis on mind and incorporates the conflictual passions of the body (to the point where his conversation seems open to the sexual horizon caught by the term 'criminal conversation'). Constraints of space mean I can only attend to one extended example of Blake's use of conversation, that is, in Book iv of *Jerusalem*.

Blake's years at Felpham brought him into close contact with the culture of polite literary conversation, not just via the company of William Hayley, but in their mutual engagement with the work of Cowper. His reaction to this culture of conversation seems to have been one of combative and transformative engagement rather than simple rejection. Of course, Blake's relationship with Hayley is one out of which he evolved the idea of 'fierce contentions of Friendship' (as opposed to the hypocrisy of the civility where 'Corporeal Friends are Spiritual Enemies' [*Milton*, 5: 26, E98]). The post-Felpham writing does seem to return thematically to the issue of conversation with more regularity and self-consciousness than before, perhaps prompted by the encounter with Hayley.[43] Although for many readers the epics seem to attempt to get beyond socialized discourse, never mind polite conversation, in a way that might jeopardize even the possibility of communication, they continually return to the utopian ideal of a fully social and sensual form of 'converse'.[44] In the process Blake seems to want to reject ordered gender divisions, perhaps because he identified these with the regulation of conversation in the eighteenth-century tradition. For conflict was precisely what Hume and Swift imagined female participation as a guarantee against. Does Blake reject the politely feminized idea of conversation he would have encountered at Hayley's in favour of a conflictual discourse gendered as masculine? In *Milton*, begun after his close contact with Hayley's world, he writes:

Altho' our Human Power can sustain the severe contentions
Of Friendship, our Sexual cannot: but flies into the Ulro.
                                        (*Milton*, 41[48]: 6–7, E143)

The flight into Ulro may suggest the stigmatization of sexual freedom as criminal conversation. Possibly it refers to the gendering of identities more generally, implying that Blake's conflictual model is hostile to the feminized culture of politeness. The Female Will's role in *Jerusalem* might even be seen as Blake's misogynistic response to the notion of woman as monarch of the empire of conversation. From this perspective, Blake would be guilty of projecting his frustrations at the regulations of polite conversation on to the agency of women (such as Montagu and More mentioned above).

Or, more encouragingly from a feminist viewpoint, does Blake actually reject the feminization of this discourse (often promoted by self-interested male entrepreneurs of polite sociability such as Hume and Hayley) rather than the idea of female participation as such? From this perspective, Blake is opening out the constriction of women's conversation that stressed polite modesty over the dangers of passion (sexual or otherwise).[45] Such a rejection would echo Wollstonecraft's attack on the dubious nature of any female mystique staked on conformity to the codes of politeness.[46] Certainly the Female Will seems involved in the sort of conversation that seeks to stabilize the limits of speech:

> Is this the Female Will O ye lovely Daughters of Albion. To
> Converse concerning Weight & Distance in the Wilds of Newton
>   & Locke.
>
> (30 [34]: 39–40, E177)

In these lines, the feminization of culture, calculations of commerce and eighteenth-century empiricism seem to be brought together, as they are, for instance, explicitly in Hume's ideas on conversation, but for Blake the conflation represents part of a conspiracy to prescribe restrictive limits to human endeavour. Yet 'converse' is not gendered as exclusively 'feminine' or 'masculine' in Blake and may remain open at the end of *Jerusalem* as a utopian possibility for both sexes:

> And they conversed together in Visionary forms dramatic which
>   bright
> Redounded from their Tongues in thunderous majesty, in Visions
> In new Expanses, creating exemplars of Memory and of Intellect
> Creating Space, Creating Time according to the wonders Divine
> Of Human Imagination.
>
> (98: 28–32, E257)

The idea of 'Visionary forms dramatic' has been a mainstay of Blake criticism for some time, licensing various discussions of the poem's dramatic and antiphonal aspects. Descriptions like Paley's 'oratorio' may seem to come closest to catching the tone of much of the dialogue in the poem, but Blake insists on 'converse'.[47] Here the world of ideology is made to drop away in favour of a more fully participatory possible future. The dream of freedom that the word 'conversation' offered but also policed in the eighteenth century is released at the end of *Jerusalem* towards what Peter Otto has called 'a universe of participation'.[48] Even the transgressive sexual possibilities captured in the phrase 'criminal conversation' are released from their position outside polite society's 'Moral Virtues' and participate in a world of sensual and intellectual commingling.

Something like this ending has been already prophesied by Los on Plate 88:

> When in Eternity Man converses with Man they enter
> Into each others Bosom (which are Universes of delight)

In mutual interchange. and first their Emanations meet
Surrounded by their Children. if they embrace & comingle
The Human Four-fold Forms mingle also in thunders of Intellect
But if the Emanations mingle not; with storms & agitations
Of earthquakes & consuming fires they roll apart in fear
For Man cannot unite with Man but by their Emanations
Which stand both Male & Female at the Gates of each Humanity.
(88: 3–11, E246)

In the shorter term, however, Los's vision of 'mutual interchange' turns out to be part of a conflictual dialogue with Enitharmon who sets out a contrary vision of 'Womans World' where 'god himself [has] a Male subservient to the Female' (88: 16 and 21, E247). Los has to face up to the fact – as in *An Island in the Moon* – that there may not always be the sympathetic answering call imagined by the sentimentalized discourse of conversation. Blake's sense of conversation as a bumpy ride is predicated on the idea of risk organized around the pause between utterances out of which may emerge contradiction or even silence.[49] Los's vision of 'mutual interchange' does not inaugurate a conversible world, not in any immediate sense anyway.

First, Los experiences rejection by Enitharmon. In a world of multiple perspectives, his prophetic vision cannot simply be called into being. It must struggle with competing points of view and take the risk of being transformed by them. Enitharmon's retort to Los concluded, she 'sat down on Sussex shore singing lulling |Cadences' (23–4). These cadences would seem a version of what Blake calls Beulah, 'a mentalized ideal vision of easeful love'.[50] Located on 'Sussex shore', Enitharmon may be speaking from the femininized 'empire of conversation' on offer to Blake in Hayley's circle in Sussex. Yet Blake represents it as an ideological position that contains its own undoing. Here is one answer to the problem of how freedom emerges from necessity for Blake. Once she enters into conversation, Enitharmon's words are open to Los and others to construe and answer in their own terms. 'Contrarious | to thy own purposes', as Los puts it, Enitharmon opens up spaces of discourse even as she attempts to shut them down (88: 26–7, E247). The collision of mind with mind is a form of knowledge production from this perspective, but one whose processes can operate via chiasmus, not simply from call and affirmative mirroring response. What characterizes the fulfilment of Los's prophecy at the end of *Jerusalem* is the endless productivity of conversation. Creative of space and time, rather than conforming to and stabilizing some pre-existing notion of politeness,

Blake radicalizes the polite vision of conversation as more fully open to difference than the polite emphasis on 'improvement' could allow. Cowper insisted to his readers that conversation was not just talk. Here at the end of *Jerusalem* we are offered a vision not just of Cowper unbound, but the conversational unbound also. Cowper's polite idea of consensus is replaced by a much less polite and more conflictual model of conversation.

Not that imagining this conversational plenitude should be mistaken for its achievement. I agree with David Simpson as to the duplicitous nature of much of our contemporary talk about conversation, but perhaps also we ought to remember with Nicholas Williams that the contradictions of ideology only make sense against the heuristic unity of utopia.[51] Moreover 'conversation' is not just a utopian possibility for Blake. Jerusalem is not only the heuristic form of liberated conversation: it is to be constituted out of all the conversations that have and will take place. Rather than separated out from talk, these visionary forms dramatic seem open to the ongoing excess of 'the daily murmur'.[52] Conversation operates as a metonym rather than as a metaphor in this regard for Blake. Like Ernst Bloch, the great Marxist theorist of utopian thought, Blake seeks to redeem an aspect of the everyday world that opens up towards a utopian possibility for the future.[53] The awakening of Albion in *Jerusalem* is both a product of and a prelude to conversation. Here Blake looks beyond the prudential limits imposed upon Godwin and his select friends. Even when he seems at his most otherworldly, Blake's predicates his Eternity on the ongoing reality of conversation, as in his description of *A Vision of the Last Judgment* which displays 'Paradise with its Inhabitants walking up & down in Conversations concerning Mental Delights' (E 562). Simpson is right to see that conversation is not a sufficient condition of freedom, but Blake's *Jerusalem* suggests that in its unbound form at least it will remain a necessary one: 'I am perhaps the most sinful of men! I pretend not to holiness! yet I pretend to love, to see, to converse with daily, as man with man, & the more to have an interest in the Friend of Sinners' (pl. 3, E145).

Notes

1. Thomas Paine, *Rights of Man*, ed. by Eric Foner (Harmondsworth: Penguin, 1969; repr. 1985), p. 237.
2. Simpson has raised this issue in a number of places in the context of a series of critical debates over the last decade, perhaps most extensively in *The Academic Postmodern and the Rule of Literature: A Report on Half Knowledge* (Chicago: University of Chicago Press, 1995), but see also 'The Cult of

"Conversation"', *Raritan: A Quarterly Review*, 16 (1997), 75–85, and, more recently, 'Politics as Such?', *New Left Review*, 30 (2004), 69–82.

3. Mary Hays, *Letters and Essays, Moral, and Miscellaneous* (1793), p. 199.

4. Jenny Davidson, *Hypocrisy and the Politics of Politeness: Manners and Morals from Locke to Austen* (Cambridge: Cambridge University Press, 2004).

5. For the difference in emphasis between *Political Justice* and the *Enquirer* see my essay on Godwin in *Romantic Difference*, ed. by Theresa Kelley (Baltimore and London: Johns Hopkins University Press, forthcoming).

6. See Jürgen Habermas, *The Structural Transformation of the Public Sphere: An Inquiry into a Category of Bourgeois Society*, trans. by Thomas Burger with the assistance of Frederick Lawrence (Cambridge: Polity Press, 1989). Habermas here has a lot to say about conversation in relation to the development of the public sphere, but only in his later work has he addressed more directly a definition of the term. See his essay 'Social Action, Purposive Action, and Communication', in Habermas, *The Pragmatics of Communication*, ed. by Maeve Cooke (Cambridge: Polity Press, 1999), pp. 105–82, (pp. 163–4).

7. See Paul Langford, *A Polite and Commercial People: England 1727–1783* (Oxford: Oxford University Press, 1992). The title phrase is taken from William Blackstone's *Commentaries on the Laws of England* (1765–9): see Langford, p. 1.

8. See Stephen Copley's excellent essay 'Commerce, Conversation and Politeness in the Early Eighteenth Century Periodical', *British Journal for Eighteenth-Century Studies*, 18 (1995), 63–77 (pp. 67–8).

9. *The Spectator*, No. 93, Saturday, 16 June 1711, ed. by Donald Bond, 5 vols (Oxford: Oxford University Press, 1965), i, 488. All subsequent references to *The Spectator* are to this edition. See the useful discussion of these national distinctions in Lawrence E. Klein, 'The Figure of France: the Politics of Sociability in England, 1660–1715', in *Exploring the Conversible World*, ed. by Elena Russo, *Yale French Studies*, 92 (1997), pp. 30–45.

10. Francis Grose, *The Olio* (London: 1792), p. 207.

11. Habermas, *Structural Transformation*, p. 42.

12. *The Tatler*, No. 225, Saturday, 16 September 1710, ed. by Donald F. Bond, 3 vols (Oxford: Oxford University Press, 1987), iii, 174. See Brian Cowan, 'Mr Spectator and the Coffeehouse Public Sphere', *Eighteenth-Century Studies*, 37 (2004), 345–66.

13. *Spectator*, No. 93, Saturday, 16 June 1711, i, 397.

14. Jonathan Swift, 'Hints Towards an Essay on Conversation', in *A Proposal for Correcting the English Tongue Polite Conversation, Etc.*, ed. by Hebert Davis with Louis Landa (Oxford: Basil Blackwell, 1957), p. 94.

15. David Hume, 'Of Essay Writing', in *Selected Essays*, ed. by Stephen Copley and Andrew Edgar (Oxford: Oxford University Press, 1993), p. 1.

16. Hume, 'Of Essay Writing', p. 3, and 'Of Refinement in the Arts', p. 169. On the identification of 'commerce' and 'conversation', see Copley 'Commerce, Conversation and Politeness'. Swift, like many others, agreed with Hume on this score at least: 'If there were no other Use in the Conversation of Ladies, it is sufficient that it would lay a restraint upon those odious Topics of Immodesty and Indecencies, into which the Rudeness of our Northern Genius is also apt to fall.' 'Hints', p. 95.

17. See Harriet Guest, 'Bluestocking Feminism', *Huntington Library Quarterly*, 65 (2002), 59–80, Emma Major, 'The Politics of Sociability: Public Dimensions of the Bluestocking Millennium', in *ibid.*, 175–92, and Elizabeth Eger ' "The noblest commerce of mankind": Conversation and Community in the Bluestocking Circle', in *Women and Enlightenment: A Comparative History*, ed. by Barbara Taylor and Sarah Knott (London: Palgrave, 2005), pp. 208–305.

18. More, 'Thoughts on Conversation', in *Essays on Various Subjects, Principally Designed For Young Ladies* (London: 1777), p. 61.

19. See the discussion in Mee, ' "Severe Contentions" ', pp. 28–9.

20. That is not to say that Barbauld did not sometimes find this atmosphere a little too far from politeness for her own comfort. Invited in 1804 to join in a project for a women's journal by Maria Edgeworth, Barbauld replied: 'Mrs Hannah More would not write along with you or me, and we should probably hesitate at joining Miss Hays, or if she were living, Mrs Godwin' ('30 August 1804', in Anna Letitia Le Breton, *Memoir of Mrs Barbauld* (London: 1874), p. 39).

21. *Works*, i, xxxi.

22. See Daniel E. White's excellent account in his *Early Romanticism and Religious Dissent* (Cambridge: Cambridge University Press, 2006).

23. Isaac Watts, *Improvement of the Mind; or, A Supplement to the Art of Logick* (London: 1741), p. 43. The book remained in print until well into the nineteenth century.

24. See 'On Conversation from Watts', in Barbauld's *The Female Speaker* (London: 1811), pp. 79–80.

25. *Political and Philosophical Writings of William Godwin*, ed. by Mark Philp, 7 vols (London: Pickering & Chatto, 1993), v: *Educational and Literary Writings*, ed. by Pamela Clemit, p. 78.

26. Godwin, III, 15.

27. Godwin II, 133. On his select clubs, see William St Clair, *The Godwins and the Shelleys: The Biography of a Family* (London: Faber and Faber, 1989), pp. 91–4.

28. On the development of the genre, see F. P. Wilson, 'Table Talk', *Huntington Library Quarterly*, 4 (1940), 27–46.

29. 'Conversation', in *Poems by William Cowper, of the Inner Temple* (London: 1782), p. 212.

30. Anthony Ashley Cooper, Third Earl of Shaftesbury, *Characteristics of Men, Manners, Opinions, Times*, ed. by Lawrence E. Klein (Cambridge: Cambridge University Press, 1999), p. 380. Shaftesbury himself was far from keen either on the commercial or feminine aspects of eighteenth-century culture.

31. Swift, *A Complete System*, in *A Proposal for Correcting the English Tongue*, p. 106. On eighteenth-century handbooks of conversation, see Peter Burke, *The Art of Conversation* (Cambridge: Polity Press, 1993) and Leland E. Warren, 'Turning Reality Round Together: Guides to Conversation in Eighteenth-Century England', *Eighteenth-Century Life*, 8 (1983), 65–87

32. I take the phrase 'open-hearted intercourse' from James Chandler's 'Moving Accidents: the Emergence of Sentimental Probablity', in *The Age of Cultural Revolutions: Britain and France, 1750–1820*, ed. by Colin Jones and Dror Wahrman (Berkeley, Los Angeles, London: University of California Press, 2002), p. 141.

33. Michael Phillips suggests it was written 'intermittently between 1782 and 1785, or perhaps even later'. See his 'Introduction', in William Blake, *An Island in the Moon: A Facsimile of the Manuscript*, introduced, transcribed and annotated by Michael Phillips (Cambridge: Cambridge University Press in Association with the Institute of Traditional Science, 1987), pp. 3–26 (p. 6).

34. See Philips, p. 7, and J. T. Smith, *Nollekens and his Times*, 2 vols (London: 1828), ii, 455.

35. Phillips, p. 6

36. Although it was a matter of debate in such circles earlier, the controversy did not really become public until 1791 with the publication of the first edition of Gilbert Wakefield's *Enquiry into the Expediency of Public or Social Worship* (London: 1791): see the discussion in Mee, *Romanticism, Enthusiasm, and Regulation: Poetics and the Policing of Culture in the Romantic Period* (Oxford: Oxford University Press, 2003), pp. 201–3, on the responses of Barbauld and Priestley. Mary Hays joined the controversy with *Cursory Remarks on an Enquiry into the Expediency of Public or Social Worship* (London: 1791) written under the pseudonym Eusabia.

37. Johnson was Blake's main employer from 1779 to 1786, but 1787 was the year when – through the good offices of Fuseli – their professional relationship intensified: see G. E. Bentley, Jr, *The Stranger from Paradise: A Biography of William Blake* (New Haven and London: Yale University Press, 2001), p. 108. Gilchrist's biography identified Johnson's shop – 'booksellers' shops were places of resort then with the literary' – as the place where Blake encountered Johnson's 'coterie': see *BR*, p. 55. The sociability surrounding Johnson's shop – rather than his famous dinners in the room above – has not been much discussed, even in the two monographs devoted to Johnson: G. P. Tyson, *Joseph Johnson: A Liberal Publisher* (Iowa City: University of Iowa Press, 1979) and Helen Braithwaite, *Romanticism, Publishing and Dissent: Joseph Johnson and the Cause of Liberty* (London: Palgrave, 2003), which focus mainly on the publications, but see Janowitz, 'Amiable and radical sociability', pp. 71–2.

38. *Nollekens*, ii, 456.

39. James Chandler, 'Blake and the Syntax of Sentiment: An Essay on 'Blaking Understanding', in *Blake, Nation Empire*, ed. Steve Clark and David Worrall (Palgrave Macmillan: Basingstoke, 2006), pp. 103–18 (p. 112). On the identification between conversational exchange and literary production as a form of 'flow', see Clifford Siskin, *The Work of Writing: Literature and Social Change in Britain 1700–1830* (Baltimore and London: Johns Hopkins University Press, 1998), especially pp. 163–70

40. For a discussion of one example of Blake's resistance to smooth substitutions, see my 'Bloody Blake: Nation and Circulation', in *Blake, Nation and Empire*, pp. 63–82.

41. Watts, p. 41.

42. See the discussion of critiques of Habermas's assumptions about what constitutes a 'proper' or 'rational' statement in Nicholas M. Williams, *Ideology and Utopia in the Poetry of William Blake* (Cambridge: Cambridge University Press, 1998), pp. 197–9.

43. Williams, p. 203, notes references to 'converse' recur throughout Book iv of *Jerusalem* with their frequency increasing as the poem nears its climax.

44. Morton D. Paley writes that it is in 'the quality of threatening to break through the forms of expression, through myth, through language itself, that Blake's most characteristic sublimity exists': see *Continuing City: William Blake's Jerusalem* (Oxford: Oxford University Press, 1983), p. 138.
45. Although the essays in *The Spectator*, for instance, are often consciously oriented to the idea of female participation in the sphere of polite conversation, they also betray a constant anxiety that their presence may license gallantry and other forms of sexual activity that distract from proper 'commerce' in both the senses of business and conversation.
46. For a reading of the Female Will in terms of Wollstonecraft's critique, see Williams, pp. 78–86. See also Davidson's *Hypocrisy and the Politics of Politeness*, p. 79, for a useful discussion of Wollstonecraft's attacks on 'modesty as a system of dissimulation, arguing that politeness oppresses both women and the politically disenfranchised working classes'.
47. Paley, p. 293.
48. Peter Otto, *Constructive Vision and Visionary Deconstruction: Los, Eternity, and the Productions of Time in the Later Poetry of William Blake* (Oxford: Oxford University Press, 1991), p. 14.
49. On the role of this 'pause' between utterances as constitutive of conversation, see Maurice Blanchot, *The Infinite Conversation*, trans. and forwd by Susan Hanson (Minneapolis and London: University of Minnesota Press, 1993), pp. 75–9.
50. Williams, p. 5.
51. *Ibid.*, p. 26.
52. See Michel de Certeau, *The Capture of Speech and Other Political Writings* (Minneapolis and London: University of Minnesota Press, 1997), p. 96.
53. See the discussion of this aspect of Bloch's work in Williams, pp. 28–9.

8
Shadows in the Cave: Refocusing Vision in Blake's Creation Myth

Sibylle Erle

In his annotations to Joshua Reynolds's *Discourses on Art*, Blake wrote that 'Men who have been Educated with Works of Venetian Artists. under their Eyes Cannot see Rafael unless they are born with Determinate Organs' (E637). What we see is not simply regulated by weight of tradition or fear of authority. Nor must we understand it to be the product of imaginative vision alone. For what we see is also the result of the physical condition of our eyes. Reynolds had related that Rafael's paintings 'frequently made "little impression" on visitors' (E637). We could interpret Blake's response and his particular mention of 'Determinate Organs' as including all the senses, though it seems more likely that he refers to Locke's theories about the mind to suggest that the visitors – not Rafael – are to blame: eyes can be active if not productive during perception.

Blake's antipathy towards Newton and disagreements with Locke have been widely recognized. This essay focuses on his more positive, if still contentious, engagement with the contemporary science of optics. The creation myth Blake evolved in the 1790s borrows from late-eighteenth-century optics in its description of the self-regulated eye. *Europe* and *The Book of Urizen* fuse two prominent optical metaphors, the *camera obscura* and the picture gallery. Sometimes the eye even behaves like an optical instrument. This essay argues that, contrary to what we might expect, contemporary optics extended Blake's range of poetic vision.

When Blake combined religious and scientific arguments about the human faculties in *Europe*, he produced the evocative image of a man residing inside a cave, left with nothing but his senses to explore the world beyond:

> Five windows light the cavern'd Man; thro' one he breathes
>   the air;
> Thro' one, hears music of the spheres; thro' one , the eternal vine
> Flourishes, that he may recieve the grapes; thro' one can look.
> And see small portions of the eternal world that ever groweth;
> Thro' one, himself pass out what time he please, but he will not;
> For stolen joys are sweet, & bread eaten in secret pleasant.
>
>   (3: 1–6, E60)

Remarkable about this passage is that it sets up the human mind as a lived-in space. Blake creates an image that renders men inhabitants of their own heads. What lies beyond the 'cavern'd man' is the forever-expanding, eternal world. Men could leave this fixed skull-space, but rather have chosen to frame their experience of the world beyond with the structures imposed by their skulls, and have all sensual experience channelled through small, anatomical holes. In other words, Blake's visual cave is not a Platonic cave nor does it work like a *camera obscura*, because to see an image created by a *camera obscura* the viewer has to be in the dark. In this passage visual experience, quite clearly, isn't rendered as men gazing at the walls of their cave but as men looking out of a house-like structure.

Blake's cave imagery tends to be read as a closing of the senses.[1] In fact, this interpretation of the body is quite conventional, and his 'cavern'd man' is part of a long tradition. Marjorie Hope Nicolson, in *Newton Demands the Muse* (1946), established the extent to which philosophers and poets used the *camera obscura* as a model for explaining the processes of human understanding.[2] Robert Gleckner has since continued this line of interpretation. To reach the full potential of divine vision, he writes, Blake's body-cave has to dissolve: 'multiplication of the senses *ad infinitum* would multiply the number of chinks in man's bodily cavern to the point where the cavern itself is annihilated, or ceases to obscure'.[3] Most arguments about Blake and optics tend to start with his rejection of Newtonian physics.[4] This rejection, moreover, was part of a wider, Europe-wide anti-Newtonian movement.[5] For many, writes Robert Essick, Sir Isaac Newton embodied the viewpoint of reason. His intense concentration on all things material symbolizes spiritual blindness, as Blake illustrated in his Large Colour Print *Newton* (*c.* 1795).[6] Donald Ault suggested in *Visionary Physics* (1974) that we should perceive Blake's notion of 'expanded and contracted vision' as an adaptation of empirical, optical theories.[7] By the end of the eighteenth century, however, research into optics had not only profited from anatomical examinations, it had also been infused with arguments about the relationship between mind and matter. Part of this context is the discovery of lens accommodation and especially the artificial eye developed by George Adams (1750–1795), possibly a Swedenborgian. What I'm suggesting is that Blake's understanding of optics was shaped by the growing philosophical awareness of the eye's inherent flexibility. The concept of the eyes as 'Determinate Organs', hurled at Joshua Reynolds in the annotations to *Discourses on Art*, transcends Newtonian optics, as it transcends the distinction between inside and outside so crucial for Locke's explanations about the mind, the senses and the world 'out there'. It focuses instead on the eye and individual perception. The mind is housed inside the body; those inhabiting it stay indoors and view the world through 'five windows'.

Blake represents the creation of the eye in his 1790s myth, but creation in Blake is never straightforward. The plot of his creation myth interlaces with Genesis, but whereas in Genesis man is created from the dust of the ground and filled immediately, it seems, with the breath of life, in *The Book of Urizen* the prototypical body evolves only gradually. In the beginning there was Urizen. Urizen decides to abandon eternity and create his own world: 'Lo, a shadow of horror is risen | In Eternity! Unknown, unprolific! | Self-closd, all-repelling' (3: 1–3, E70). While the reader is prepared by the *Book*'s 'Preludium' to expect insurrection, those in heaven are unable to understand what is going on: 'Some said | "It is Urizen", But unknown, abstracted | Brooding secret, the dark power hid' (3: 5–7, E70). Urizen tries to hide and as he is digging a hole for himself, he acquires the first body: 'And a roof, vast petrific around, | On all sides He fram'd: like a womb; | Where thousands of rivers in veins | Of blood pour down the mountains to cool | The eternal fires beating without' (5: 28–32, E73). The poem describes, several times, the growth of this prototypical body into its human anatomy, as if propelled by an inner logic, and with Los, the second creator figure, adding finishing touches. When Urizen's creation commences, he observes how his creatures manifest themselves, piece by piece, just as we, the readers, witnessed the formation of his body:

> his world teemd vast enormities
> Frightening; faithless; fawning
> Portions of life; similitudes

Of a foot, or a hand, or a head
Or a heart, or an eye, they swam mischevous
Dread terrors! delighting in blood.

(23: 1–7, E81)

Recognizing that creation in Blake is really a demonstration of man's fall from perfection is nothing new. Less often noted is that the manifestation of the eye's anatomy marks a crucial stage of this fall.[8] During the creation-fall all the senses shrink, but it is especially the shrinking eyes, growing 'small like the eyes of a man', that define what is human (25: 29–36, E82). Nobody is in control, and creation simply happens, as the body seems to assume its shape of its own accord.

The complexity of Blake's 1790s' creation myth is the result of his tentative, possibly incompetent dabbling in natural philosophy. In common with the associationist thinking of the early 1790s, it uses the *camera obscura* and the picture gallery as analogies for the working of the human mind, but in both *Europe* and *The Book of Urizen* these metaphors lose the cause and effect relationship they would imply within an empiricist context. The question for Blake is how visual experience of the body gets translated into knowledge about that body, rather than knowledge about the world.

About a century earlier, John Locke argued that humans were born without innate ideas and that the mind resembled a 'tabula rasa'. As they grow up, Locke believed, humans acquire ideas not through reason but through experience.[9] To understand, Locke wrote, humans have continually to reflect on newly acquired data; to be able to think clearly, they have to pay close attention to how their minds operate:

> Men then come to be furnished with fewer or more simple ideas from without, according as the *objects*, they converse with, afford greater or less variety; and from the operation of their minds within, according as they more or less *reflect* on them.[10]

As Locke moves on to the next point, his language loses some of its precision. He seems to emphasize that man has to 'turn his eyes to', that is look at, the objects inside his mind, 'and all that may be observed therein'. Because '[a] picture, or clock', he wrote:

> may be so placed, that they may come in [a man's] way every day; but yet he will have but a confused idea of all the parts they are made up

of, till he *applies himself with attention,* to consider them each in particular.[11]

Locke here hints at understanding as introspection. He presents it, however, as a product rather than a process: all man has to do is to put visual experiences into order and identify 'clear ideas'. The *camera obscura* is a central analogy for Locke, because in empiricist thinking eyes are referred to as passive receptors that allow the external world to enter the mind and imprint itself onto the retina. Locke compared the mind to a 'dark room', stacked with pictures:

> For, methinks, the *understanding* is not much unlike a closet wholly shut from light, with only some little opening left, to let in external visible resemblances, or ideas of things without; would the pictures coming into such a dark room but stay there, and lie so orderly as to be found upon occasion, it would very much resemble the understanding of a man, in reference to all objects of sight, and the ideas of them.[12]

The empiricist approach to the philosophy of mind, in the first instance, hinged upon the fact that the eye transmits images into the space of the mind. Empiricist thinkers perceived the content of the mind to be a mirror of external objects. According to Locke, the acquisition of knowledge is a two-stage process and it involves sensory perception as well as reflection. Blake's attitude to this kind of closed-off mind space was ambivalent. *Europe* moves from the idea of man as 'cavern'd', to the idea of 'someone' inside the mind-cave moving around freely and doing the looking. As pointed out earlier, being 'cavern'd' is not such a bad thing. Those inside the cave experience it as a safe hiding place. When Blake started to work on *The Book of Urizen*, he opted for a more complex description of man's relationship with his body.

In *The Book of Urizen* we witness the creation of the body – not the world. First, the skeleton manifests itself; second, the heart casts out a net of blood vessels; third, the nervous system grows into position and weaves this body together (12: 5–7, E76). It is during the third stage of the seven ages of creation that the eyes appear:

> In harrowing fear rolling round;
> His nervous brain shot branches
> Round the branches of his heart.
> On high into two little orbs

And fixed in two little caves
Hiding carefully from the wind,
His Eyes beheld the deep,
And a third Age passed over:
And a state of dismal woe.
                    (11: 10–18, E76)

In this passage, the nerves spread and weave the human form. They go to the head, stop and transform themselves into eyes which then look out of a still incomplete body to survey 'the deep'. No doubt, the image of 'looking' eyes clashes with the very idea of the *camera obscura* apparatus. The authority of creation is undermined, because it is impossible to pinpoint when exactly the body becomes visible. In addition, there isn't just one body in Blake's creation myth. Los, who decided to rescue Urizen, gets embodied too.

Newton, famously, sat inside a dark room when researching light. He contemplated its physical qualities while looking at reflections, generated by a prism, on the walls of his study. Newton explained human perception by analogy:

In like manner when a Man views any Object [...] the Light which comes from several Points of the Object is so refracted by the transparent skins and humours of the Eye, (that is by the outward coat [...] called the *Tunica* Cornea, and by the crystalline humour [...] which is beyond the Pupil [...]) as to converge and meet again at so many Points in the bottom of the Eye, and there to paint the Picture of the Object upon that skin (called the *Tunica Retina*) with which the bottom of the Eye is covered.[13]

Newton identified retina-images as pictures painted onto the retina-canvas by rays of light, and emphasized that the ultimate single picture was located beyond the retina. This argument culminates in 'Query 15' of the *Opticks* where he contends that, on their way to the brain, the optic nerves merge into one to 'make but one entire Species or Picture'.[14] Newton's explanations were contested by Dr William Porterfield (*c.* 1696–1771), Scottish physician and inventor of the optometer, a device for measuring the far and near points of distinct vision. Porterfield, one of many late eighteenth-century ophthalmologists working on single and binocular vision, argued that there was no anatomical proof for the junction of the optic nerves.[15] With this experimental confutation, the idea of the mind as an optic cave began to lose its conceptual coherence: because whereas the cave metaphor implies that there is one opening, the skull one suggests two. So, if each eye transmitted an image from the outside world, what fused these two images into one? The answer came from another Scot, the philosopher Thomas Reid (1710–1796). Reid argued that the perception of single objects with two eyes was brought about by habit. Reid believed that sensation was based on an actual transfer of data from the eye to the brain. For two images to manifest in exactly the same place on the retina, the eyes' movement had to be parallel, and the eyes had to be able to adjust naturally to distance and movement. The mind, according to Reid, perceived a single object because it was unable to distinguish between two images.[16] The final blow to Newton, in this argument, came from Joseph Priestley. Priestley revisited the concept of imprinted reality by pointing out that the eye-cavern couldn't possibly contain pictures from the external world, because 'the retina [...] presents no particular surface'. It was impossible precisely and unambiguously to locate the pictures on the retina.[17]

In the past, the picture gallery had been used to explain the working of memory. Within the context of the debates about single and binocular vision, the Lockean notion of clear and distinct ideas had become an impossibility. In order to think as well as to act, man had to be able to associate new and old ideas. If empiricist thinkers, despite anatomical evidence, continued to use the picture gallery as a metaphor, they would also have had to accept that each concept or idea existed in two versions and that there was room for confusion. Blake's works might also be read according to Lockean associationism. For example, the 'golden compasses' used by Urizen in *The Book of Urizen* to explore his world (20: 39, E81) remind one of at least two images: *The Ancient of Days*, the frontispiece to *Europe*, and *Newton*, the Large Colour Print.

Another context for Blake's understanding of contemporary optics is Swedenborgianism. Blake himself had links to the Swedenborgians. He was, for instance, present at the New Church General Conference discussed in David Worrall's contribution to this volume. Through the Swedenborgians he could have met George Adams who wrote about eyes, electricity, microscopes and magnetism, and published with Robert Hindmarsh, a founding member and chronicler of the Swedenborgian Church.[18] Adams had been apprenticed to his father, whom he succeeded in the office of mathematical instrument maker to King George III. Later, he also became optician to the Prince of Wales. He was particularly interested in the systematic instruction of laymen. In the preface of his five volume *Lectures on Natural and Experimental*

Philosophy (1794), he wrote that he wanted to lead his readers 'from a Consideration of the Works of God, to acknowledge and reference his Power, Wisdom, and Goodness' and also prove to them that 'natural philosophy affords no support to the wretched system of materialism'.[19] In the late eighteenth century the impact of new, more powerful optical instruments was enormous, enabling professional as well as lay persons to see star constellations that had never been seen before. In his *Astronomical and Geographical Essays* (1789) Adams reasoned that discoveries made with new optical devices enlarged the boundaries of the known universe. He emphasized that Sir Frederick William Herschel, astronomer and telescope maker, discovered Uranus only after he redesigned his telescope.[20] Adams tried to develop an optical technology which would allow its users to be more inquisitive about everyday matters. He was especially fascinated by the human eye and his most significant invention, offered for sale from 1789, was the artificial eye.[21] His instructions read as follows:

> If the artificial eye be turned towards any bright object, at a moderate distance, and the lens for the natural sight be brought before the pupil, a lively and distinct, though inverted, picture of the object will be exhibited on the greyed glass. If either of the other lenses be placed opposite the pupil, the picture becomes confused; but it is again rendered distinct, by placing the corresponding lens before it.[22]

Adams wanted to demonstrate how reading glasses and 'opake [*sic*] shades to candles' impacted on the eye.[23] Blake might have been one of those who held the artificial eye in his hand and marvelled at how sight could be improved by changing and inserting different, more powerful lenses. The artificial eye was a toy and Adams conceded that he could not explain why objects appeared upside down.[24] Five years later, in *Lectures on Natural and Experimental Philosophy*, Adams again sang the praises of his invention – which meant, at the very least, that no one needed to cut open ox eyes any more. The artificial eye, he said, offered a clean and pleasant demonstration of optical effects.[25] It could be disassembled, its mechanisms could be followed layer by layer, and different lenses could be inserted in order to produce the effects of long- or short-sighted vision. In the *Lectures*, Adams discussed the physiological operations taking place in and around the body of the eye. Yet while he presented the eye initially as a *camera obscura*, he ended up declaring it a masterwork of divine wisdom.

When it came to explaining the connection between mind and matter, Adams drew on the Swedenborgian notion of influx, claiming that the correspondences 'manifest in the internal and external motions' of the eye were intended to encourage man to transfer his 'words and ideas from earthly to heavenly subjects'.[26] Adams not only speculated about the relationship between sight and vision, he explained how and when sight could be preserved. It was Adams, not Swedenborg, who visualized or rather externalized optical effects that would normally occur inside the body.

The Swedenborgian idea of a visible *spiritual* world is something several of Blake's contemporaries picked up on. It is, for example, mocked by Henry Fuseli in his review of Swedenborg's *Wisdom of Angels* in 1789: 'More news from the spiritual world! If this be not angelic wisdom, it is something so wholly beyond the comprehension of our weak intellects, that it must needs relate to beings of a very different order.'[27] Another important critic of Swedenborg was Joseph Priestley. Priestley didn't reject Swedenborgianism because of its 'imaginative nature', but because it 'lacked the confirmation of independent testimony, or the verification of miracle'.[28] The Swedenborgians not only insisted that there were two worlds; they also claimed that Swedenborg was unique in travelling between them. Priestley mocked the Swedenborgians for accepting something so unscriptural and argued that Swedenborg's spiritual journeys were nothing but dreams.[29]

In his creation myth, Blake seems to have adapted optic theory to explain the *visible* existence of the spiritual world. Considering Priestley's objection we might argue that Blake combines dreamed with seen images.[30] For example, in both *Europe* and *The Book of Urizen*, he uses dream imagery to describe man's relationship with history: 'Enitharmon slept, | Eighteen hundred years: Man was a Dream!' (9: 1, E63). It is one thing to say that human history isn't real; it is another to maintain that man has been incapacitated by history:

> Enitharmon laugh'd in her sleep to see (O womans triumph)
> Every house a den, every man bound; the shadows are filld
> With spectres, and the windows wove over with curses of iron:
> Over the doors Thou shalt not; & over the chimneys Fear is
>   written:
> With bands of iron round their necks fasten'd into the walls
> The citizens: in leaden gyves the inhabitants of suburbs
> Walk heavy: soft and bent are the bones of villagers.
>
> (12: 25–31, E64)

Leaving gender issues aside, the implied opposition between dreaming and consciousness is that human history and all its achievements are the nightmare man needs to awake from. If they could really see what has been going on, they would understand that they are enslaved. The idea of history being a string of nightmarish images taking possession of the human mind recurs at the beginning of *The Book of Urizen* with the narrator preparing to write down 'dark visions of torment' (2: 7, E70). When the first body is crafted onto Urizen, he falls into a deep, 'stony sleep'. His body changes when 'Ages on ages roll'd over him!' (6: 7, 10: 1, E74). As the dream world takes over, Urizen awakes as a different person. He awakes as a man.

One commentator has suggested that the brain's anatomy and the apparent lack of space for the soul within it motivated Swedenborg to develop the notion of influx, that is, of spirit acting on matter and turning visual experience into something the brain could process.[31] Swedenborg draws on Locke, but his argument about internal knowledge is in conflict with Locke's point about ideas being acquired through external experience only. Swedenborg, like Locke, stresses that humans need really to 'look' at what materializes inside their minds, and argues that some parts of the ideas accumulated inside the mind may not be seen very clearly:

> nothing is distinctly perceived in the internal organs, without some general knowledge; but particular ideas remain in the shade, just so far as the general knowledge under whose intuition, as it were, they exist, does not shine upon them to give light. In all cases, therefore, the corresponding universal must be present, if an inferior general or universal is to be distinctly perceived. And the general must be present, if the special is to be perceived; and the special if the particular, and the particular if the individual. Therefore, from a knowledge of that which is more universal, we can know what the perception of particulars is, whether distinct or obscure.[32]

Swedenborg takes Locke's conception of the mind as a dark chamber in a new direction. For Swedenborg, however, ideas inside that chamber are obscure when they are not illuminated by their 'corresponding universal'. Swedenborg's use of light as a means of intellectual clarification implies that light inside the mind gets reflected from general to specific, from specific to particular and from divine to human. The human and the divine are naturally separate, but thanks to divine influx they can coexist. Understanding, for Swedenborg, depends on the accumulation of divine wisdom. He displaces the Lockean idea of reflection with a dynamics of internal experience. Priestley attacked the belief that there existed a space in the mind the spiritual could flow into and enable visionary experience.[33] Blake's appropriation of optic theory follows Swedenborg in that it foregrounds internal experience and delineates perception as recognition. He would have encountered this idea in his copy of Swedenborg's *The Wisdom of Angels*: 'It is from Appearance that the Eye sees, but it is the Understanding that sees through the Eye, wherefore also to see is predicated of the Understanding.'[34]

The debate between Priestley and the Swedenborgians is usually considered in terms of a polar opposition between the Joseph Johnson circle and those gathered around Robert Hindmarsh. The politics of the early New Jerusalem Church were by no means uncomplicated and the initial power struggle between two of its leading members, Robert Hindmarsh and Joseph Proud, minister of the Birmingham Swedenborgian temple, has been written out of Hindmarsh's *Rise and Progress of the New Jerusalem Church* (1861).[35] The tensions within the Swedenborgian Church manifest themselves in differing responses to Priestley's *Letters to the Members of the New Jerusalem Church* (1792). Almost immediately Proud published *A Candid and Impartial Reply to the Rev. Dr Priestley's Letters*.[36] Hindmarsh's response appeared later that year.[37] Hindmarsh's *Letters* completely ignored Proud and emphatically restated the increasingly regulative principles of the Swedenborgian Church.[38]

It has been argued that Blake rejected Swedenborgianism when he wrote *The Marriage of Heaven and Hell*, and it seems likely that this rejection coincided with Priestley's narrow escape of the Birmingham riots.[39] In London, Blake and Priestley's paths may have crossed at Joseph Johnson's, because in 1791 when Blake was hoping to publish *The French Revolution*, Priestley was getting his *Letters* ready. The Swedenborgians, as it emerges from Proud's *Reply*, consisting of careful combination of close readings, engaged with the developments in contemporary optics. Proud, to repudiate Priestley, stressed that Swedenborg 'knew of' the planet Uranus.[40] The planet had been known as a star since 1670, but was officially rediscovered and reidentified by William Herschel in 1781. Proud, of course, suggests that Swedenborg had foretold the future: he had been able to see the star for what it was (a planet) without having to resort to using optical instruments. This point provides another example of the shift from perception to vision within the Swedenborgian discourse, because Swedenborg's vision of

Uranus can be explained in terms of his two-world model. When Proud claims that Swedenborg was able to 'see' Uranus, he essentially blurs the concepts of material and spiritual. Similarly, Blake combines and fuses different worlds in his creation myth. He has different characters, eternal and non-eternal, interact and, as the story progresses, lose sight of each other. Only the reader remains all seeing. In view of the text-image relationships of *The Book of Urizen* Blake gives readers an advantage over the poet, who listens to the 'call' of the Eternals (2: 5, E70). As well as visualizing the images, described by the poet, readers have simultaneously to try and match textual with printed images. To understand what the eternal body looks like the work has to be attentively perused.

There has been much controversy about a passage from *The Marriage of Heaven and Hell*: 'If the doors of perception were cleansed every thing would appear to man as it is: infinite. | For man has closed himself up, till he sees all things thro' narrow chinks of his cavern' (pl. 14, E39). Blake again makes a statement about the mind, the senses and the world 'out there', but this is the only time the word 'chinks' is used to explain the connection between them. In all other instances 'windows' or 'doors' link the inside with the outside. Some have argued that Blake meant that mankind had to do away with these gateways; others have pointed out that eternal vision cannot be taken for granted.[41] That there are classical sources for Blake's metaphor, equating 'doors' with windows to the soul, has been acknowledged too. Yet so far, not enough thought has been given to the optical dimension of this passage.[42] What if Blake's metaphor revolves around the idea that 'cleansing' means clearing of the eyes' lenses? This would introduce a new way of interpreting these lines, because in using the lens-as-eye as a metaphor for perception Blake would question the reliability of optic instruments as well as the stability of meaning systems based on visual experience.

Next to these philosophical and religious debates, feeding into the popular appropriation of optic theory, there is yet another context that may have shaped Blake's conception of the human eye: ophthalmology. Eye treatment was established as a branch of clinical practice at the beginning of the nineteenth century, much earlier than any other formal treatment.[43] What if we read Blake's statement 'If the doors of perception were cleansed every thing would appear to man as it is: infinite' as a comment on surgical intervention? Blake could have encountered speculation about eye surgery in the work of Erasmus Darwin. Not only may Blake have known Darwin through Joseph Johnson, who published his books, but he had also been involved with the engraving work for *The Botanic Garden* (1791).[44]

Substantial information on how diseases affected vision was in Darwin's *Zoonomia* (1796). Darwin writes that the most common reason for blindness was an obfuscation of the cornea.[45] In the second volume, he talks about a risky experiment concerning the restoration of sight, the hitherto unattempted trephination of the cornea: 'if the scar should heal without losing its transparency, many blind people might be made to see tolerably well by this slight and not painful operation'.[46] The dates don't match, but Blake's lens metaphor could imply loss of sight or blindness due to an opaque cornea. Blake uses the words 'window' and 'door' almost interchangeably. His metaphor is built around eyes as 'doors of perception' that can be cleaned like windows as well as opened up. This, again, implies the restoration of a literal, direct connection between the inner and outer spaces of human existence.

In the early 1790s, eyes and in particular crystalline lenses were the talk of the town. John Hunter, the most famous, London-based surgeon of the late eighteenth century, died in October 1793. Hunter's brother-in-law Everard Home reported to the Royal Society about Hunter's plans for experiments on the nature of the crystalline lens of the eye.[47] However, the race for the discovery of the muscular nature of the lens had already been won. Porterfield, for example, had argued that an object appeared single, because visual location was innate and lens accommodation depended on the muscular structure of the crystalline.[48] Considerable progress in the research into binocular visual direction was made by the physician and American-born Scotsman William Charles Wells. In his *Essay on Single Vision with Two Eyes* (1792)[49] Wells acknowledged that Porterfield was one of the few who had based optical speculation on experimentation. Next he outlined how Porterfield's claims about innate visual location oversimplified a rather complex process. Wells argued that the ability to see one object with two eyes depended on two factors: visual direction, which he says was innate, and comprehension of distance, which he says was learned.[50] Next is Thomas Young's work. He studied with John Hunter and is probably best known for his involvement in the deciphering of the Rosetta stone in 1814.[51] When Young presented his first paper on the muscular structure of the crystalline before the Royal Academy in May 1793, he was just twenty-one years old, and had only been studying medicine for a year. In other words, both Hunter and Young were working on the same project. Young's paper, outlining how the crystalline adapted its focus in relation to the objects before it, was published in the

Philosophical Transactions in the same year. Young's extraordinary discovery made a big impact. Johnson's *Analytical Review*, as part of its annual review of the *Philosophical Transactions*, summarizes the significance of Young's work in August 1794.[52] We don't know who wrote this review. Its argument evidences a high degree of familiarity with the subject: 'Various have been the conjectures and inferences among opticians to explain the manner in which the eye varies it's [*sic*] focal distance [...]. After enumerating most of them, Mr Y. explains the fact, by showing, that the crystalline humour is muscular throughout.'[53] Could its author be Priestley who had argued, twenty years earlier, that the crystalline was more or less solid and that the muscles of the eye moved the lens to focus on objects?[54]

1794 is an important year for developments in understanding perception and mind–matter relationships. The issue of *The Analytical Review* that reviewed Young's discovery also had an article on Darwin's *Zoonomia*. Darwin claimed that the crystalline consisted of fibres and the reviewer emphasizes that for Darwin

> the *immediate organs of sense* are asserted to consist like the muscles of moving fibres. [...] An *idea* is defined to be a motion of the fibres of some immediate organ of sense, and hence is frequently termed also a *sensual motion*. Perception comprehends both that motion, or the idea, and attention to it.[55]

For Darwin, the eye can no longer be viewed as a passive recipient of visual experience. It is actively involved in the shaping of visual perception. That Young's discovery was important for Johnson emerges from the opening paragraph of the review. It presents Darwin as an original genius whose work is significant but vulnerable. What follows is a very long and detailed review. Emphasis is put on the long gestation time of the work and the fact that Darwin should have published a lot sooner.[56]

During this period, Blake was preoccupied with the notion of the inherent flexibility of the eyes. In *The Book of Urizen* he equips his main creator figure with senses, flexible and regulated through will-power: 'The will of the Immortal expanded | Or contracted his all flexible senses' (3: 37–8, E71). In *Europe* Blake delineates how man's 'fluxile eyes' change, during the sleep of eighteen hundred years, into 'two stationary orbs, concentrating all things' (10: 11–12, E63). He also explains how, once the senses are 'barr'd and petrify'd against the infinite', 'Thought chang'd the infinite to a serpent', his symbol for evil (10: 15–16, E63).

As mentioned earlier, a conflicting image is that in *The Book of Urizen* the quality of Urizen's eyesight changes once he acquires a body. Only Los, Blake's second, still-eternal creator figure, realizes what is happening to Urizen:

> 2. All the myriads of Eternity:
> All the wisdom & joy of life:
> Roll like a sea around him,
> Except what his little orbs
> Of sight by degrees unfold.

> 3. And now his eternal life
> Like a dream was obliterated.
>   (13: 28–34, E77)

Eternity, once forever expanding, is now like a sea, a simile often used in materialist writing. The 'eternal life' can no longer be enjoyed, because it has dispersed 'like a dream'. The reason is that Urizen has been equipped with a human body. Throughout the poem, the acts of looking, seeing, identifying, or recognizing are linked with the idea that eyes are not only flexible, but have different kinds of capacities, because in order to see Urizen's newly created world the remaining Eternals have to make extra efforts: 'As glasses discover Worlds | In the endless Abyss of space, | So the expanding eyes of Immortals | Beheld the dark visions of Los' (E78). The Eternals' expanding eyes are like optic devices. What is disturbing about this scenario is that these eternal eyes can penetrate the human body and see Los's projected visions. With the creation myth progressing, Los also acquires a human body and assumes the role of Adam. His 'dark visions' may suggest, on the one hand, depression about his new mode of being. However, he doesn't seem to realize what is happening to him. It is essentially the space of the eye in which the transition from eternal vision to fallen sight takes place. Los has quite literally become blind to what is going on around him. Those in power, however, have retained the capacity to see into the barred-off inner-space and monitor all of Los's movements and thoughts.

Unlike the Swedenborgians, Blake doesn't subscribe to the idea of two, parallel worlds. In his creation myth, Blake maps out a world in which the material and the spiritual coexist, or rather visually interpenetrate. When Urizen sets off to explore his world, Blake fuses the material and eternal worlds by means of a travel narrative. It is with the sun as a lantern that Urizen lights his way:

> 1. Urizen explor'd his dens
> Mountain, moor, & wilderness,
> With a globe of fire lightening his journey
> A fearful journey, annoy'd
> By cruel enormities: forms
> Of life on his forsaken mountains
>
> 2. And his world teemd vast enormities
> Frightning; faithless; fawning
> Portions of life; similitudes
> Of a foot, or a hand, or a head
> Or a heart, or an eye, they swam mischievous
> Dread terrors! delighting in blood
>
> 3. Most Urizen sicken'd to see
> His eternal creations appear
> Sons & daughters of sorrow on mountains
> Weeping! wailing!
>
> $\qquad\qquad\qquad$ (22: 22–23: 11, E81)

Swedenborg once declared how a single vision had changed his whole life: 'The Lord himself hath called me: who was graciously pleased to manifest himself to me his unworthy servant, in a personal appearance, in the year 1743; to open to me a sight of the spiritual world.'[57] He used metaphors of travel, and claimed that in order to bridge his two modes of existence he had to relocate his spirit.

> I am in a natural state, and at the same time in a spiritual state, in a natural state with men of the earth, and in a spiritual state with you; and when I am in a natural state, I am not seen by you, but when I am in a spiritual state, I am seen; that such should be my condition, was given of the Lord. [...] a man of the natural world doth not see a man of the spiritual world, nor *vice versa*; wherefore when I let my spirit into the body, I was not seen by thee, but when I let it out of the body, I was seen.[58]

We could, of course, say that Blake's creator figure is a Gnostic God and as such responsible for the poor quality of creation which seems to lack a coherent telos. But through his body Urizen has become part of that world. Images access his mind-space through his eyes, and it is the physicality of these eyes that mediates his connection with his created world. The histories of the divine and human bodies have been intertwined and the inner and outer spaces of human experience compete with one another. Urizen is appalled and admits to himself that his creation is a failure. The divine and the human become intertwined when Urizen, guided by his human eyes, identifies body fragments and decides to cast 'The Net of Religion' to make the fragments hold together (25: 22, E82).

Blake emphasizes the importance of the mind-cave in *Europe*, where he has it protect man from the overwhelming variety of the eternal life. The idea of man as 'cavern'd' implies a mind-space in which all the senses can mix, mingle and amalgamate ideas. Once this interplay gets replaced by organic sense organization, as *The Book of Urizen* illustrates, the pictures themselves become active. *The Book of Urizen* with its different perspectives and body images continues to be a challenge, because it forces its readers, time and again, to compare as well as juxtapose body objects with body images and thus reexperience the overly familiar shapes of the human body. Blake makes staring impossible. Against the background of the creation story, he explores the dimensions of the human body by means of the opposition between Urizen's fixed stare and the reader's flexible glance.

Notes

1. Joseph Viscomi, 'In the Caves of Heaven and Hell: Swedenborg and Printmaking in Blake's *Marriage*', in *Blake in the Nineties*, ed. by Steve Clark and David Worrall (New York: St Martin's Press; Basingstoke: Macmillan, 1999), pp. 27–60.
2. Marjory Hope Nicolson, *Newton Demands the Muse: Newton's Opticks and the Eighteenth Century Poets* (Westport, CT: Greenwood Press, 1979), p. 144.
3. Robert F. Gleckner, 'Blake and the Senses', *Studies in Romanticism*, 5 (1965), 1–65 (p. 13).
4. Frederick Burwick, *The Damnation of Newton: Goethe's Color Theory and Romantic Perception* (Berlin: Walter de Gryter, 1986), p. 8.
5. Stuart Peterfreund, 'Blake and Anti-Newtonian Thought', in *Beyond the Two Cultures: Essays in Science, Technology, and Literature*, ed. by J. W. Slade and J. Y. Lee (Ames, IA: Iowa State University Press, 1990), pp. 141–60 (p. 142).
6. Robert N. Essick, 'Blake's Newton', *Blake Studies*, 3 (1971), 149–62.
7. Donald D. Ault, *Visionary Physics: Blake's Response to Newton* (Chicago, IL: University of Chicago Press, 1974), pp. 141–60.
8. Many critics have discussed Blake's notion of 'fallen vision' in relation to the fall from paradise. See, for example, Thomas Frosch, *The Awakening of Albion: The Renovation of the Body in the Poetry of William Blake* (Ithaca, NY: Cornell University Press, 1974), p. 17.

9. John Locke, *An Essay Concerning Human Understanding* (Harmondsworth: Penguin Books, 1997), p. 147 (Book ii, Chapter 9, para. 15).
10. *Ibid.*, p. 111 (Book ii, Chapter 1, para. 7).
11. *Ibid.*, pp. 111–2 (Book ii, Chapter 1, para. 7), emphasis in original.
12. *Ibid.*, p. 158 (Book ii, Chapter 11, para. 17).
13. Isaac Newton, *Opticks; or, a Treatise of the Reflections, Refractions, Inflections and Colours of Light* (London: 1704), p. 10.
14. *Ibid.*, p. 136.
15. William Porterfield, *A Treatise on the Eye, the Manner and Phaenomena of Vision*, 2 vols (Edinburgh: 1759), i, 191. See R. Ruston James, *Studies in the History of Ophthalmology in England Prior to the Year 1800* (Cambridge: Cambridge University Press, 1933), pp. 109–12 on the context of Porterfield's work.
16. Thomas Reid, *An Inquiry into the Human Mind, on the Principles of Common Sense* (Edinburgh: 1764), p. 365.
17. Joseph Priestley, *The History and Present State of Discoveries Relating to Vision, Light, and Colours*, 2 vols (1772), i, 199.
18. In the 1780s the Swedenborgians had regular meetings: 'the untranslated writings of Swedenborg were read from the Latin either by Mr George Adams or myself'. See Robert Hindmarsh, *Rise and Progress of the New Jerusalem Church, in England, America, and Other Parts*, ed. by E. Madeley (London: 1861), p. 25. Blake attended some of these meetings (see John Howard, 'An Audience for *The Marriage of Heaven and Hell*', *Blake Studies*, 3 (1970), 19–52 (p. 23)). Adams was a patron of Blake's friend John Birch (*c.* 1745–1815), who treated Blake's wife for rheumatism in 1804. See *BR*, p. 98.
19. George Adams, *Lectures on Natural and Experimental Philosophy*, 5 vols (London: 1794), i, ix–x.
20. George Adams, *Astronomical and Geographical Essays*, 3rd edn (London: 1795), p. 57.
21. George Adams, *A Catalogue of Mathematical and Philosophical Instruments* (London: *c.* 1789).
22. George Adams, *An Essay on Vision, Briefly Explaining the Fabric of the Eye, and the Nature of Vision* (London: 1789), p. 51.
23. *Ibid.*, pp. 1, 2.
24. *Ibid.*, p. 51.
25. Adams, *Lectures*, ii, 292–3.
26. *Ibid.*, ii, 141, 146.
27. *The Analytical Review*, 5 (1789), 352–3 (pp. 352, 353).
28. Martin Fitzpatrick, 'Joseph Priestley, Politics and Ancient Prophecy', *Enlightenment and Dissent*, 10 (1991), 104–9 (p. 106).
29. Joseph Priestley, *Letters to the Members of the New Jerusalem Church, Formed by Baron Swedenborg* (Birmingham: 1791), pp. xiv–xvi, 52–4.
30. For the developments in materialist thinking, see John W. Yolton, *Thinking Matter: Materialism in Eighteenth-Century Britain* (Minneapolis, MN: University of Minnesota Press, 1983), pp. 107–26.
31. Martin Priestman, *Romantic Atheism: Poetry and Freethought, 1780–1830* (Cambridge: Cambridge University Press, 1999), p. 87.
32. Emanuel Swedenborg, *Cerebrum: Three Transactions on the Cerebrum, a Posthumous Work*, trans. by A. Acton, 2 vols (Philadelphia, PA: Swedenborg Scientific Association, 1938), i, 149–50.

33. Priestley, *Letters to the Members of the New Jerusalem Church*, pp. 47–9.
34. Emanuel Swedenborg, *The Wisdom of Angels, Concerning Divine Love and Divine Wisdom* (London: 1788), p. 342.
35. David George Goyder, *A Concise History of the New Church* (London: 1827); David Bogue and James Bennett, *History of Dissenters, from the Revolution in 1688 to the Year 1806* (London: 1809–12).
36. Priestley planned to present the manuscript to Proud ahead of publication, but it was destroyed in the riots of July 1791. See also Robert Schofield, *The Lunar Society of Birmingham: A Social History of Provincial Science and Industry in Eighteenth-Century Britain* (Oxford: Clarendon Press, 1963), pp. 357–63.
37. The third reply is John Bellamy's *Jesus Christ the Only God* (London: 1792).
38. Robert Hindmarsh, *Letters to Dr Priestley: Containing Proofs of the Exclusive Divinity of Jesus Christ, [...] And of the Divine Mission of Emanuel Swedenborg* (London: 1792), p. v. For the growing conservatism within the Swedenborgian movement, see Thompson, *Witness*, pp. 135, 142–4, 166–7.
39. See Howard, 'An Audience for *The Marriage of Heaven and Hell*', pp. 19–52.
40. Joseph Proud, *A Candid and Impartial Reply to the Rev. Dr Priestley's Letters* (Birmingham: 1791), pp. 12–13.
41. Harold Bloom, *Blake's Apocalypse* (Garden City, NY: Doubleday, 1963), pp. 88–9; Donald A. Dike, 'The Difficult Innocence: Blake's Songs and Pastoral', *ELH*, 28 (1961), 353–75 (p. 358).
42. '[Blake] writes first of "doors" but in developing the metaphor he is clearly thinking of (glass) windows, whose cleansing will obviously improve perception.' See Howard Jacobson, 'Blake's Doors of Perception', *Notes and Queries*, 49 (2002), 454–5 (pp. 454–5).
43. James, *Studies in the History of Ophthalmology*, pp. 89–131; Roy Porter, *The Greatest Benefit to Mankind: A Medical History of Humanity From Antiquity to the Present* (London: HarperCollins, 1997).
44. Robert N. Essick, *William Blake's Commercial Book Illustrations: A Catalogue and Study of the Plates Engraved by Blake after Designs by Other Artists* (Oxford: Clarendon Press, 1991), pp. 45–7.
45. Erasmus Darwin, *Zoonomia; or, the Laws of Organic Life*, 2 vols (London, 1796), i, 23. Volume i appeared in 1794. See *Analytical Review*, 19 (1794), 225–34, 337–50, 449–63.
46. Darwin, *Zoonomia*, ii, 48. S. Louise Moffatt, Victoria A. Cartwright and Thomas H. Stumpf, 'Centennial Review of Corneal Transplantation', *Clinical and Experimental Ophthalmology*, 33 (2005), 642–57.
47. Everard Home, 'Some Facts Relative to the Late Mr John Hunter's Preparation for the Croonian Lecture', *Philosophical Transactions of the Royal Society of London*, 84 (1794), 21–7.
48. William Porterfield, 'An Essay Concerning the Motions of our Eyes', *Edinburgh Medical Essays and Observations*, 3 (1738), 191–2.
49. See *Analytical Review*, 11 (1792), 166–8.
50. Nicholas J. Wade, 'Porterfield and Wells on the Motions of our Eyes', *Perception*, 29 (2000), 221–39.
51. *The History of Ophthalmology*, ed. by Daniel M. Albert and Diane D. Edwards (Cambridge, MA: Blackwell Science, 1996), pp. 68, 71–2, 110, 116, 117–18.

52. Geoffrey N. Cantor, *Optics After Newton: Theories of Light in Britain and Ireland, 1704–1840* (Manchester: Manchester University Press, 1983), p. 129.
53. See *Analytical Review*, 19 (1794), 365–9 (p. 368).
54. Joseph Priestley, *The History and Present State of Discoveries Relating to Vision, Light, and Colours*, 2 vols (1772), i, 184–5.
55. Darwin, *Zoonomia*, i, 18. *Analytical Review*, 19 (1794), 225–34 (p. 226).
56. See *Analytical Review*, 19 (1794), 225, and *Analytical Review*, 20 (1794), 225–37 (p. 236).
57. *Conjuror's Magazine*, 1 (1791), 130.
58. Emanuel Swedenborg, *The Delights of Wisdom Concerning Conjugial* [*sic*] *Love* (London: 1794), p. 314.

9
A Minute Skirmish: Blake, Hayley and the Art of Miniature Painting

Mark Crosby

On 12 August 1803, a month before Blake was due to return to London from the coastal village of Felpham, he was involved in a scuffle with a soldier that began in the garden of his cottage and spread to the local public house. A few days after this incident the soldier, Private John Scolfield, made a formal complaint against Blake to the local magistrate, identifying him as a 'Miniature Painter' and accusing him of, amongst other things, uttering seditious expressions.[1] This was an extremely serious accusation and, if found guilty, Blake would have been imprisoned for at least three months or, in the context of the French invasion threat, transported to Botany Bay. In response, Blake denied the accusations and also claimed that Scolfield had described him as a French spy. According to Blake, Scolfield said:

> That it would be right to have my House Searched, as I might have plans of the County which I intended to Send to the Enemy; he called me a Military Painter; I suppose mistaking the Words Miniature Painter, which he might have heard me called.[2]

Scolfield's apparent confusion of Blake's profession tapped into the widespread fear of French invasion. Rumours of French spies roaming the English countryside, particularly on the south coast of England, were prevalent during this period. According to Blake, it appears that Scolfield had used Blake's profession as a miniature painter to draw him into the war between Britain and France. As Blake's refutation of Scolfield's complaint implies, the confusion of 'Miniature Painter' for 'Military Painter' configured Blake as an active participant in this conflict.³ Blake's brief foray into miniature painting, and more precisely the painting techniques used in this genre, was the site of an earlier, more localized conflict between Blake and his Sussex patron, the poet, biographer and man of letters, William Hayley. In this instance, it was Blake's creative independence that was at stake.

Blake's relationship with Hayley appears to have been a fractious affair. In July 1800, Blake accepted Hayley's invitation to move to Felpham with the promise of at least 'twelve months work [...] & a great deal more in prospect'.⁴ Blake had been struggling for commercial engraving work in London since 1798. In 1800, with Britain suffering from an acute wheat shortage, rampant inflation and outbreaks of civil unrest in urban areas, Hayley's offer of work combined with the tranquil surroundings of rural Sussex proved impossible for Blake to resist. The relationship between the two men seems have begun promisingly with Blake describing his new patron and his new home in enthusiastic terms.

By November 1802, however, Blake informed his London patron, Thomas Butts, that he had been 'very Unhappy' in Felpham (E719). It was not until January 1803 that Blake elaborated on the causes of his unhappiness, claiming that the 'unhealthiness' of the village had greatly affected him and his wife, Catherine. Blake also alluded to his relationship with Hayley, telling Butts that 'the mere drudgery of business' had prevented him from pursuing his visionary work (E724). Blake's complaint was probably aimed at Hayley's engraving commissions, which, paradoxically, had been one of the factors that had initially attracted Blake to Sussex in 1800. In a letter to his brother, James, of 30 January 1803, Blake is more explicit in his criticism of Hayley, claiming that his patron was 'Envious' and 'frightend' [*sic*] of him (E725). In his correspondence, as well as a number of manuscript epigrams, Blake interprets his growing resentment at Hayley's patronage as a spiritual conflict. While Hayley's patronage was financially rewarding, Blake came to regard it as creatively debilitating, possibly due to the quantity of work Hayley had commissioned. This apparently contradictory view of Hayley, as economic benefactor yet creative hindrance, is suggested in an epigram Blake addressed to 'H-----' in his manuscript notebook: 'Thy Friendship oft has made my heart to ake | Do be my Enemy for Friendships sake' (E506). In a letter to Butts of 25 April 1803, Blake elaborates on this position: 'If a Man is the Enemy of my Spiritual Life while he pretends to be the Friend of my Corporeal. he is my Real Enemy' (E728). This change of attitude can be traced to a poem included in one of two letters Blake addressed to Butts on 22 November 1802.

The poem was composed during a walk from Felpham to Chichester, 'a twelvemonth ago' (E720), which dates it to October–November 1801, and includes the following lines: 'Remembering the verses that Hayley sung | When my heart knocked against the root of my tongue' (E720–1). In the context of the poem, the remembrance of Hayley's verses results in a disturbance of the rural realm, with 'Silver Angels and Golden Demons' suddenly appearing to hinder the narrator's progress. The silent indignation Blake feels, and the frustration he experiences at his own lack of verbal agency, is reflected by the turbulence affecting the rural idyll. This would suggest that around October–November 1801, Blake had begun to resent Hayley's patronage. An examination of the miniature paintings Hayley commissioned Blake to execute earlier that year, however, suggests that this resentment began much sooner and manifested itself as an aesthetic reaction to Hayley's patronage. This essay discusses the painting techniques Blake used in the extant miniature portraits he produced in Sussex to argue that they not only constitute a form of non-verbal resistance to Hayley's patronage, but also were the opening salvo in Blake's spiritual conflict with his new patron.

Blake's brief career as a miniaturist appears to have begun less than four months after he had arrived in Felpham. In a letter to his close friend, the portrait painter George Romney, of 5 February 1801, Hayley, referring to Blake, claims: 'I have taught Him he says to paint miniature, & in Truth he has made a very credible Copy from yr admirable Portrait of the dear departed Bard'.[5] Hayley is describing Romney's 1792 crayon portrait of Cowper, after which Blake made two copies in miniature.[6] At the end of February, Hayley also informed Cowper's cousin, Lady Hesketh, of Blake's newly acquired ability:

> He says I have taught him to paint in miniature & in Truth He has improved his excellent versatile Talents very much in this retired scene, where he has access to several fine works of art by my Friend Romney.

Two months later, in a letter to Romney of 21 April 1801, Hayley again claims to have taught Blake 'to paint miniature, with considerable success'.[7] It is possible that the initial promise Blake had demonstrated as a miniaturist, coupled with his enthusiasm towards the genre, encouraged Hayley to attempt to establish him in a fashionable and profitable profession.

The popularity of miniature portraiture in Britain reached its high point during the second half of the eighteenth century. Miniature portraits offered a visual representation of the social and political ties that formed the nexus of polite society.[8] The popularity of miniature portraits, and the concomitant financial rewards to miniaturists, is evident in contemporary financial records of the period. The account books of notable miniaturists such as Ozias Humphry and George Engleheart demonstrate the levels of remuneration miniature painters received, with both painters charging between 8 and 12 guineas per portrait between 1780 and 1810.[9] According to the miniaturist Andrew Robertson, Richard Cosway, the highest-earning and most fashionable miniaturist of the period, charged between 20 and 30 guineas for his miniature portraits in 1802.[10] In this context, Hayley's attempt to direct Blake towards miniature painting may have been an astute economical move. On 1 September 1800, Blake had told George Cumberland that the move to Felpham would allow him to be 'independent'.[11] Hayley's network of connections, including members of the Sussex gentry, might indeed have given Blake a platform to establish his independence as an artist. Hayley's attempt to direct Blake towards miniature painting fulfilled the basic duty of a patron, to obtain work for his client, and was probably influenced by his friendship with one of the most innovative and successful miniaturists of the eighteenth century.[12]

In a letter to Romney of 21 April 1801, Hayley claims to have instructed Blake, 'with the aid of Meyer'.[13] It is likely that Hayley was referring to his friend, the miniaturist Jeremiah Meyer, whom he described elsewhere as 'the most eminent painter in miniature'.[14] A German émigré, Meyer arrived in England when he was twelve and studied enamel painting under another German miniaturist, Christian Frederick Zincke. The growing popularity during the eighteenth century of miniatures painted in watercolour on oval ivory supports persuaded Meyer to experiment with the luminescent qualities of the ivory. Commercial success with his innovative techniques led to Meyer being appointed 'miniature painter to the Queen' and 'painter in enamel to the King' in 1764.[15] Meyer's increasing popularity, as well as his standing among contemporary artists, is evident in John Singleton Copley's letter from New York in 1771, where he describes seeing 'a miniature of Governor Martin by Miers [*sic*] which cost 30 guineas', adding 'I think it worth the Money'.[16] Meyer was also a member of the Society of Artists and later a founder member of the Royal Academy, featuring in Zoffany's *Founders of the Royal Academy of Arts* (1771–2). In 1774, an anonymous review of Meyer's miniature portraits exhibited at the Royal Academy exhibition states:

These miniatures excel all others in pleasing Expression, Variety of Tints, and Freedom of Execution, being performed by hatching, and not stippling as most Miniatures are. Indeed, in this branch of Art Mr Meyer seems to stand unrivalled, and I believe he may be justly reckoned the first miniature painter in Europe.[17]

The review emphasizes Meyer's use of hatching, a technique that employs bisecting lines to render the portrait. This technique is given as 'the most expeditious manner of working in miniature' in two pages of manuscript notes titled: *A Few Hints For Painting Watercolour From My Dear Friend Mr Meyer*. The notes are appended to the end of Meyer's sketchbook, held by the Ashmolean Museum, Oxford, and are dated 1767.[18] Meyer's hatching technique sought to exploit the surface of the ivory support, and departed significantly from the techniques of the early eighteenth-century 'modest school' of miniaturists. An examination of Meyer's miniature portraits, as well as his sketchbook, which contains numerous preparatory drawings, reveals his distinctive style.

Like many of his contemporaries, Meyer uses opaque colours, albeit sparingly, to depict clothing, which was executed in a linear style, consisting of densely painted vertical lines. Opaque white is used on cravats, neckties, fichus and the decorative trimmings of ladies' dresses. It was Meyer's use of regular lines on the background and on the face that marked him out from other miniaturists. Rather than layering colour onto the ivory so as to obliterate the support, or using small dots created with the tip of a very fine brush, a technique known as stippling, Meyer employed narrow bisecting lines to cover the surface of the ivory. A partial drawing of George III's wife, Queen Charlotte, in Meyer's sketchbook reveals him experimenting with hatching on the left cheek, chin nose and eyes.[19] An unfinished miniature based on this sketch, showing the subject in a pale blue dress, again reveals Meyer's extensive use of hatching to delineate the face.[20] This linear style produces several distinctive features, including protruding lips and sunken eyes. The hatching technique is more pronounced after 1770, where it becomes much denser in areas of shadow: under the chin, for instance, and around the ear. While he employed hatching to render shaded areas, Meyer was also careful to retain the luminous surface of the ivory.[21] To avoid subduing the ivory's luminosity Meyer advised his titular friend in *A Few Hints for Painting* that 'black never [...] be used in flesh'.[22]

While studying at Cambridge, Hayley formed a lifelong friendship with Meyer and, according to his *Memoirs*, spent his 'daylight hours in painting miniature'. Among the subjects he painted were 'small heads of our Saviour and St John after Raphael, minutely finished in watercolours, for a pair of bracelets' as well as 'a diminutive portrait, in a ring' of a relation. No extant examples of his miniature portraits have been identified, and indeed Hayley ceased painting altogether in 1772, due to an inflammation of the eyes. Nonetheless, through 'his friendship with Meyer' Hayley claimed to have 'acquired knowledge in the management of waters, as enabled him to instruct'.[23] *A Few Hints of Painting*, which dates from this period, indicates the kind of advice that Meyer was dispensing at the time.[24] It seems that as far as Hayley was concerned the friendship and guidance of Meyer legitimated his attempt to direct Blake towards miniature painting.[25]

This attempt was initially greeted with enthusiasm. On 10 May, Blake told Butts that 'Miniature is become a Goddess in my Eyes & my friends in Sussex say that I Excell in the pursuit. I have a great many orders and they multiply' (E715). There are references to at least ten miniatures by Blake, but only six have so far been identified.[26] Four are undated and have hitherto been attributed to the three-year period in Felpham, which considering Blake's claim to have 'a great many orders' is a relatively small amount, even taking into account the untraced miniatures and the other work Blake was doing, such as the portraits for Hayley's library.[27] In comparison, between 1775 and 1813 George Engleheart produced 4,853 miniature portraits, at a rate of 124 per year, and in 1800 Andrew Robertson produced 85 miniature portraits.[28] Furthermore, despite the comparatively small number of miniatures by Blake that have so far been discovered, Private John Scolfield's identification of him as a 'Miniature Painter' suggests that he was known locally by this profession.[29]

The first miniatures Blake executed in Felpham were probably of Hayley's friend, the poet William Cowper. In 1801, Hayley wrote to Cowper's cousin, Lady Hesketh, concerning the biography of Cowper he was working on and also to discuss the frontispiece engraving of the poet for the biography. Hayley predicted that Blake 'will produce a Head of Cowper that will surprise and delight you'.[30] In order to realize this prediction it seems that Hayley instructed Blake to produce at least four renderings of Cowper after Romney's 1792 portrait, including two miniatures.[31] Hayley considered Romney's portrait 'the nearest approach [Romney] had ever made to a perfect representation of life and character', which is probably the reason that it was chosen as the basis for the engraving.[32] It is therefore likely that Blake's two miniatures of Cowper were the first he painted under Hayley's guidance.[33] Hayley gave the more finished miniature to Romney and the other was sent to Cowper's nephew, Johnny Johnson.[34]

Figure 9.1   William Blake, *William Cowper* (1801). Reproduced with kind permission from the Trustees of the Ashmolean Museum, Oxford.

Both Cowper miniatures are watercolour on card.[35] The more finished miniature is held in the Ashmolean Museum and depicts the subject's head and shoulders, with the head facing slightly left, in an oval measuring 7.3 x 6 cm (Figure 9.1).[36] The background is a brown wash in which vertical brush strokes are evident. The clothing is executed using linear strokes to delineate the jacket. Opaque white is used on the necktie and morning cap. Blake's rendering of Cowper's face initially appears linear, using fine lines to delineate the neck, chin and nostril,

Figure 9.2   William Blake, *Thomas Butts Senior* (*c*.1801–9). Reproduced with kind permission from the Trustees of the British Museum.

but under magnification a number of major departures from Meyer's hatching technique can be discerned. Blake uses a delicate stippling technique on the face. This is particularly noticeable around the ear, lips, nose, eyes, cheeks and forehead. Fine red dots are evident on the cheeks and lips and, contrary to Meyer's advice in *A Few Hints*, Blake uses black pigment to enhance skin tone and for areas of shadow, such as under the chin, below the ear, under the left eye, and under the nose and bottom lip. Blake's extensive use of stipple on the face is also evident in his miniature of John Johnson, executed in watercolour on card in 1802, and in the miniature of Thomas Butts, which has also been dated to this period.[37]

When precisely Blake produced the miniature of Butts is not known, but Martin Butlin tentatively dates it *c*.1801, based on Blake's letter to Butts of 11 September 1801: 'by my sisters hands I transmit to Mrs Butts an attempt at your likeness which I hope she who is the best judge will think like' (E716).[38] Unlike the miniatures of Cowper and Johnson, the Butts miniature is a watercolour on an oval ivory support, measuring 8.5 × 6.3 cm and is set in a gilt oval frame (Figure 9.2).[39] If Butlin is correct in his dating then it is the first instance of Blake using ivory as a support. Blake depicts Butts with close-cropped, dishevelled hair, in what was known as the Brutus style. He is dressed in a blue uniform with a gold epaulette. His head is turned slightly to the left and his shoulders are visible; he holds a book in his right hand.[40] The background is predominantly blank with faint traces of blue above and around the sitter's head and hair. The clothing is drawn using linear brush strokes, with opaque white on the necktie and gold on the epaulette. Blake employs several linear brush strokes to portray the eyebrows, chin and jowls, but the majority of the face is rendered with carefully worked stippling, which is achieved by using densely interspersed red and black dots. As in the Cowper and Johnson miniatures, Blake also uses black for shadow, under the nose, right ear and chin. The hand holding the book is painted using carefully worked stippling combined with linear brush strokes. The colouring of the skin is extremely light because rather than using opaque white on the face Blake leaves areas unpainted, using the surface of the ivory support to achieve tone and reflection, which is noticeable on the tip and bridge of the nose. Blake does use a small amount of opaque white on the pupils for a reflective effect. The skin tone is far lighter than in the Cowper and Johnson miniatures, and accentuates the luminous qualities of the ivory support. This delicate stippling technique is also evident in Blake's miniatures of Mrs Elizabeth Butts and Thomas Butts junior, which have been dated 1809.[41]

The extensive use of stippling in all Blake's extant miniatures differs significantly from the hatching techniques employed by Meyer. Indeed, Meyer explicitly advises against stippling as well as the use of black pigment on the face. It was Meyer who, Hayley claimed, taught him miniature painting, and according to Hayley, he taught Blake. But the disparity between Meyer's hatching technique and Blake's delicate stippling appears to cast doubt on Hayley's claim that he taught Blake to paint miniatures.

There were, of course, painters other than Hayley or Meyer to whom Blake might have turned for instruction. A number of contemporary miniaturists, including Richard Cosway and Ozias Humphry, were friendly with Blake and could have influenced his style. Richard Cosway succeeded Meyer in becoming the most successful and fashionable miniaturist of the period.[42] It is likely that Cosway had known Blake from as early as 1768. Cosway was a student at William Shipley's drawing academy in the Strand and later became a tutor when Henry Pars became principal of the academy around 1765.[43] According to Benjamin H. Malkin, Blake 'was put to Mr Pars's drawing-school in the Strand' at the age of ten, that is, in 1767.[44] Cosway was teaching at the academy at this time, although there is no extant evidence to indicate that he taught Blake.[45] As a miniaturist, Cosway developed a number of key stylistic features that make his work recognizable, including round, clear eyes, elongated necks and distended heads.[46] From 1770, Cosway, following Meyer, layered transparent colours in bisecting linear brush strokes onto the support, which allowed the luminescence of ivory to suggest light on the face. Cosway models the features of his subjects using short grey brush strokes and creates an almost three-dimensional illusion by employing long strokes around the contours of the face, especially the cheeks and the chin. He also uses loose hatching on the face, particularly in areas of shadow. In a letter to his sister, Andrew Robertson describes Cosway's technique:

> In Cosway, I had my principle of colouring confirmed; he does all with ink – sketching in drapery etc. light and pretty, – no blue in the face – very little red on cheeks, lips and eyes, and it is done.[47]

Cosway draws the sitter's clothing using linear brush strokes with opaque white used to highlight neckties and drapery. His hatching technique is much looser than Meyer's more precise style and differs significantly from Blake's stippling technique.

Like Cosway, Ozias Humphry also attended Shipley's drawing academy, and later became a moderately successful miniaturist, competing with

John Smart for commissions while in India. In 1792, Humphry was forced to give up the profession due to deteriorating eyes and between 1794 and 1796 he commissioned Blake to print two books of designs derived from the early illuminated books.[48] It is clear that Humphry knew Blake, but an examination of his painting style suggests that he did not influence Blake's distinctive style. Humphry's early miniature portraits are characterized by heavy, rich colouring, achieved by using fine interlocking brush strokes that are difficult to discern.[49] His later style follows that of Meyer and Cosway, using hatching and flowing lines to delineate the face. Unlike Cosway, Humphry did not enlarge the eyes, preferring to depict them slightly slanted.[50] One of the key features of Humphry's miniatures is his extremely detailed backdrops.[51] Blake, however, on the evidence of his extant miniatures, executed only one portrait with a discernable backdrop: the miniature of John Johnson in 1802.

Another contemporary miniaturist to consider, due to his friendship with Hayley, is George Engleheart.[52] Like Meyer, Engleheart was a German émigré who became a very successful miniaturist. There are three distinct phases to Engleheart's career. The early phase is dominated by the use of fine vertical brush strokes on the background and extensive use of lead white to provide tone to the face. During the middle phase Engleheart used diagonal grey lines to delineate the eyes and mouth and fine hatching for tone and shadow. After 1800 larger rectangular ivory supports became fashionable and Engleheart adjusted his style, using thicker brush strokes to bring greater realism to his portraits.[53] Engleheart's methods involve the heavy application of paint onto the ivory, and the final aesthetic differs significantly from Blake's delicate stipple technique. It is evident that Blake's stippling technique was not derived from the styles employed by Cosway, Humphry or Engleheart.[54] Indeed, Blake's use of stipple differed from that of other contemporary miniaturists, such as Archibald Robertson. In his *Treatise of Miniature Painting*, dated 25 September 1800, Robertson instructs his younger brother on the methods of shading:

> To proceed with fair hatches, throwing the blot either out of the picture, or into dark shade, crossing in all directions in the dark, and only as little as possible in the lights.[55]

Robertson also emphasizes that for the face: 'leave nothing, if possible to stippling'.[56] The remainder of this essay discusses other possible influences on Blake's distinctive stipple technique.

Stippling was frequently employed by miniaturists in the sixteenth and early seventeenth centuries. By 1627, however, the miniaturist Edward Norgate was advising that skin tone should be rendered by using 'severall redds' [sic] worked by hatching rather than 'with stips, points or pricks'.[57] Miniaturists such as Bernard Lens and his sons used stippling intermittently at the beginning of the eighteenth century, but by 1770 it had been replaced by the more fashionable hatching methods of Meyer and Cosway.[58] It is possible that Blake learned stippling from Claude Boutet's *The Art of Painting in Miniature* (1752), which claims to teach 'the speedy and perfect acquisition of that art without a master'.[59] Boutet discusses different techniques of stippling, or dotting, but advocates the use of the 'hatch by little strokes, that cross each other every other way' and further advises 'such as would paint in miniature to use it'.[60] After 1800 the increasing popularity of rectangular frames resulted in the tendency to cover 'as much of the ivory as possible, especially in the hair, clothing and backgrounds, with sonorous, thickly layered and gummed pigments'.[61] Blake's use of stipple appears inconsistent, even anachronistic, when set alongside this aesthetic. It was, however, a technique he was familiar with from his training as an engraver.

Blake was predominantly a line engraver, but during his apprenticeship to James Basire, engraver to the Society of Antiquaries, he learned a variety of engraving and etching techniques, including stippling.[62] A number of his commercial engravings, including *The Fall of Rosamund* (1783), *The Idle Laundress* (1788), *The Industrious Cottagers* (1788) and *Edmund Pitts Esq.* (1793–6), are rendered using stipple.[63] For example, the skin tone in the colour print of *The Idle Laundress* has been achieved, as Michael Phillips notes, by 'very little red ink being left in the recesses made on the surface of the plate by the points of' an engraving tool known as a roulette, which produced a stippling effect.[64] There are two engravings that date from the Felpham period which are also rendered using stipple: the engraving of Thomas Alphonso after Flaxman's medallion in *Essay on Sculpture* (1800) and the engraving of Cowper after Thomas Lawrence in the second volume of the *Life of Cowper* (1804). Both demonstrate Blake's use of stippling on the face for tone and shadowing. To achieve this effect, Blake probably used an engraving tool with a sharp point such as a burin or graver to make dot-like indentations into the surface of the copperplate. The engraving of Thomas Alphonso is set in a circular frame, with a diameter of 6.5 cm (Figure 9.3). The face and background have been rendered entirely with stipple, with a combination of line and stipple for the hair and clothing. Like the aesthetic Blake achieves in his miniature paintings, he leaves

Figure 9.3 Thomas Alphonso Hayley (1800), designed by Henry Howard after a medallion by John Flaxman, engraved by William Blake. Reproduced with kind permission from the Bodleian Library, University of Oxford, N. 280 d. 489.

areas blank in both engravings, using the paper support to provide light for the face. This is noticeable on the upper cheek, nose and above the eye on the Thomas Alphonso engraving, and on the chin, cheeks, tip and bridge of the nose, and the forehead of the Cowper engraving.[65] Apart from the use of stipple in engravings, there is also a pencil and watercolour portrait by Blake dating from the Felpham period that makes extensive use of stipple.

Robert Essick has persuasively demonstrated that the *Portrait of William Blake* in his collection is a self-portrait executed from 1802 onwards, probably during Blake's residence in Felpham. The portrait appears to be related to Blake's brief career as a miniature painter, as both G. E. Bentley, Jr, and Robert Essick suggest.[66] Blake depicts his head and shoulders, facing towards the viewer, in an oval frame measuring 24.3 x 20.1 cm. He draws his clothing using pencil and black watercolour wash, and uses opaque white on his necktie. As he does in his miniature portraits, Blake, as Essick recognizes, uses fine stippling to delineate 'the contours of [the] face'.[67] Stipple is used to add tonality to the skin, such as the shading around the mouth, cheeks and nose. The white of the paper support has been used to provide reflective light on the chin, tip, bridge and sides of the nose, and the forehead. Blake's use of stippling in this portrait is consistent with his extant miniature portraits.[68]

Despite Blake's initial enthusiasm, Hayley's attempt to establish him as a miniaturist did not succeed. This was not due to any lack of ability on Blake's part. Contemporary accounts of Blake's miniatures are favourable, for example, the generally critical Lady Hesketh concedes that the Cowper miniature is 'well executed'.[69] Hayley's friend, the composer, John Marsh, was slightly more equivocal, noting in his journals that he saw 'a striking Miniature of Mr Hayley' by Blake in 1801.[70] It is possible that Blake used a delicate stippling technique in his miniatures because of its association in contemporary engravings with a softer, more feminized aesthetic. At the beginning of the nineteenth century stipple engravers, such as Caroline Watson, became very popular because of their softer style. Indeed, Hayley preferred Watson's stipple engravings to Blake's more linear engraving style, commissioning her to produce, among other things, the frontispiece engraving that appeared in the second, third and fourth editions of his biography of Cowper.[71] Also, Blake's use of stippling in his miniatures differed significantly from the popular aesthetic developed by miniaturists after 1800, which involved covering the surface of the ivory with heavy layers of paint.

The few extant miniatures, as well as manuscript references to miniatures executed by Blake during the Felpham period, appear to contradict his claim to 'have a great many orders and they multiply' (E715). The delicate stippling used on the faces of all Blake's extant miniatures appears to contradict Hayley's statement: 'He says I have taught him to paint in miniature'.[72] While Blake may have initially followed his patron's advice by executing a number of miniature portraits, it seems he did not, for the most part, follow Hayley's instructions for miniature painting. Blake uses linear strokes and opaque white to depict clothing and, like Meyer and Cosway, takes advantage of the luminescence of the support, but eschews contemporary miniature techniques to achieve this effect by using a delicate stippling technique that was probably adapted from the engraving techniques he learned during his apprenticeship.

Blake's apparent rejection of Hayley's presumed advice is fully expressed in a letter to his brother of 30 January 1803, where he states: 'as a Painter his views and mine are opposite; he thinks to turn me into a Portrait Painter as he did poor Romney' (E725).[73] Blake's criticism of Hayley is in stark contrast to his initial response to miniature portraiture, which suggests, perhaps, that he felt an initial enthusiasm that subsequently waned, or, alternatively, that he dissimulated his fondness for miniature painting in order to please his patron. Indeed, Blake's statement to Butts in a letter of 10 May 1801 that 'Miniature is become a Goddess in my Eyes' is qualified by the claim that he has 'a great many orders' (E715), which suggests that he primarily saw the commissions in an economic context. The evidence presented here that Blake's use of stippling was contrary to contemporary miniature painting techniques, particularly those of Hayley's friend and painting instructor, Jeremiah Meyer, suggests that in early 1801 Blake considered his patron's attempt economically helpful, yet creatively limiting. Put most forcefully, the use of stippling undermines Hayley's role as patron and, as such, marks the beginning of Blake's eventual rejection of Hayley's patronage. During his three-year residence in Felpham, Blake would find other ways to articulate a response to Hayley, but it appears that the first skirmish in Blake's spiritual conflict with his corporeal friend was the delicate stippling technique evident in all his extant miniature portraits.

Notes

The author wishes to thank G. E. Bentley, Jr, Robert Essick, Stephen Lloyd and Michael Phillips for reading early drafts of this essay.

1. *The Information and Complaint of John Scofield*, West Sussex County Record Office: Add MS 1607. There are a number of variant spellings for Scolfield's name on the legal documents and the military records. I have used the most common form.
2. *Blake's Memorandum in Refutation of the Information and Complaint of John Scolfield*, West Sussex Country Record Office: Add MS 1607.
3. Scolfield's ambiguous account of what Blake and Catherine said in the garden implied that they would join Napoleon's army when it landed. For more on the historical context of Blake's trial, see Mark Crosby and Jon Mee, 'This Soldierlike Danger: The Trial of William Blake for Sedition', *Resisting Napoleon: The British Response to the Threat of Invasion 1797–1815*, ed. by Mark Philp (Aldershot: Ashgate, 2006), pp. 111–24.
4. *BR*, p. 95.

5. *BR*, p. 104.
6. Romney's portrait of Cowper was executed during the poet's visit to Sussex in 1792. In a letter written from Eartham of 26 August 1792, Cowper states: 'Romney has drawn me in crayons, and in the opinion of all here, with the best hand, and with the most exact resemblance possible', see William Cowper, *Letters and Prose Writings*, ed. by James King and Charles Ryskamp, 5 vols (Oxford: Clarendon Press, 1979–86), iv (1984), pp. 180–3 (p. 182).
7. *BR*, pp. 104, 107.
8. For a discussion of the social significance of miniatures in Hanoverian society, see Marcia Pointon, 'Surrounded with Brilliants: Miniature Portraits in Eighteenth Century England', *Art Bulletin,* 83 (2001), 48–71.
9. In 1768 Ozias Humphry charged 12 guineas per miniature and George Engleheart 8 to 10 guineas. See Graham Reynolds, *English Portrait Miniatures* (Cambridge: Cambridge University Press, 1998), pp. 134, 140–1.
10. Quoted in Basil Long, *British Miniaturists* (London: Geoffrey Bless, 1929), p. 99.
11. *BR*, p. 95.
12. It is possible that Hayley had seen some copies of Blake's early illuminated books. The scale of the relief-etched designs are, in some instances, similar to contemporary miniature paintings and may have also influenced Hayley's attempt to establish Blake as a miniaturist.
13. *BR*, pp. 106–7.
14. William Hayley, *Memoirs of the Life and Writings of William Hayley with Extracts from his Private Correspondence and Unpublished Poetry*, ed. by John Johnson, 2 vols (London: 1823), i, p. 53. Hayley's regard for Meyer is also reflected in *An Essay on Painting* where he calls for 'a Myrtle Leaf for Meyer's Brow!' and his epitaph for Meyer, which reads: 'Age after age may not one artist yield/Equal to thee in painting's nicer field'. See Hayley, *An Essay on Painting, in a Poetical Epistle to an Eminent Painter* (London: J Dodsley, 1781), p. 37. For epigraph, see Meyer's memorial, St Anne's Church, Kew, Richmond. My claim that Hayley is referring to Jeremiah Meyer in the letter to Romney is contrary to Robert Essick's suggestion that it must be Meyer's son, William, as his father 'died in 1789'. See Robert Essick, 'Corrigendum', *Blake, An Illustrated Quarterly*, 39.4 (Spring 2006), 182. There is no extant evidence, including miniature portraits, to support Essick's claim that William Meyer was a miniature painter. According to Hayley's *Memoirs*, William Meyer was employed as a 'secretary to a British resident in Corfu' from some point after Thomas Alphonso's death in 1800 until 1807. See Hayley, *Memoirs* II, p. 65.
15. Daphne Foskett, *Collecting Miniatures* (London: Antiques Collector's Club, 1979), p. 374.
16. Quoted in Long, p. 293.
17. Quoted in *ibid*., p. 294.
18. Ashmolean Museum: Acc. No. 1361.
19. *Ibid*., fol. 4, No. 5.
20. Ashmolean Museum: Min. 1920, 60, 157.
21. Patrick J. Noon, 'Miniatures on the Market', *The English Miniature*, ed. by John Murdoch and others (New Haven, CT: Yale University Press, 1981), 176–97 (pp. 180–1). For other descriptions of Meyer's style, see: Daphne Foskett, *British Portrait Miniatures: A History* (London: Methuen, 1963) p. 132;

Reynolds, pp. 84–9; Christopher Lloyd and Vanessa Remington, *Masterpieces in Little: Portrait Miniatures from the Collection of Her Majesty Queen Elizabeth II* (London: Boydell Press, 1996), p. 154; Katherine Coombs, *The Portrait Miniature in England* (London: Victoria and Albert Museum Publications, 1998), pp. 84–90; and Ann Summer and Richard Walker, *Secret Passion to Noble Fashion: the World of the Portrait Miniature* (Bath: Holburne Museum of Art, 1999), p. 86.

22. Ashmolean Museum: Acc. No. 1361.

23. Hayley, *Memoirs,* I, p. 57.

24. It is unlikely that the titular friend of *A Few Hints* was Hayley, as the handwriting differs considerably from Hayley's distinctive hand.

25. Hayley cultivated friendships with a number of painters, including Joseph Wright of Derby, Richard Westall and George Romney. It is possible that these friendships also influenced his decision to direct Blake towards miniature portraiture.

26. As well as the six extant miniatures discussed in this essay, there are also epistolary and journal references to miniatures of Hayley and his wife Eliza and two miniatures of Romney executed by Blake in Felpham. In a letter to George Romney of 21 April 1801, Hayley claims to have taught Blake miniature painting using 'the two infinitely best Resemblances of yrself, that I am so happy to possess. – one he will copy exactly, – the Head from the large unfinsh'd sketch he shall reduce to the same size as its companion'. In his journal entry for 9 May 1801, Hayley's friend, the composer John Marsh, recalls seeing 'a striking Miniature of Mr Hayley' by Blake, and in a letter to Daniel Parker Coke of 13 May 1801, Hayley refers to a miniature of his wife Eliza that his son, Thomas Alphonso, was planning to execute, but which Blake appears to have painted: 'My dear Tom intended to execute for you such a Resemblance of Mrs H – His own calamitous illness & Death precluded Him from that pleasure – I have recently formed a new artist for this purpose by teaching a worthy creature (by profession an Engraver) who lives in a little Cottage very near me to paint in miniature – accept this little specimen of his Talent as a mark of Kind Remembrance' (cited in *BR*, pp. 107–8).

27. See Martin Butlin, *The Complete Paintings and Drawings of William Blake*, 2 vols. (London: Yale University Press, 1981), *Text Volume*, Cat. Nos. 346, 348, 353, 376, 377 and 378 (pp. 303–4, 306, 316 and 317).

28. Archibald Robertson, *Letters and Papers of Andrew Robertson*, ed. by Emily Robertson, (London: Eyre and Spottiswoode, 1898), pp. 18–19. Also see Reynolds, pp. 140–1.

29. West Sussex County Record Office: Add MS 1607.

30. British Library Add. MS 30803A, fol. 108.

31. Butlin speculates that only the unfinished miniature was undertaken as a preparatory work for Blake's engraving of Cowper for the first volume of Hayley's *Life of Cowper* (1803). See Butlin, *Text Volume*, Cat. No. 353 (p. 306). There is also a pencil sketch of Cowper attributed to Blake in a copy of the first edition of Cowper's *Poems* (1782) – see Charles Ryskamp, 'Blake's Cowperian Sketches', *Review of English Studies*, 9.33 (February 1958), 48–9.

32. Hayley, *Memoirs*, i, p. 181.

33. G. C. Williamson believes that the most finished Cowper miniature, now in the Ashmolean Museum, 'may have been painted to conciliate Romney's

son John'. See Butlin, *Text Volume*, Cat. No. 354 (p. 306). This would date the miniature *c*.1803–4, when Hayley was involved in negotiations to write Romney's biography, rather than 1801. This supposition is, according to Butlin, based on a reference to Romney's portrait in Blake's letters to Hayley on 27 January and 23 February 1804. Blake does not refer to Cowper in either letter; rather he mentions 'my portrait of Romney' (E740). Butlin records two untraced miniatures of Romney by Blake mentioned in Hayley's letter to Romney of 21 April 1801. Hayley tells Romney that he has 'two of the best Resemblances of yrself' which Blake will copy in miniature (*BR*, p. 107). From the epistolary evidence it seems obvious that both Blake's miniatures of Romney were executed *c*.1801.

34. The unfinished painting is reproduced in Thomas Wright, *The Life of William Cowper* (London: Farncombe and Sons, 1921), p. 336. Also see Morton D. Paley, 'Cowper as Blake's Spectre', *Eighteenth-Century Studies*, 1 (1968), 236–52 (pp. 237–8).

35. There are a number of notable differences between Romney's 1792 portrait and Blake's two miniatures. Blake softens the eyes, presumably a request from Hayley in an attempt to pacify Lady Hesketh, who seems to have objected to Romney's original being used as the basis of the engraving because it hinted at Cowper's fragile mental state. In a letter to Hayley of 19 March 1801, Hesketh states, 'I have no doubt the Original from which this fatal Miniature is taken is a very fine Picture, considered as a Picture, & I even believe the miniature is very well executed [...] you will not be so cruel as to multiply this fatal resemblance, by having the picture engrav'd!' See British Library Add. MS 30803A, fol. 114/5. For other differences between Blake's miniatures of Cowper and Romney's original, see Robert Essick, 'A (Self?) Portrait of William Blake', *Blake: An Illustrated Quarterly*, 39.3 (Winter 2005–6), 126–39 (p. 136).

36. Ashmolean Museum: Min. 385.

37. The miniature of Johnny Johnson is also in an oval frame, and shows the sitter's head and shoulders. Johnson is depicted facing slightly to the left with his left arm resting on top of a book. Rather than a watercolour wash, Blake has painted a church steeple in the background, a reference to Johnson's profession. See Butlin, *Text Volume*, Cat. No. 347 (pp. 303–4).

38. See Butlin, *Text Volume*, Cat. No. 376 (p. 316). The author has questioned Butlin's speculative dating of this miniature on stylistic grounds and epistolary evidence. See Mark Crosby, 'William Blake's Miniatures of the Butts Family', *Blake: An Illustrated Quarterly* (forthcoming).

39. British Museum Prints and Drawings: Acc No. 1942, 1010.4.

40. Thomas Butts senior was chief clerk in the office of the Muster Master General. The uniform he is wearing in the miniature may be related to that office, but as G. E. Bentley, Jr, points out: 'Thomas Butts, Sr was never either an artillery officer or Muster-Master General'. See G. E. Bentley, Jr, 'Thomas Butts, White Collar Maecenas', *PMLA*, 71 (1956), 1052–66 (p. 1056). It was fashionable for men to wear military-style uniforms from around 1800 until 1820. See C. Willett Cunnington and Phillis Cunnington, *Handbook of English Costume in the Nineteenth Century* (London: Faber and Faber, 1970), p. 75.

41. British Museum Prints and Drawings: Acc No 1942, 1010.6 and 1942 1010. 5. Also see Butlin, *Text Volume*, Cat. Nos. 377 and 378 (pp. 316–17) and

Ada E. Briggs's discussion of the three Butts miniatures in 'Mr Butts, the Friend and Patron of Blake', *The Connoisseur*, XIX.74 (October 1907), 92–6.

42. For an in-depth examination of Cosway's career, see Stephen Lloyd and Aileen Ribeiro, *Richard and Maria Cosway: Regency Artists of Taste and Fashion*, (Edinburgh: Trustees of the National Galleries of Scotland, 1995).

43. See Lloyd and Ribeiro, p. 22, and Gerald Barnett, *Richard and Maria Cosway: A Biography*, (Tiverton: West Country Books, 1995), p. 32.

44. *BR*, p. 562.

45. Cosway and Blake were later neighbours in South Molton Street. Cumberland describes a visit to both men on 3 June 1814, remarking: 'Called Cosway by Daley N 51 South Molton Street facing Poor Blake where he has been 3 Years' (*BR*, p. 316).

46. Jim Murrell claims that Cosway 'worked carefully with stipple in the features'. See Jim Murrell, 'The Craft of the Miniaturist', in *The English Miniature*, Murdoch and others 1–24 (pp. 19–20). A close examination of Cosway's miniatures in the Ashmolean Museum, Fitzwilliam Museum and Victoria and Albert Museum, however, reveals the extensive use of hatching and not stipple. Also see Richard Walker, *Miniatures: A Selection of Miniatures in the Ashmolean Museum* (Oxford: Ashmolean Museum, 1997), pp. 46–7 and Robert Bayne-Powell, *Catalogue of Portrait Miniatures in the Fitzwilliam Museum* (Cambridge: Cambridge University Press, 1985), pp. 156–8. Cosway's techniques are also described in Foskett, *British Portrait Miniatures*, p. 106; Noon, pp. 181–6; Reynolds, pp. 90–9; Lloyd and Remington, pp. 37–8; and Torben Holck Colding, *Aspects of Miniature Painting* (London: Thomas Nelson & Sons, 1953), p. 161.

47. See Robertson, pp. 69–73.

48. These were colour printed plates from the early illuminated books with the texts masked. See Butlin, *Text Volume*, Cat. Nos. 261–2 (pp. 132–45) and David Bindman, *Blake as an Artist* (Oxford: Phaidon, 1977), pp. 96–8. For biographical details, see George Charles Willliamson, *Ozias Humphry* (London: 1918).

49. For more on Humphry's style, see Foskett, *British Portrait Miniatures*, p. 118; Reynolds, pp. 104–5; Long, p. 230; Lloyd and Remington, p. 37; and Noon, p. 192.

50. Daphne Foskett suggests that Humphry gave his subjects 'an almost sleepy look'. See Foskett, *British Portrait Miniatures*, p. 118.

51. For a brief discussion of Humphry's 'elaborate backdrops', see Noon, p. 192.

52. For biographical details, see George Charles Williamson and Henry Engleheart, *George Engleheart 1750–1829: Miniature Painter to George III* (London: 1902).

53. For more on Engleheart's style, see Foskett, *British Portrait Miniatures*, p. 121, Reynolds, pp. 108–13, and Long, p. 142.

54. As well as the obvious stylistic differences between the miniatures executed by Blake and Engleheart, the biographical evidence also suggests that Engleheart's did not influence Blake's miniature painting techniques. Hayley's biographer, Morchard Bishop, claims that Engleheart and Hayley became friends during the period of Hayley's second marriage. This was between 1809 and 1812. Bishop's supposition appears to be based on Hayley's correspondence in the Fitzwilliam Museum and the British Library.

See Morchard Bishop, *Blake's Hayley: The Life, Works, and Friendships of William Hayley* (London: Victor Gollancz, 1951), p. 324. There is no mention of Engleheart in Hayley's *Memoirs* or manuscript autobiography. Although, as Hayley's editor John Johnson reveals, Hayley ceased to keep a diary from the period of his second marriage. See Hayley, *Memoirs*, II, p. 194.

55. Robertson, p. 31.

56. *Ibid.*, p. 32.

57. Edward Norgate, *Miniatura; or, The Art of Limning*, ed. by Jeffrey M. Muller and Jim Murrell (London: Yale University Press, 1997), p. 74.

58. For Bernard Lens, see Lloyd and Remington, p. 30, and Coomb, pp. 78–83.

59. Claude Boutet, *The Art of Painting in Miniature* (London: 1752), p. 1. There is no record of Boutet's text in the sale catalogue of Hayley's library.

60. *Ibid.*, pp. 17–18.

61. Noon, p. 197.

62. For biographical details of Blake's apprenticeship to Basire, see *BR*, pp. 11–17. Essick also recognizes that Blake was 'an expert stipple engraver'. See Essick, 'A (Self?) Portrait', p. 137.

63. See Robert Essick, *The Separate Plates of William Blake* (Princeton, NJ: Princeton University Press, 1983), pp. 134–8, 158–69, 178–80. Blake also used stipple in the two frontispiece engravings of *The Poems of Caius Valerius Catullus* (1795): see Robert Essick, *William Blake's Commercial Book Illustrations* (Oxford: Clarendon Press, 1991), p. 66.

64. When applied to the surface of the copper plate the roulette tool made small, dot-like indentations. See Michael Phillips, *The Creation of the Songs: From Manuscript to Illuminated Printing* (Princeton, NJ: Princeton University Press, 2000), p. 95.

65. Blake's use of the support to add tonality is also evident in his early illuminated books, which are coloured in thin, translucent watercolour washes that allow the white paper to provide luminescence to the design. See Phillips, pp. 26–7, and Robert Essick, *William Blake: Printmaker* (Princeton, NJ: Princeton University Press 1980), pp. 124–5.

66. See G. E. Bentley, Jr, *The Stranger from Paradise: A Biography of William Blake* (New Haven: Yale University Press, 2001), plate 88, and Essick, 'A (Self?) Portrait', p. 130.

67. Essick, 'A (Self?) Portrait', p. 137.

68. Essick has shown that the features of the portrait have been reversed suggesting that Blake executed the portrait by copying his reflection in a mirror. See Essick, 'A (Self?) Portrait', pp. 138/9

69. *BR*, p. 105.

70. John Marsh, *Journals*, Huntington Library MS 54457, vol. XX, p. 116. This miniature has yet to be identified.

71. The second, third and fourth editions of Hayley's *Life of Cowper* were published in four volumes, in a quarto format, in 1806, 1809 and 1812, and contain Watson's engraving of Romney's 1792 portrait. The smaller format of these editions precluded Blake's folio-sized plates being reused, although Hayley was aware that Blake could reduce his engravings to fit any format, as he had done with 1805 edition of the *Ballads*. Hayley also commissioned Watson to execute seven of the twelve plates for his biography of Romney. In a letter of 9 January 1810, Edward Garrard Marsh complimented Hayley

on the Romney biography, adding 'Watson's engravings are beautiful in the extreme; and you never made a happier exchange than when you employed her instead of Blake' (*BR*, p. 295). For a discussion of Watson's softer, more feminine aesthetic as the antithesis of Blake's linear style, see Robert Essick, 'William Blake's "Female Will" and Its Biographical Context', in *Studies in English Literature, 1500–1900*, 31.4 (August 1991), 615–30.

72. *BR*, p. 104.
73. Blake may have also been influenced by the shifting attitude towards miniaturists that occurred after 1802. The status of miniaturists as artists came under attack by a number of critics, including Martin Archer Shee, who claimed that miniature painting was the 'refuge of imbecility'. See Martin Archer Shee, *Rhymes on Art, or the Remonstrance of a Painter* (London: 1805), p. 30. See also Noon, p. 197.

10
Blake and the Literary Galleries

Luisa Calè

> Conflict lies at the basis of every art. (a unique figurative transformation of the dialectic).
>
> Sergei Eisenstein, 1929

> O Society for Encouragement of Art – O King & Nobility of England! Where have you hid Fuseli's Milton? Is Satan troubled at his Exposure.
>
> Anns to Reynolds, E636

With these words Blake overwrites Edmond Malone's triumphal address to the King in his edition of Sir Joshua Reynolds's works.[1] In the annotations to Reynolds, Blake's confrontation with Malone, Reynolds and the field of art takes on epic proportions through a series of references to *Paradise Lost*. Against Malone's celebration of Reynolds and the new scene of British art, Blake conjures up Fuseli's Milton Gallery and casts Fuseli and himself in a Satanic pose: 'Fuseli Indignant <almost> hid himself – I [*was*] <am> hid' (E636). If Reynolds is the anointed son of God, Fuseli and Blake take on the position of marginalized Satans, reiterating Homer's image of the stars who hide their diminished heads in front of the sun.[2] Another symptom pointing to the failure of the field of art to foster the right artists is the career of James Barry. It was Barry whose paintings for the Society for the Encouragement of the Arts failed to lead to patronage; hence Blake's contrast between Barry living on 'Bread & Apples' and Reynolds wallowing in riches (E636). Blake's conflation of Barry and Fuseli is revealing. Neither enjoyed financial success, but after Barry's expulsion from the Royal Academy, Fuseli took over his place as Professor of Painting (1799) and later became Keeper (1804). Although the Milton

Gallery was a failure from a financial point of view, it enjoyed both support and recognition from the Royal Academy. So Fuseli hardly qualified as an indignant Satan challenging institutional patronage of the arts. On the contrary, he sought to appeal to different publics, such as the radical dissenters who funded him on the one hand, and official art milieus on the other. To do so, Fuseli had to play down the radical edge of some of his pictures. For instance, in *Satan Encount'ring Death, Sin Interposing*, Death's seemingly headless crown, a dark form set against a black background, was barely perceptible; it was, in any case, no more than a shadowy possibility or a visual illusion, rather than a clear reference to regicide.[3] Blake's strong misreading, then, makes his identification with Fuseli and the Milton Gallery all the more indicative of his conflictual relationship with the field of art.

This essay examines Blake's engagement with the literary galleries. While Blake's production of illuminated books has been thoroughly researched, Blake Studies has yet to engage with the literary galleries as a cultural form with specific practices of reading, viewing and collecting. In what follows, I suggest how Blake responded to the rhetoric and aesthetics of the literary galleries. These venues generated an intermedial and interactive relationship between the exhibition space, the exhibition catalogue and illustrated books. This aesthetic experience reconfigured the practices of reading and viewing in ways that help us rethink Blake's textual practice. His visual allusions to literary gallery pictures show us how he rearticulated their aesthetic through the forms of the illuminated and the extra-illustrated book. Extra-illustration is a practice of collecting and book production, whereby extraneous materials such as prints, drawings, watercolours are pasted onto or inserted in-between the pages of already existing editions. Between 1795 and 1798 Blake extra-illustrated editions of Edward Young's and Thomas Gray's poetry with watercolours. Blake's illuminated and extra-illustrated books engage with the literary galleries in different ways. I explore these differences through Blake's dialogue with Fuseli's *Satan Bursts From Chaos*, a Milton Gallery picture which Blake was commissioned to engrave for Joseph Johnson's Milton edition, which he went on to emulate in both illuminated and extra-illustrated formats in the mid- and late 1790s.

Literary Gallery Conflicts

Conflict characterized not only personal attitudes to the art world, but also the relationship between different groups, institutions and venues.

An entry entitled 'The Miltons' published in the *Oracle* newspaper in January 1792 outlines the site of contest:

These grand Designs display so well the Taste and Talents of a Nation, that we say the more rivalry the better. The arrangements run thus:

Johnson,	*versus*	Boydell.
Fuseli,	———	All England.
	Literary department	
Cowper,	———	Hayley.

Readers wishing to add Blake to this sketch of enemy lines would place him in the camp of Johnson, Fuseli and Cowper. Three days after this announcement, another article in the same newspaper publicized the work in progress at the Milton Gallery, featuring prints of *Satan Opposing Death, and Sin Intervening* to be engraved by William Sharp, and *Satan Starts From Chaos*, intended for Blake.[4] The format of Johnson's and Boydell's Miltons followed the model of Boydell's Shakspeare Gallery (announced in 1786, opened in 1789), which combined an exhibition of newly commissioned paintings with the sale of the prints engraved from those paintings and the subscription to a nine-volume edition of Shakespeare's works. This initiative, Boydell claimed, offered an answer to the lack of patronage of grand-style English art and would thus support the birth of an English School of Painting financed through subscription. By the time Boydell's and Johnson's editions of Milton were announced, the literary-gallery format had been followed by Thomas Macklin's Poets (1788) and his Bible (1790), while Robert Bowyer published prospectuses for his Historic Gallery in 1792 and opened it to the public in 1793.

The 'rivalry' between the competing Milton publications defines the illustrated book market as a site of conflict. In the heated public sphere of the 1790s, the Joseph Johnson imprint was associated with publications by Joseph Priestley, Mary Wollstonecraft, Gilbert Wakefield and Tom Paine. By contrast, John Boydell joined the counter-revolutionary efforts of the Society for the Preservation of Liberty and Property against Republicans and Levellers.[5] Both literary galleries were distinguished from the Royal Academy. A vocabulary of conflict defined the place of the literary galleries in the field of art in prospectuses, advertisements and catalogue introductions. These publications, however, shun conflict and reconfigure the commercial public sphere around the more peaceful connotations of competition to suit a liberal vision of the market as a self-regulating mechanism. For Immanuel Kant commerce contributes to a condition of perpetual peace rather than conflict between nations.[6] Literary-gallery advertisements and puffs argue that commerce promotes the free circulation of goods across borders rather than protectionist measures against the import of foreign luxuries. Thanks to the market of prints, pictures now offered to the public a new generation of artists to enlist in 'the first Aera of competition in Painting', which summons art to the 'first English olympiad'.[7] The civic humanist argument that associates art with freedom is reshaped to make space for commerce. If the progress of art can be taken as a sign of English liberty, this is because commerce is thought to stimulate comparison and competition. Entrepreneurs like Boydell, the 'commercial Maecenas',[8] represent the English answer to the Medici of Italy by stimulating the patronage of the people rather than the monopoly of the King or the aristocracy.[9] Such a liberal view of competition clashes with Blake's charges against 'Contemptible Counter Arts' (E580).[10] His relationship with the literary galleries was ambivalent and polemical.

Blake's ambivalence can be detected through the echoes of literary-gallery puffing that can be heard in his writing. On the frontispiece of Blake's copy of Emanuel Swedenborg's *Treatise Concerning Heaven and Hell* (1784) a previous annotator had inscribed the famous passage in *Midsummer Night's Dream* in which Theseus defines the imagination as that which 'gives to airy Nothing a local habitation & a name' (V. i. 18–19). Beside it Blake penned the following comment: 'Thus Fools quote Shakespeare The Above is Theseus's opinion Not Shakespeares You might as well quote Satans blasphemies from Milton & give them as Miltons Opinions' (E601).[11] Prominent among those who appropriated Theseus's definition under Shakespeare's name was John Boydell. In his preface to the Shakspeare Gallery catalogue, the quotation is turned into a question and a concession to his critics: 'what pencil can give to his airy beings "a local habitation and a name"?'. Indeed, the task of 'giving a local habitation and a name' to Shakespeare's 'airy beings' would defeat the powers of Michelangelo and Raphael, let alone Boydell's artists.[12] By contrast, a few years later, a puff for the Milton Gallery used the same passage to celebrate Fuseli's visual embodiments of Milton's incorporeal inventions.[13]

Theseus's definition of the imagination and its literary-gallery context reemerge twice in Blake's *Milton*. The first instance celebrates the activities of the sons of Los. The 'Printing Press of Los', or 'War on

Earth', is located eastward of Golgonooza, 'namd Art & Manufacture by mortal men'. Human arts and sciences are divided between Bowlahoola ('namd Law. by mortals') and Allamanda, a cultivated land 'calld on Earth Commerce', situated around the city of Golgonooza (27 [29]: 1, 8–9, 42–3, E125; 24 [26]: 50, E120). In this symbolic topography:

> Some Sons of Los surrounded the Passions with porches of iron
> & silver
> Creating form & beauty around the dark regions of sorrow,
> Giving to airy nothing a name and a habitation.
> (28[30]: 1–3, E125)

Their work echoes the artistic endeavours of the fallen demons in Book ii of *Paradise Lost*. Like Milton's demon-builders, the Sons of Los turn 'airy nothing' into an architectural 'habitation'. This demonic 'habitation' draws out an important dimension of the literary galleries. By giving visual form to 'airy nothings' the literary galleries claimed to 'give a local habitation and a name' not just to the inventions of Shakespeare or Milton, but to British art itself. For one of the obstructions to the development of British art had been the lack of physical spaces where artists could show their works and thus make a name for themselves. Reference to a 'local habitation and a name' resurfaces at the beginning of the second book of *Milton*. This time it is a request for a 'Temporal Habitation' advanced by the emanations in Beulah, the place 'where Contrarieties are equally True', 'a pleasant and lovely Shadow | Where no dispute can come' (30[33]: 1–3, E129). Such a place seems to embody a type of patronage and a form of politeness that Blake would hardly ascribe to if 'Without Contraries is no progression' (*Marriage*, pl. 3, E34).

Blake complained that the literary gallery printsellers had ignored his talents. Although he was initially listed among the engravers engaged in Henry Fuseli's Milton Gallery and Robert Bowyer's Historic Gallery, nothing came of either.[14] On the other hand, he did receive minor commissions from Boydell and Macklin.[15] Macklin's most prominent engraver was the Italian émigré Francesco Bartolozzi, who was at the heart of the visual culture that Blake attacks in the Notebook satires (see Morton Paley's essay in this volume). However, despite Blake's ambivalence towards Bartolozzi's visual aesthetic, it would be wrong to underestimate the impact that the literary galleries had on Blake's engagement with the book as a medium.

'Turning readers into Spectators': the Gallery and the Book

In an article of 1788, Fuseli argued that 'the excellence of pictures or of language consists in raising clear, complete, and circumstantial images, and turning readers into spectators'.[16] This claim was not new. Similar claims, deriving from Aristotelian rhetoric, can be found in Joseph Addison's *Spectator*, Lord Kames's *Elements of Criticism* and Joseph Warton's *An Essay on the Genius and Writings of Pope*, which was Fuseli's immediate source.[17] What was new was the moment. For Fuseli's article inaugurated the new 'Arts' section of the *Analytical Review* by writing about Macklin's Poets Gallery, the first literary gallery to open to the public. In Fuseli's words the claim became literal: the readers' spectatorship was no longer a virtual production of the act of reading; rather, literary texts were literally turned into galleries of pictures and literally appealed to readers to become spectators and see/read literature in the form of sequences of pictures.

The relationship between pictures and words, the gallery and the book, is crucial to the literary galleries. In these exhibition spaces pictures hung one beside another could be perceived as a visual sequence independent of or different from the articulations of the verbal source. Readers could also complement their visual skills with their memory or their powers of invention to link together the episodes depicted into a narrative continuum. On the other hand, books were prominent at the literary galleries. Indeed, the pictures on view had been commissioned to provide engravings for illustrated editions and these exhibitions functioned as showrooms to promote subscriptions and sales. As a result, relevant references to the illustrated editions could be found in titles, catalogue excerpts and inscriptions at the bottom of the prints. This practice of quotation and anthologization inevitably interrupted and put into question the linear cohesion of the source, while it asked readers to reconstruct the story drawing on their memory or imagination. Outside the exhibition space, readers could recall the visual experience they had at the gallery through the prints, which they were invited to bind either with the letterpress produced for the purpose as part of the gallery or into editions they already owned. Readers could, in other words, customize their volumes by combining prints from different sources – produced individually, in series, or culled from other books. This practice of extra-illustration combined the acts of reading, viewing and collecting. The literary galleries fostered a dynamic relationship between viewing and reading. The gallery functioned as a spatial repository hung with pictures, a paper gallery and a retail outlet where buyers could examine the prints and buy them as parts of books, separate plates, or in series.

This dynamic is relevant to Blake's illuminated work in the first half of the 1790s. Martin Butlin has noted a progressive increase in the scale of Blake's illuminated printing until 'the despairing, agonized protagonists of *Urizen* almost break out of the bounds of the page, and the next step was literally [...] the production of some of the illustrations from the books as separate color-printed designs without text'.[18] Full-page illustrations emulate the format of picture reproductions. Because they are less bound by a textual sequence they offer a more dynamic relationship between text and images within the bindings of the book. Their autonomy made them easier to move from their original context and to insert into the Large and Small Books of Designs. Joseph Viscomi argues that Ozias Humphry commissioned the Large and Small Books of Designs as samplers of Blake's colour-printing technique, complementing the illuminated books he already owned.[19] According to Butlin, there is a coherent development from the full-page illustrations to the large separate colour prints of 1795.[20] The themes of some of these prints recall the subjects of the literary galleries. Compare, for instance, Blake's *The House of Death* with Fuseli's Milton Gallery picture *The Lazarhouse* (1791–5).[21] More interesting in terms of scale is Blake's *The Good and Evil Angels*. The compositional structure comes from Fuseli's *Satan Starts at the Touch of Ithuriel's Lance* (1780), later the basis for picture XIV of the Milton Gallery. Robin Hamlyn argues that *The Good and Evil Angels* is an enlarged version in reverse of plate 4 of *The Marriage of Heaven and Hell*, which Blake produced after colour printing copies of *Marriage* around 1794.[22] The difference in scale suggests the differences between literary-gallery formats: a larger image to be seen on a wall and smaller one to be perused in a book. However, the display at the literary galleries emphasized the distinction between media, which stood for the distinction between invention and execution, intellectual and mechanical faculties, viewing and reading. Indeed, oil paintings had pride of place in the exhibition space, whereas prints were mostly part of the experience of the illustrated book, a distinction that Blake's large colour plates of 1795 challenged.

Jean Hagstrum and W. J. T. Mitchell define *The Book of Urizen* as a picture gallery.[23] 'Gallery' was a slippery term, used not only to refer to an architectural space, but also to books of engravings reproducing paintings or frescoes, often as a series from famous galleries. These paper 'galleries' functioned as a repository of memory but also as paper surrogates for those who did not have access to the originals. Through such paper galleries, Blake was introduced to Michelangelo, Raphael and Rubens. However, the experience of prints as traces of an absent architectural space was different from the combined experience of the gallery and the book fostered by the literary galleries. As Blake used the artist book as a form of exhibition through publication, he initiated the route of autonomy that the artist book movement of the 1960s took as a reaction against the institutionalized spaces of the art world. In both cases, however, the book as gallery worked insofar as it was read as a response to the art world that fostered the viewing practices and exhibition politics it left behind.

Blake's use of the book as gallery is evident in some of the illustrations that he produced for the illustrated edition of Young's *Night Thoughts* published by Richard Edwards in 1797. Blake worked on pages from the first and second editions of *Night Thoughts*, which he pasted on to much larger sheets; he asterisked the lines he intended to illustrate and then painted in watercolour around the letterpress. The technique might feel domestic, yet through this homely medium Blake engages with the more public dynamics of gallery competition. Consider his extra-illustration for Night i of Young's *Night Thoughts*:

> Know, Smiler! At thy peril art thou pleas'd;
> Thy pleasure is the promise of thy Pain.
> Misfortune, like a Creditor severe,
> But rises in demand for her Delay;
> She makes a scourge of past Prosperity,
> *To sting thee more, and double thy Distress.[24]

The visual composition Blake chooses to illustrate this passage alludes to Philippe Jacques de Loutherbourg's *The Deluge*, which had been on view as part of Macklin's Bible since 1790.[25] An additional source for the composition is Fuseli's 1781 Royal Academy exhibit *The Death of Dido*.[26] This picture exemplifies Fuseli's rivalry with Reynolds in that it tried to outdo the painting of the same subject that Reynolds had painted for the same exhibition. As the serpent coming from de Loutherbourg turns Fuseli's Dido into a Cleopatra, Blake's image offers a literal referent for the 'sting' of misfortune. In reading Young's words and looking at Blake's illustration the reader might visualize the two gallery pictures in an inter-medial practice of reading that connects Young's *Night Thoughts* with the visual culture and the conflicts of the contemporary exhibition scene.

Yet exhibition culture rearticulates the act of reading in a more radical way. A dynamic tension exists between the multidirectional possibilities of the exhibition space and the continuities of the text, when the eye alternates between viewing a picture and reading a catalogue entry or when the textual sequence on the page is interrupted by extra-illustrated pages added to the book. In other words, the exhibition does not stand alone as a mode that invokes pictorial protocols of experience divorced from the work's status as a book.[27] Rather, the relationship between exhibition and book, book and print, bound and unbound forms, and spatial and temporal orders of experience rearticulates the practices of reading and viewing in a way that questions textual continuities and produces an aesthetics of the book radically unbound. Unbound forms have been an important way of conceptualizing Blake's books. According to Paul Mann, Blake's mode of production should be taken as the meaning or aesthetic of his books.[28] Blake did not print his books one copy at a time: in a printing session he produced a number of copies of each print. Later the prints would be coloured and assembled into sometimes unique configurations. This process leads Saree Makdisi to argue that 'the category of the book as such seems almost an organizing fiction, a convenient rubric or packaging, a useful mode to try and contain what turn out to be uncontainable images'. Makdisi claims that for Blake the book is 'almost an afterthought [...] rather than the organizing and guiding rubric for the process of production itself'.[29] A different interpretation of what Blake's printing sessions reveal about his idea of the book can be detected in Viscomi's decision to call the copies produced during a printing session an 'edition'.[30] The importance of the book as a form is further suggested by the fact that some of Blake's illuminated works are entitled 'books' and emulate the experience of an open book by printing plates on the pages' rectos and versos. Nonetheless, Makdisi's model can be fruitfully read as part of a gallery aesthetic in which the narrative possibilities of images are indeed uncontainable in the sense that their multiple positions in different copies of a book offer multiple inventive options. Indeed, in Blake's time no reader was in a position to collate all versions and copies of Blake's images. Yet Blake's contemporaries would be versed in actual and virtual imaging through the practices of reading, viewing, collecting and customizing books generated by the confluence of the book and print market in late eighteenth-century exhibition culture. Such a dynamic only works, however, if virtual imaging participates in a dialectical tension with the book as an aesthetic category.

The act of reading has often been thought of in terms of production, process, or performance. In a provocative article, Harold Bloom called on the Russian film director Sergei Eisenstein to suggest that 'Blake [...] wants his reader to be more of a film-script reader or even a director than a film-viewer'.[31] While Bloom paradoxically used Eisenstein to foreclose the materiality of Blake's visual aesthetic, it is tempting to use Eisenstein to think about the intermedial gallery environment as a model for the act of reading. In their intermedial functioning, the gallery and the book offer discontinuous syntactic articulations of words and images along the lines that Eisenstein identified with film montage.[32] At first Blake's choice of medium seems to foreclose the discontinuities produced by the tension between the experience of the exhibition and the book. Illuminated printing reacts to the division of labour that characterizes the literary galleries by way of an alternative 'method of Printing which combines the Painter and Poet' (E692). While this description fails to account for Catherine Blake's contribution to the colouring process, Blake's suggestion that painter, poet and engraver are unified in the same person is confirmed by a design in which letters turn into foliage and images venture in between the lines of the text. Thus challenging the distinction between letterpress and illustration, words and images, Blake emphasizes the uniformity of his medium. As a result, this method offers less scope for the verbal and visual intervention of readers to invent or remember words to accompany the pictures in front of them, or a mental image for the text encountered on the page. Nor is there much scope for extra-illustrators to supplement such homogeneous works with prints from extraneous sources and thus turn them into a record of collecting and personal taste. On the other hand, much as extra-illustration discovers in a book the potential for a dynamic and unique personal object, so too do Blake's illuminated books reveal an unstable and unpredictable dynamism. Not only do they lack synchronization between the text and image on the same plate or across subsequent plates, but plates are placed in different sequences in different copies of the same book. Such a dynamic form can be fruitfully investigated through Eisenstein's reading of the 'contrapuntal design of non-coincidences' between pictures and words. To illustrate how such a reading might work, I will now turn to Blake's allusions to Fuseli's *Satan Bursts From Chaos*.

Satan Bursts From Chaos and *The Book of Urizen*

While Joseph Johnson's edition of Milton folded and Blake's commission to engrave Fuseli's *Satan Bursts From Chaos* did not result in an illustration to *Paradise Lost*, a trace of Fuseli's picture can be detected in plate 10 of Blake's *Book of Urizen*. Before Fuseli's picture was exhibited at the

Figure 10.1 Henry Fuseli, *Satan Bursts from Chaos* (1799). Reproduced with kind permission from Private Collection, Switzerland, copyright Schweizerisches Institut für Kunstwissenschaft.

Milton Gallery, those who had a chance to see it at Fuseli's were free to recall or invent words to go with it. By the time the Milton Gallery opened in 1799, they had the option to complement their memory or invention with the corresponding extract from *Paradise Lost* excerpted

Figure 10.2   William Blake, *The First Book of Urizen*, copy C, pl. 9: 'Chap: IV / 1
Ages on ages roll'd over him ...' (1794). Reproduced with kind permission from the
Yale Center for British Art, Paul Mellon Collection, B1978.43.1428.

in the gallery catalogue, which describes how Satan 'springs upwards like a pyramid of fire'.[33] Although, of course, fewer people had access to *Urizen*, Blake's book emulates some aspects of the exhibition culture of the time. One of the 'gallery' features of *Urizen* is that it was printed on the rectos only, which means that readers opening the book are confronted with a single plate at a time.[34] So they are encouraged to halt and peruse plate 10 autonomously the way they might peruse a picture, because they are less conscious that the plate is one in a sequence as when an open book shows two pages at a time. Nonetheless, the fact that plate 10 is inscribed with text reminds them that it is part of a book and encourages them to join the plates into a narrative continuum. This oscillation between the book seen as a gallery and as a text is reinforced by the appearance of plate 10 in the two Small Books of Designs assembled between 1794 and 1796. In these collections, instead of the text of *Urizen*, which is masked, plate 10 is inscribed with the words 'Does the Soul labour thus | in Caverns of the Grave'.[35] While Fuseli's catalogue entry selects words that convey Satan's kinetic impetus, this inscription and the text of plate 10 amplify the effort required in traversing Chaos as a work of ages. A comparison of the two figures confirms their contrary emphases on dynamism and interminable labour. In Blake's counter-reading, instead of Fuseli's highly dynamic sequence of Satan's fast-moving pace through Chaos we see a more static figure, a tired old Titan tense with effort.

Urizen has as many plate sequences as there are copies. This dynamism has teased the desire for narrative closure in several critics. G. E. Bentley attempted to 'establish' the text by selecting the copy that seemed most consistent in its narrative sequence and used it as a basis for his eclectic reading text.[36] Full-plate illustrations are deemed responsible for most of the variation, while the critic aims to anchor them to the narrative so as to achieve maximum continuity.[37] Such attempts have a Urizenic feel, as if trying to stabilize the illuminated book into that 'solid without fluctuation' that Urizen seeks to achieve with his book of brass (4: 11, E71), a self-reflective parody of Blake's own book-making. However, the fact that Blake had numbered copies with different sequences suggests that there may be other ways of reading *Urizen*.[38] Indeed, Jerome McGann reads it as a response to late eighteenth-century developments in biblical scholarship. As a parody of the Bible, *Urizen* exhibits its condition as a fragmentary, miscellaneous work through its textual inconsistencies, repetitions and non-sequiturs.[39]

A cinematic reading adds a further dimension to McGann's argument for textual discontinuity. According to Eisenstein, montage is a dialectical form which operates through 'conflict between two neighbouring fragments. Conflict. Collision.'[40] Visual cues invite us to view plate 10 as part of a visual continuum, one in a sequence of movements represented in plates 9, 13 and 14, which feature a naked figure against a dark background opening up a path through an unfathomable dark waste by pushing against rocks. A cinematic reading may tend to blend these poses into the stages of a movement, but that tendency is no sooner satisfied than undone. For these plates are only occasionally contiguous: depending on the copy consulted, they are interrupted by a varying number and sequence of other plates:

Erdman	A	B	C	D	F	G
9	23	15	8	8	11	4
10	13	9	9	9	9	12
13	16	14	10	12	13	15
14	15	13	14	13	8	8[41]

Visual and narrative continuums are reversible and temporary forms within a dynamic conception of the book as a montage of words and images. Blake's book thus reunites in one medium what is an intermedial practice of reading and viewing at the gallery. In a literary gallery viewers could turn into readers and back again as their eyes alternated between a view of the pictures and a reading of relevant catalogue excerpts. In the three dimensions of the gallery space spectators could look at pictures ignoring the viewing sequence suggested by the catalogue. The different arrangements of prints across different copies retain some of that freedom for the medium of the book, which is thus liberated from the need to conform to a single arrangement of the plates in a sequence. Viscomi argues that the presence or absence of plates 4 and 16 have significant impact in shaping different narrative paths, but follows Geoffrey Keynes in considering the alternative arrangements of full-plate illustrations as 'probably insignificant'.[42] Yet these full-plate illustrations have a significant role in the dynamic relationship with the text written on contiguous plates. For instance, the 'Preludium' invokes the Eternals to 'unfold [...] dark visions of torment'; this injunction has different effects depending on whether it is followed by full-plate visualizations of Urizen crouching in chains (pl. 22) and his sons (pl. 24) as in Copy A, or by Chapter 1 (pl. 3) as in copies B, C, D, F and G. In the first case, the full plates interrupt the narrative continuum and the flow of reading, opening up other possibilities. Not only does the anchoring of images and words change and with it their allusive potential, but so too does the way the book addresses its public as readers and/or spectators. When the injunction to see is followed by full-page illustrations of the 'visions of torment', the readers are engaged in the process of invention and encouraged to anticipate the plot; when it is followed by Chapter 1 the visions are further defined as an 'abominable void', a 'soul-shudd'ring vacuum' (pl. 3, E70), which some attribute to Urizen. This time the reader is left to visualize this expanded Miltonic chaos materialized through the text's words. In each case the reader is confronted with a different task and the rhythm of the story is different.

Satan Bursts from Chaos vs The Christian Triumph

Satan Bursts From Chaos also resurfaces in the watercolour illustrations with which Blake extra-illustrated Young's *Night Thoughts*. Blake scholars have pointed out that Blake's illustrations express a competitive relationship with Young's poem. This critical distance takes the shape of a personal visual appropriation. For Walter Benjamin the age of technical reproducibility marks the transition from an aesthetic based on distance to a much more personal and tactile relationship with art, which enables viewers to take hold of objects and manipulate them.[43] This tactile dimension is central to extra-illustrated books. Pasting the text onto larger sheets opens up a space for the readers to add materials of their choice to the text. In the case of Blake's extra-illustration of Young, a preparatory phase towards a commission, this space is limited by the sequence of pages, which dictates a one-to-one relationship between the page of text and the number and sequence of illustrations, whereas extra-illustrated books often multiply in bulk when they are rebound with the additional materials added by their owners. As they paused to decorate the moments or turns in the text which particularly captured their attention with prints, drawings, or watercolours, readers were free to add extra pages, and were therefore no longer bound to the rhythm of reading produced by the book's printed layout.

Through his allusions to a Miltonic iconography, Blake's illustrations to *Night Thoughts* appeal to the visual paradigms of Edwards's prospective buyers. Indeed, the volume's declared aim was to give 'to the great work of Young some of those advantages of dress and ornament which have lately distinguished the immortal productions of Shakspeare and of Milton'.[44] The book's circulation, format and intertextual network locate *Night Thoughts* at the crossroads between the literary gallery ventures, medieval book illuminations and the visual format of the alternative printing techniques that Blake described in his 1793 prospectus. The unusual layout of Blake's illustrations suggests that he was looking for alternatives to the formats of the printed book. By surrounding the text, the illustrations evoke the visual aesthetic of medieval illuminated

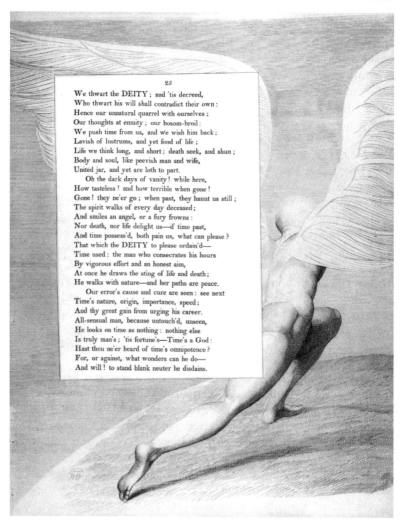

Figure 10.3 William Blake, Extra-illustration of Night II lines 145–63, in Edward Young, *The Complaint, and, The Consolation; or, Night Thoughts* (London, 1797), p. 25. Reproduced with kind permission from the Bodleian Library, University of Oxford, Arch A b. 11, p. 25.

books. The Bedford Book of Hours, which had already influenced Blake's *Songs of Innocence and of Experience*,[45] was on display at the shop of Edwards's brother, James, in Pall Mall. James Edwards was a partner in Robert Bowyer's *History of England*; the prospectus for *Night Thoughts* indicates that specimens of the work were on display at both Bowyer's Historic Gallery and at James Edwards's shop in Pall Mall.[46] Visual references to the literary galleries suggest that *Night Thoughts* participated in the publishing circuit of the literary galleries and addressed the same public.

Consider the elongated limbs of Time's flight with which Blake extra-illustrated Night ii, lines 145–63. Young's text is asterisked on a line which invites the reader to visualize Time: 'Behold him, when past by; what then is seen | But his broad Pinions swifter than the Winds?'[47] Visualizing Young's Time through *Satan Bursts From Chaos* means reading Fuseli's picture emblematically and turning Satan's journey out of Chaos and towards Eden into an image of Time and impending Death.[48] In this case, Blake emphasizes the kinetic effects of Fuseli's picture to the point of generating a cinematic sequence out of it. A previous and a subsequent motion visualize the lines '*Time*, in advance, behind him hides his Wings' and 'Measuring his Motions by revolving Spheres'.[49] As it is surrounded by the visual action, the block of text acquires an iconic dimension: Time can first be seen to the left of the letterpress, then on the subsequent page his 'passing by' is visualized through a 180-degree rotation to the right of the letterpress. Blake's depiction of movement and Edwards's manipulation of the typeface make the most of the medium of the book, taking advantage of the cinematic effect produced by turning the pages. In the engraved edition the relationship between the three moments of Time's flight is tightened by the smaller letterpress used by Edwards. The text is compressed to fit the three illustrations onto three subsequent pages. This layout involves the elimination of two extra-illustrated sheets, which interrupt the transition between the second and third movement in Blake's extra-illustrated volume of watercolours.[50] While the two intervening sheets in watercolour illustrate the tension that Young outlines between kinetic Time and Time interminable, the engraved edition emphasizes the speed at the expense of the alternation of contrasting paces which characterizes Young's perception of time.

Following Janet Warner we may also see Fuseli's elongated limbs in the leaping figure of Christ resurrected which Blake painted as a frontispiece to *Night Thoughts* iv, 'The Christian Triumph'.[51] The shape of the clouds also recalls Fuseli's *Satan Bursts From Chaos*. The idea of

Figure 10.4   William Blake, 'The Christian Triumph', frontispiece to Night IV, in Edward Young, *The Complaint, and, The Consolation; or, Night Thoughts* (London, 1797), p. 65. Reproduced with kind permission from the Bodleian Library, University of Oxford, Arch A b. 11, p. 65.

reading Young through Milton is intriguing. Yet in 1797 'the dress and ornament [...] of Shakspeare and of Milton' would inevitably point the reading public to Boydell's Shakespeare and to his newly published Milton, rather than to the by then defunct Milton edition planned by

Figure 10.5 Richard Westall, Illustration for Book III of *Paradise Lost*, in *The Poetical Works of John Milton*, 3 vols (London, 1794–7), I, opposite p. 77. Reproduced with kind permission from the Bodleian Library, University of Oxford, 27980 b. 1–3 vols, opposite p. 77.

Joseph Johnson. Boydell's publication of Milton roughly coincides with Blake's work on *Night Thoughts*. So it would make more sense if the iconography of *Night Thoughts* alluded to the more successful Milton published by Boydell. Leaving aside Fuseli's elongated limbs, let us turn to Richard Westall's illustrations to Boydell's Milton. Indeed, as G. E. Bentley pointed out in his edition of *Vala*, Blake's 'Christian Triumph' alludes to Westall's illustration for Book III in Boydell's edition of *Paradise Lost*.[52] Christ appears as a figure of mediation ascending in mid-air, following the iconography of a Transfiguration.

Blake's reading of Young is much more Christological than Young's text justifies.[53] This Christological interest is confirmed by the choices Blake made for the *Paradise Lost* plates he produced for Joseph Thomas and Thomas Butts in 1807–8: 'Christ Offers To Redeem Man' for Book iii and a Crucifixion for Book xi instead of the Fuselian 'House of Death' of 1795. By contrast, Book iii of Milton's epic is absent from Fuseli's corpus: Christ the redeemer would have found little favour with the Unitarian milieu of Joseph Johnson that funded Fuseli's work. So it is all the more significant to see Blake turn to the rival Milton edition for his figure of mediation. In August 1799 Blake complained to George Cumberland that even Johnson and Fuseli had ignored his graver since the Young edition (E704). The lack of commissions may be explained by entirely different reasons: by that time Richard Edwards had retired, Johnson was awaiting a jail sentence and Fuseli was dejected because of the disappointing turnout at the Milton Gallery. Even so, Blake had grounds to be concerned that they might be displeased with the Christological iconography of his Young illustrations.

Yet, despite the iconographic and theological differences between Westall's Christ and Fuseli's Satan, a kinetic trace of Fuseli's elongated *Satan Bursts From Chaos* might well inhabit the body of Christ triumphant in Blake's *Night Thoughts*. An allusion to both Fuseli's Satan and Westall's Christ in the same image might act as a source of energy. If Blake's reference to Westall's Christ suggests that *Night Thoughts* interpellates the horizon of expectation of the Boydell reader, a tension of contraries that refuses a neat partition into Good and Evil is a fit dialectical image to disturb the iconography of Boydell's edition.

Blake's allusion to Boydell's Milton confirms evidence that in 1796–7 he was experimenting with different book formats in an attempt to access the literary-gallery market.[54] In 1797 and 1798 he was listed in directories addressed to the subscribers of illustrated books such as Boydell's Milton and Edwards's *Night Thoughts*.[55] Rather than one 'Local Habitation and a Name', his texts advocate a plurality of places or 'gates' to experience. Trying to cross the class boundaries of the artisan-engraver, Blake tried to incorporate in his works the freedoms of reading and viewing experienced in the exhibition space. In a public sphere held together by modes of sympathy predicated on politeness and the toning down of individual differences, Fuseli could move between the different publics of rational dissent and the Royal Academy; he would dine at Joseph Johnsons's or visit him in jail, but also exhibit at Boydell's and take up positions in a royal institution. By contrast, Blake emphasized dialectical tensions: in his work he despised 'soft dissimulation', focused on forms of 'corporeal strife' (*Milton*, pl. 8, 31[34]), and argued for the clash of contraries and a friendship based on opposition (*Marriage*, pl. 3, 20). It is questionable whether his audience was fit, but it was certainly too few.

Notes

1. *Works of Sir Joshua Reynolds*, ed. by Edmond Malone, 2nd edn, 3 vols (London: 1798), i, i: annotated copy held in British Library, sig. C.45.e.18–20.
2. For Satan's image of the stars hiding their diminished heads in front of the sun, see *Paradise Lost*, iv. 32–5, which William Hayley applied to Homer in *An Essay on Epic Poetry* (London: 1782), p. 11, ll. 177–84, whereas James Gillray quoted it to caricature the Royal Academicians in *Titianus Redivivus* (1797), where the stars hiding their diminished heads are Rubens, Correggio, Michelangelo, Raphael and Parmigianino falling onto the cracked façade of the Royal Academy.
3. See Luisa Calè, *Fuseli's Milton Gallery: 'Turning Readers into Spectators'* (Oxford: Clarendon Press, 2006), pp. 142–83.
4. 'The Miltons', *The Oracle*, 10 January 1792, and 8, 10, 11, 13 February 1792. I am grateful to Jon Mee for these references.
5. Michael Phillips, 'Blake and the Terror 1792–93', *The Library*, 16 (1994), 263–97.
6. Immanuel Kant, 'Perpetual Peace: A Philosophical Sketch', in *Political Writings*, ed. by H. S. Reiss, 2nd edn (Cambridge: Cambridge University Press, 1991), p. 114. Kant's essay was first translated as *Project for a Perpetual Peace, A Philosophical Essay* (London: 1796).
7. *St James's Chronicle*, 5–7 May 1789.
8. *Ibid.*
9. *The World*, 5 May 1789; *The Times*, 7 May 1789; see also Calè, *Fuseli's Milton Gallery*, pp. 18–20.
10. See Morris Eaves, *The Counter-Arts Conspiracy: Art and Industry in the Age of Blake* (Ithaca, NY: Cornell University Press, 1992).
11. The edition Blake owned was published in 1784, but his marginalia contain a reference to a Swedenborg text published in 1787, and Morton Paley concurs with G. E. Bentley in a tentative dating of 1788 for Blake's marginalia. See G. E. Bentley, *Blake Books* (Oxford: Clarendon Press, 1977), p. 696; Morton Paley, ' "A New Heaven is Begun": William Blake and Swedenborgianism',

BIQ, 13 (1979), 64–90 (pp. 65, 67, 87, n. 13). Susan Matthews suggests that Blake's rejection of the definition of the imagination in *Midsummer Night's Dream* is part of a rejection of the 'territorialization' of the imagination and with it the colonial, African localizations cherished by the Swedenborgians: see Matthews, 'Africa and Utopia: Refusing a "Local Habitation"', in *The Reception of Blake in the Orient*, ed. by Steve Clark and Masashi Suzuki (London: Continuum, 2006), pp. 104–20 (pp. 104–5).

12. See Preface, in *A Catalogue of the Pictures in the Shakspeare Gallery* (London: 1789), pp. ix–x, also reprinted in *The Diary; or Woodfall's Register*, 5 May 1789, p. 4.

13. See *Morning Chronicle*, 17 June 1799. The Boydell-Fuseli context is discussed in Calè, *Fuseli's Milton Gallery*, pp. 17, 30, 45, 55.

14. 'I was alive & in health & with the same Talents I now have all the time of Boydells Macklins Bowyers & other Great Works. I was known by them & was look'd upon by them as Incapable of Employment in those Works' (letter from Blake to Hayley, 11 December 1805, E766–7). For listings of Blake in the Milton Gallery and Historic Gallery prospectuses, see *BR*, p. 62.

15. A variation print for Boydell's *Romeo and Juliet*, published in 1799, bears the signature of Blake: see *Boydell's Graphic Illustrations of the Dramatic Works of Shakspeare* (London: 1803); and *The Dramatic Works of Shakspeare Revised by George Steevens* (London: 1802), ix; see also Bentley, *Blake Books*, nos. 437 and 497, pp. 535–6 and 614–17; Robert Essick, *The Separate Plates of William Blake, A Catalogue* (Princeton, NJ: Princeton University Press, 1983), pp. 252–3; and Robert Essick, *William Blake's Commercial Book Illustrations* (Oxford: Clarendon, 1991), p. 83. For Macklin, Blake engraved *The Fall of Rosamund* in 1783, and also works by Meheux and Watteau: see *Poetic Description of Choice and Valuable Prints, Published by Mr Macklin at the Poets' Gallery, Fleet Street* (London: 1794), 62, 68, 70, and *BR*, pp. 305, 814–15n.

16. *Analytical Review*, 1 June 1788, 216–18 (p. 216).

17. Calè, *Fuseli's Milton Gallery*, pp. 58–64, 89, 100, 106–7.

18. Martin Butlin, 'The Evolution of Blake's Large Color Prints of 1795', in *William Blake, Essays for S. Foster Damon*, ed. by Alvin H. Rosenfeld (Providence: Brown University Press, 1969), pp. 109–16 (pp. 111, 114).

19. Joseph Viscomi, *Blake and the Idea of the Book* (Princeton, NJ: Princeton University Press, 1993), pp. 302, 304.

20. Butlin, 'The Evolution of Blake's Large Color Prints', p. 115.

21. Copies of Blake's 1795 colour print *The House of Death* are at the Fitzwilliam Museum, the British Museum and at Tate Britain; see Anthony Blunt, *The Art of William Blake* (Oxford: Oxford University Press, 1959), p. 41. Both pictures derive from the bounding horizon figure delineated in *The Fertilization of the Nile*, which Fuseli designed and Blake engraved for Erasmus Darwin's *The Botanic Garden* (1791). Their collaboration dates back to their joint work on the English translation of Johann Caspar Lavater's *Essays in Physiognomy*, trans. by Henry Hunter, 3 vols (London: 1789–98).

22. See Robin Hamlyn and Michael Phillips, *William Blake* (London: Tate, 2000), p. 218 and pl. 252.

23. J. H. Hagstrum, 'Blake and the Sister-Arts Tradition', in *Blake's Visionary Forms Dramatic*, ed. by D. V. Erdman and J. E. Grant (Princeton, NJ: Princeton

University Press, 1970), pp. 82–91. Although W. J. T. Mitchell maintains that Blake's books do not invite the reader to visualize his icons, he nonetheless defines *Urizen* as a picture gallery: see his *Blake's Composite Art: a Study of the Illuminated Poetry* (Princeton, NJ: Princeton University Press, 1978), pp. 1–2, 137.

24. Edward Young, *The Complaint; or, Night-Thoughts on Life, Death, & Immortality. Night the First*, 2nd edn (London: 1742), Night I, ll. 314–40, p. 22. Blake's watercolours and prints are reproduced in *William Blake's Designs for Edward Young's Night Thoughts: A Complete Edition*, ed. by D. V. Erdman and others, 2 vols (Oxford: Clarendon Press, 1980).

25. De Loutherbourg's *The Deluge* was engraved on 27 October 1797, one month after the publication of Edwards's *Night Thoughts*, but the painting was on show among the Scripture Pictures at Macklin's Poets Gallery from 1790 onwards: see *Catalogue of the Fifth Exhibition of Pictures, Painted for Mr Macklin by the Artists of Britain, Illustrative of the British Poets, and the Bible* (London: 1792), no. XXIX; Morton D. Paley, *The Apocalyptic Sublime* (New Haven: Yale University Press, 1986), p. 14 and fig. 7 on *The Deluge*, and pp. 54–68 on de Loutherbourg's contributions to Macklin's Bible.

26. Yale Center for British Art, Paul Mellon Collection, reproduced in *Art on the Line: The Royal Academy Exhibitions at Somerset House 1780–1836*, ed. by David Solkin (New Haven: Yale University Press, 2001), p. 87, fig. 56.

27. Many critics observed of the Blake exhibition at Tate Britain in 2001 that the display of *Jerusalem*'s prints hanging one beside the other encouraged spectators to perceive *Jerusalem* through 'pictorial modes of attention', thus 'turning down the volume on the words. *Jerusalem* becomes a bizarrely beautiful array of visual elements to be eyed rather than read'. See Morris Eaves, 'National Arts and Disruptive Technologies in Blake's Prospectus of 1793', in *Blake, Nation and Empire*, ed. Steve Clark and David Worrall (Basingstoke: Palgrave, 2006), pp. 119–35 (pp. 130–1).

28. Paul Mann, 'Apocalypse and Recuperation: Blake and the Maw of Commerce', *ELH*, 52 (1985), 1–32.

29. Saree Makdisi, *William Blake and the Impossible History of the 1790s* (Chicago: University of Chicago Press, 2003), pp. 191–2.

30. Viscomi, *Blake and the Idea of the Book*, pp. 153–8.

31. Harold Bloom, 'The Visionary Cinema of Romantic Poetry', in *Essays for Foster Damon*, ed. by Alvin H. Rosenfeld (Providence, RI: Brown University Press, 1969), pp. 18–35 (pp. 18–19). Bloom's essay draws on Sergei Eisenstein's montage readings of poets with particular reference to Milton: see Eisenstein, *The Film Sense*, trans. by Jay Leyda (London: Faber, 1986), pp. 34–7, 51–8, first published in 1943. See also Calè, *Fuseli's Milton Gallery*, pp. 1–5, 123, 131–6.

32. Eisenstein, *The Film Sense*, pp. 47, 51–8. On Blake's syntactic interruptions, see James Chandler, 'Blake and the Syntax of Sentiment: An Essay on "Blaking" Understanding', in *Blake, Nation and Empire*, pp. 102–18.

33. Henry Fuseli, *Milton Gallery: A Catalogue of the First Series of Pictures and Sketches, From the Poetic Works of John Milton* (London: [1799]), p. 7; *Paradise Lost*, ii. 1013.

34. Viscomi, *Blake and the Idea of the Book*, p. 280.

35. William Blake to Dawson Turner, 9 June 1818 (E771), and Martin Butlin, *Paintings and Drawings of William Blake*, 2 vols (New Haven: Yale University Press, 1981), i, 135, 139 (nos. 260.15 and 261.6), and ii, plates 319 and 355.

36. *William Blake's Writings*, ed. by G. E. Bentley, Jr, 2 vols (Oxford: Clarendon, 1978), i, 715–17.

37. David Erdman, 'Textual Notes', E804.

38. On the imagery of the book in *Urizen*, see Paul Mann, '*The Book of Urizen* and the Horizon of the Book', in *Unnam'd Forms: Blake and Textuality*, ed. by Nelson Hilton and Thomas Vogler (Berkeley: University of California Press, 1986), pp. 49–68.

39. Jerome J. McGann, 'The Idea of an Indeterminate Text: Blake's Bible of Hell and Dr Alexander Geddes', *Studies in Romanticism*, 25 (1986), 303–24.

40. Eisenstein, 'Beyond the Shot' (1929), in *Selected Works, Vol 1: Writings, 1922–34*, ed. and trans. by Richard Taylor (London: BFI, 1988), pp. 138–50 (p. 144).

41. For ease of reference, I follow the numbering established by Bentley (*William Blake's Writings*, i, 715–17) and accepted by Erdman, which is listed in the first column on the left and juxtaposed horizontally to the number indicating the place that plate has in the sequence of other copies, as consulted on: <http://www.blakearchive.org>

42. Viscomi, *Blake and the Idea of the Book*, p. 283.

43. Walter Benjamin, 'The Work of Art in the Age of its Technological Reproducibility: Third Version', in *Selected Writings*, ed. by Howard Eiland and Michael W. Jennings, 4 vols (Cambridge, MA: Belknap Press, 1996–2003), iv, 255.

44. 'Advertisement', in Edward Young, *The Complaint, and, the Consolation; or, Night Thoughts* (London: 1797), p. iii.

45. Jean Hagstrum, *William Blake Poet and Painter: An Introduction to the Illuminated Verse* (Chicago: University of Chicago Press, 1964), p. 31.

46. Quoted in John E. Grant, Edward J. Rose and Michael J. Tolley, 'Introduction', in *William Blake's Designs for Edward Young's Night Thoughts*, i, 7.

47. *William Blake's Designs for Edward Young's Night Thoughts*, NT 46 (Night II, p. 13), ll. 146–7. In this edition, '*NT*' indicates the watercolour designs to *Night Thoughts*, and 'E' designates the engraved designs. Full-page reproduced illustrations are not otherwise numbered.

48. *William Blake's Designs for Edward Young's Night Thoughts*, NT46, 15E.

49. *Ibid.*, NT45 (Night II, p. 12), l. 144, and NT49 (Night II, p. 16), l. 220; see also 14E–16E.

50. *Ibid.*, NT45, 46 and 49; cfr 14–16E.

51. J. A. Warner, *Blake and the Language of Art* (Kingston, NY: McGill-Queen's University Press, 1984), pp. 138–46.

52. See *The Poetical Works of John Milton*, 3 vols (London: 1794–7), i, opposite p. 77; *Vala; or, the Four Zoas*, ed. by G. E. Bentley (Oxford: Clarendon Press, 1963), p. 183n.; *Blake's Night Thoughts*, i, 89 n. 42. For a discussion of 'The Christian Triumph' and its substitution of the original title page of NT4, see also Grant *et al.*, 'Introduction', *Blake's Designs for Edward Young's Night Thoughts*, i, 30.

53. Grant *et al.*, 'Introduction', *William Blake's Designs for Edward Young's Night Thoughts*, i, 35.

54. On *Vala* and *The Four Zoas* as experiments in the book format of *Night Thoughts*, see Paul Mann, 'The Final State of *The Four Zoas*', and Robert Essick, '*The Four Zoas*: Intention and Production', *BIQ*, 18 (1985), 204–15, 216–20.

55. See Angus Whitehead, 'William Blocke: New References to Blake in *Boyle's City Guide* (1797) and *Boyles' City Companion* (1798)', *Blake Journal*, 8 (2004), 30–46, and Mark Crosby, 'Sparks of Fire: William Blake in Felpham 1800–1803' (unpublished doctoral thesis, University of Oxford, 2007), chapter 1. I am grateful to Mark Crosby for these references.

11
Blake's Poems on Art and Artists
Morton D. Paley

My subject is Blake's conflict with the artistic values of his own time as expressed in certain writings of the years 1798 to 1811. These comprise his annotations to the second edition (1798) of *The Works of Sir Joshua Reynolds* with a very long Introduction by Edmond Malone, his *Descriptive Catalogue* of 1809, the *Public Address* of 1809–10, the *Vision of the Last Judgment* of 1810 and a number of Notebook poems written from perhaps 1807 until 1812.[1] The first four have been given considerable attention by scholars, while the last has not. Perhaps because of their free-and-easy manner, doggerel rhyming and frequently outrageous humour, Blake's poems about art and artists have never been given serious – or even flippant – consideration in their own right. I want to argue that they have great interest both as satire and as expressions of Blake's views about art, artists and the art market, and also that a major impetus for them was Blake's reaction to an event that has also been little discussed in relation to him: the Orléans Sale of 1798, the greatest sale of Italian, French and Spanish paintings that had ever taken place in London. First, I will address the question of why Blake did not express his views about art earlier, especially when there had been a previous Orléans sale, of the Dutch and Flemish paintings in the collection, in 1793.

The mid-1790s were one of the most wonderfully productive periods of Blake's life, years full of activity and hope. On 10 October 1793 he issued a prospectus entitled 'To the Public' in which he offered for sale copies of six illuminated books – *Songs of Innocence, Songs of Experience, America, The Book of Thel, Visions of the Daughters of Albion* and *The Marriage of Heaven and Hell*, plus two large examples of 'Historical Engraving' – *Job* and *Edward and Elinor* – and two small books of engravings – *The History of England* and *The Gates of Paradise*. Of these ten items, all but *The History of England*, which was evidently to be based on a number of drawings, most of which Blake had already executed, were published.[2] In 1793 Blake also engraved twelve plates for John Gay's *Fables*, and twelve for John Stedman's *Surinam* (first published in 1796). In the following year he issued two more impressive illuminated books, *Europe* and *The First Book of Urizen*, and the large *Ezekiel* plate, and also contributed six engravings to his friend George Cumberland's *Thoughts on Outline* (1796). His new illuminated books of 1795 – *The Song of Los*, *The Book of Los* and *The Book of Ahania*, were less ambitious than their immediate predecessors, but in that same year Blake was working on his great sequence of colour-printed drawings or mono-types. 1795 was indeed, to use Joseph Viscomi's phrase, Blake's *annus mirabilis*, not only for the ambition and size of his achievement in that year, but also for his experiments in colour printing. Before these were completed, Blake received a commission from Richard Edwards to illustrate Edward Young's Graveyard poem *Night Thoughts*, a commission that would result in his drawing 597 watercolours and then, in 1796–7, in engraving forty-three folio-sized plates. It is hard to see how Blake could have found the time or energy to address the artistic values of his time when he himself was making so much art. Another reason may be simply that in the early and mid-1790s Blake had not yet arrived at what we think of as his characteristic views about art and artists. None of these is known to have been expressed before 1798. Indeed, for a period he was far more eclectic in his views of art and artists than he was to be later. In 1799 he wrote to the Rev. John Trusler:

> I would rather Paint Pictures in oil of the same dimensions than make Drawings. & on the same terms. by this means you will have a number of Cabinet pictures. which I flatter myself will not be unworthy of a Scholar of Rembrant & Teniers. whom I have Studied no less than Rafael & Michael angelo. (E701)

Of course this may, at least in part, be a matter of telling Trusler what Blake thought Trusler wanted to hear. But that Blake was seriously affected by types of art he later rejected is clear in the *Descriptive Catalogue* of 1809, where he writes of being tempted by 'Venetian and Flemish Demons; whose enmity to the Painter himself, and to all Artists, who study in the Florentine and Roman Schools may be removed by an exhibition and exposure of their vile tricks'. The chief tempters were Titian and that 'most outrageous demon' Rubens. Of Rubens, Blake says: 'though the original conception was all fire and animation, he loads it with hellish brownness, and blocks up all its gates of light except one, and that one he closes with iron bars, till the victim is obliged to give up the Florentine and Roman practice, and adopt the Venetian and Flemish' (E547). Interestingly, when Blake describes the renewal of his vision the day after visiting the Truchsessian Gallery in 1804, it is in terms of the removal of barriers to light: 'I was again enlightened with the light I enjoyed in my youth, and which has for exactly twenty years been closed from me as by a door and by window-shutters.'[3]

As we can see, for these two reasons Blake may not have reacted immediately against the Dutch and Flemish Orléans pictures exhibited in 1793 at the Old Academy Rooms in Pall Mall, and seen by as many as two thousand people a week.[4] There seven paintings by Rubens were sold, among which was *The Judgment of Paris* (now National Gallery 194), bought by Lord Kinnaird for 2,000 guineas. Four pictures by Philips Wouvermans including *The Stable*, valued at 200 guineas, were sold, and nine by Teniers, with William Beckford paying 500 guineas for Teniers's *The Ale-House and Smokers* and *Le Cabaret*.[5] And there were six paintings by or attributed to Rembrandt, including *The Mill* (now National Gallery of Art, Washington DC), which sold for 500 guineas, and *The Cradle*, afterwards bought by Richard Payne Knight for 1,000 guineas.[6] As Blake's circumstances changed and his optimism faded, he may well have been mindful of the large sums brought by Dutch and Flemish pictures in this 1793 sale, as well as the results of the later one.

After 1797 and the failure, through no fault of Blake's, of the first part of the *Night Thoughts* edition (there was no second), there came a period of few engraving commissions and no new illuminated books. His only steady source of income was the one guinea each he received from Thomas Butts for fifty small pictures from the Bible, starting no later than 26 August 1799 and continuing after his removal to Felpham in September 1800.[7] With the exception of these drawings for Butts, Blake's imaginative life became highly polarized during his self-described 'three years slumber on the banks of the Ocean' (*Jerusalem*, pl. 3, E145). On the one hand he did have commercial work – commissions for William Hayley's projects and miniatures for Hayley's circle; on the other he was writing (and drawing) *Vala*, a work for which the intended audience remains unclear. Back in London, he made a beginning on both *Milton* and *Jerusalem* in 1804 (as the dates on their title pages signify), and subsequently he was no doubt elated by the prospect of illustrating a new edition of Robert Blair's *The Grave* and executing the engravings for it. We know the outcome. After the publisher Robert Hartley Cromek deprived Blake of his engraving commission, very likely as a consequence of showing his magnificently 'primitive' relief etching *Deaths Door*, Blake realized that he had become marginalized both as artist and as engraver. 'Tuesday Janry. 20. 1807', he wrote in his Notebook, 'between Two & Seven in the Evening – Despair'(E 694).

The circumstances of the 1798 Orléans Sale, a prodigious event in the art world, were well known, one might even say well publicized. Three wealthy noblemen – Francis Egerton, 3rd Duke of Bridgewater, George Granville Leveson-Gower, Earl Gower (later 2nd Marquess of Stafford and 1st Duke of Sutherland) and Frederick Howard, 5th Earl of Carlisle – clubbed together to buy the cream of the French and Italian pictures, through the agency of William Bryan, reserving the pictures for the sum of £43,500.[8] Bryan, although known to us principally for his *Biographical and Critical Dictionary of Painters and Engravers* (1816), was one of the most important art dealers of his time. 'The Orleans exhibition', William Buchanan wrote, opened on 26 December 1798 and continued for six months 'in the rooms belonging to Mr Bryan, in Pall-Mall, and at the Lysceum [*sic*], in the Strand, neither of these places being individually sufficient to contain the collection'. Among the admirers of the exhibition was the young William Hazlitt, who would shortly say he aspired to paint in the manner of Titian.[9] 'A new sense came upon me,' Hazlitt wrote, 'a new heaven and earth stood before me [...]. From that time on I lived in a world of pictures.'[10] Blake's reaction is likely to have been considerably less adulatory. In his view the art market had elevated Titian, Rubens and Rembrandt above Michelangelo and Raphael. It is true that the Duke of Bridgewater paid 1,200 guineas for *The Madonna and the Infant Christ* (National Gallery of Scotland), but Raphael's madonnas were never as important to Blake as his frescoes, especially the group from the Vatican loggie known in engraved form as the 'Raphael Bible'.[11] The originals of these and of Michelangelo's were for obvious reasons unavailable to the market (though one has the impression that dealers like Bryan and Buchanan would have torn them from the walls if they could have).

Characterized by a spirit of aggression, the satirical poems that Blake consequently wrote employ punning and other forms of double meaning to bring out the assumed duplicity of their targets, which are fashionable foreigners (both words and people), pretentious collectors and artists who 'could not draw' ('Annotations to Reynolds', E646). Language is used very inventively in these poems, as in the creation of names for identifiable people, names that have the flavour of the eighteenth-century theatre and of Hogarth's narrative engravings. Blake had long been taken with satirical naming, as in 'Steelyard the Lawgiver', 'Obtuse

Angle' and 'Mrs Nannicantipot' in *An Island in the Moon* (1784). Now Blake's sometime friend Thomas Stothard becomes 'Stewhard', Cromek, 'Bob Screwmuch' and Louis Schiavonetti, who engraved Blake's *Grave* designs, 'Assassinetti'. Prince Hoare, editor of *The Artist*, is 'trembling Hare', who 'sits on his weakly paper'. Proper nouns can be used as verbs – Fools 'never can Rafael it Fuseli it nor Blake it' and the puns are deliberately outrageous. 'The Cunning sures & the Aim at yours' (E510), Blake wrote as a single line in his Notebook, punning on 'connoisseurs' and 'amateurs' (as Erdman notes, E869). Of these two words of French derivation, 'amateur' was a relative newcomer to the language: the *OED*'s first recorded uses, both from the *European Magazine*, were in 1784 and 1786; the word was still unusual enough *c.* 1803 for Rees's *Cyclopedia* to gloss it: 'Amateur, in the Arts, is a foreign term introduced and now passing current amongst us, to denote a person understanding, and loving or practicing the polite arts of painting, sculpture, or architecture, without any regard to pecuniary advantage' (*OED, s.v.*). 'Connoisseur' was an earlier arrival, dating to 1714. Elsewhere Blake transforms it into a verb, as in 'every man [...] who has not been connoisseured out of his senses'.[12] Blake assumes a pugilistic Hogarthian stance towards things – or at least words – from France.

In one of these poems Blake parallels the 'Ignorant Savage' with the 'taught Englishman' who 'spends his whole Fortune'| On a smear or a squall to destroy Picture or Tune', concluding:

> And I call upon Colonel Wardle
> To give these Rascals a dose of Cawdle.
>
> (E514)

This poem has been dated to the spring of 1809, as Lieutenant Colonel Gwyllym Lloyd Wardle, MP, was eminent only in that year, when his exposure of corruption in army promotions and contracts led to a trial that resulted in the Duke of York's resignation as commander-in-chief (*DNB, s.v.*). Wardle's political career effectually ended later in 1809 when he was successfully sued by his chief witness, the Regent's former mistress Mrs Clarke, and lost credibility. In April 1809, when Wardle's popularity was at its height, Thomas Rowlandson published a print entitled *Colonel Wardle's Exhibition*, showing Wardle using the 'Wand of Perseverance' to point out bubbles emanating from a chamber pot labelled 'Mrs Clarke's Reservoir'. Among these bubbles are 'The Virtue of a General', 'The Honor of a House Keeper' and 'The Faith of an Agent'; the largest is reserved for 'the Word of a prince'.[13] Blake wants to employ a like strategy to expose the bubbles of the art market. The dose of Cawdle that he wants English collectors to take has a double meaning. Caudle then as now was a hot gruel mixed with ale and spices, with which the sick were often dosed, but in an older sense caudle of hemp-seed was gallows-humour for hanging, as in *2 Henry VI*:

Say. [Lord Say]

Long sitting to determine poor men's causes
Hath made me full of sickness and diseases.

Cade. [Jack Cade]
Ye shall have a hempen Caudle then, and the help of hatchet.
(iv. 8. 78–80)

The fate Blake imagines for English connoisseurs may be more unsavoury than drinking spiced gruel.

The title of the 'Cawdle' poem may also bear some consideration: 'On the Great Encouragement Given by English Nobility & Gentry to Correggio Rembrandt Reynolds Gainsborough Catalani DuCrowe & Dilberry Doodle'. We recognize the four famous painters, but what do the last three names signify? Angelica Catalani was the most famous soprano in England from her arrival there in 1806 to her departure in 1813. Coleridge reviewed her performance in Paisello's *Elfrida* in June 1812, praising her acting as well as her singing, and she was Susanna in the first British performance of *The Marriage of Figaro* that same year.[14] In December 1806 Robert Dighton published what became a celebrated hand-coloured portrait of her – the National Portrait Gallery owns no fewer than ten examples – in costume for *Semiramide* by Marcus Portogallo.[15] Her performance became all the rage, to the point that a cap modelled on the one she wore on stage was pictured in *Le Beau Monde, or Literary and Fashionable Magazine* for 6 April 1807, and described as 'IL BERRETTA ALLA SEMIRAMIDE full dress cap, with drapery of plain white patent net, trimmed round with silver silk fringe, and a silver tiara in front'.[16] Blake includes Catalani here not for any quality of her voice (which in all probability he never heard) but because she represents to him one of a pretentious high society's more expensive fads, as did the castrato Farinelli to Hogarth in *A Rake's Progress* 2, where an enormous scroll is headed: 'A list of the rich Presents Signor Farinelli the Italian singer condescended to accept of the English Nobility and Gentry for one Night's Performance in the

Opera *Atarexes'*. As for 'DuCrowe', he was the Swiss artist Louis Ducros (1748–1810), still living when Blake wrote these lines. Ducros had, in partnership with the engraver Giovanni Battista Volpato, produced numerous views of Rome popular with tourists. He also painted large watercolours, for example *View at Tivoli* and *The Arch of Constantine* (both National Trust, Stourhead, Wilts.), and *The Waterfalls of Tivoli* (National Gallery of Art, Washington DC).[17] Collected by Sir Richard Colt Hoare of Stourhead, Ducros had remarkable success in his chosen field, thus drawing the wrath of an artist he had probably never heard of, one unsympathetic to picturesque views, even more unsympathetic to aristocratic patronage and no doubt resentful at his own friend George Cumberland's suggesting in 1808 that he publish his 'new Method of engraving' accompanied by 'a few Specimens of Plates for subscribers of it – as Du Crow did of his Aqua tinta'.[18] Last, 'Dilberry', is a piece of outrageous scatalogical slang; 'dilberries' are defined in Francis Grose's *Classical Dictionary of the Vulgar Tongue* as 'Small pieces of excrement adhering to the hairs near the fundament';[19] and while 'doodle' did not acquire its meaning of 'aimless drawing' until 1937 (*OED, s.v.*), in Blake's time it could refer to a child's penis (*Classic al Dictionary, s.v.*). This jarring descent from the high-toned to the vulgar is of course another of the satirist's stratagems.

Another poem employing what Blake regards as foreign cant terms is 'To Venetian Artists' (E515). In it Blake tells the fable of a dog who swims across a river with a stolen bone:

> As he swam he saw the reflection of the bone
> This is quite Perfection, one Generalizing Tone
> Outline Theres no outline Theres no such thing
> All is Chiaro Scuro Poco Piu its all Colouring
> Snap. Snap! he has lost shadow & substance too
> He had them both before now how do ye do.

In this Aesopian story, the dog is the viewer who is taken in by illusionist art, and thus loses the reality that can be embodied in outline. 'Chiaroscuro', which aids the deception with its lights and darks, is of course a word of Italian origin, while 'Poco Piu', as Morris Eaves points out, is a common term in connoisseurship standing for *poco più o pocomeno*, 'the little more or less that makes the difference'.[20] (The *OED's* earliest example of the phrase is 'the Poco piu and the Poco meno of the Italian artists', from *Tristam Shandy*, 1760; however, *poco più* occurs on its own in 1724.)

Colouring is of course one of the subjects on which Blake differs most from Reynolds, particularly with Reynolds's dictum in the Eighth Discourse that 'the masses of light in a picture be always of a warm mellow colour, yellow, red or a yellowish-white; and that the blue, the grey or the green colours be kept almost entirely out of these masses, and be used only to support and set off these warm colours; and for this purpose, a small proportion of cold colours will be sufficient'.[21] For Blake this was too formulaic and mechanical. 'Colouring formed upon these Principles', he wrote in the margin, 'is destructive of All Art because it takes away the possibility of Variety & only promotes Harmony or Blending of Colours one into another' (E661). Reynolds continued: 'Let this conduct be reserved; let the warm be Cold, and the surrounding colours warm, as we often see in the works of the Roman and Florentine painters, and it will be out of the power of art, even in the hands of Rubens or Titian, to make a picture splendid and harmonious'.[22] Blake did not extend his own remarks here, but instead wrote (or had already written) a four-line poem on Reynolds's title page, under the inserted title 'Advice of the Popes who succeeded the Age of Rafael'. It begins:

Degrade first the Arts if you'd Mankind degrade,
Hire Idiots to Paint with cold light & hot shade.

(E635)

What Blake meant by this has found a recent exposition in the script of the movie *Dangerous Minds*, in this conversation between a teacher (played by Michelle Pfeiffer) and a student named Raul:

[Student]: So what's 'Hire idiots to paint
with cold light and hot shade'?

[Teacher:] They're being sarcastic, Raul.
I mean, 'cause you know that light
is supposed to be warm, right?

And shade is supposed to be what?
Cold?

Exactly. But if you go and hire an idiot
to do the job, he's gonna do it backwards.[23]

At the time Blake wrote, as well as in Reynolds's own time, Reynolds's views on cold and hot colours were far from universally accepted. A contemporary anecdote to the effect that Gainsborough painted *The Blue Boy* to contradict Reynolds was almost certainly untrue, but the fact that some believed it shows that Blake was not alone in his objection.

Reynolds himself is the subject, or rather the butt, of several of the poems, including 'Florentine Ingratitude' (E511–12), which concerns the Reynolds self-portrait in the Uffizi (then the Royal or Ducal) Gallery. The poem begins by referring to Sir Joshua's gift of the painting (1775) to the Gallery at the invitation of the Reale Accademia di Belle Arte, of which Reynolds had been elected a member while still in Italy.[24] (Two mezzotint engravings after this self-portrait, one by Charles Townley (1777) and the other by John Keyes Sherwin (1784) had been published, so Blake would have had ample opportunity to see the image in monochrome.) Reynolds shows himself wearing his Oxford doctoral cap and gown – he had been made a Doctor of Civil Law in 1773 – as he does in an earlier version (Tate) and in his famous self-portrait with a bust of Michelangelo (*c.* 1779–80, Royal Academy). This emphasis on the academic accords with a theme frequently expressed in the *Discourses* – that the painter is a practitioner of one of the liberal arts. Michelangelo is present in the Uffizi picture not as a bust but as a rolled-up set of drawings in Reynolds's right hand, marked 'Disegni del Divino'. The warm reds of the gown and the contrast between the very dark background and the flesh tones of his face and his white cravat give expression to Reynolds's views of the centrality of warm colour masses and of chiaroscuro. The Tate Britain display caption for the early version is indeed accurate, but we can imagine what interpretation Blake would have given it: 'In this picture, his costume, his pose, and the dramatic contrasts of light and dark all refer to the work of Rembrandt. Even the shape of his face is made to resemble the Dutch artist's distinctive, jowly features.'[25]

Blake begins:

> Sir Joshua sent his portrait to
> The birth place of Michael Angelo
> And in the hand of the simpering fool
> He put a Dirty paper scroll
> And on the paper to be polite
> Did Sketches by Michel Angelo write.

Blake probably knew enough Italian to be aware that 'Disegni' did not mean 'sketches'. In Renaissance Italian art theory Design was closely related to Drawing. As Harold Osborne puts it in *The Oxford Companion to Art*:

> Its primary sense was drawing, as, for example, when the 15th-c. theorist Franceso Lancillotti in his *Trattato di pittura* (1509) distinguished *disegno, colorito, compositione,* and *inventione* as the four elements of painting. So too Cennini made *disegno* and *il colorire* the bases of painting and Vasari set design over against invention as the father and mother of all the arts. In its wider meaning *disegno* came to imply the creative idea in the mind of the artist (as this was often thought to be bodied forth in the preliminary drawing).[26]

Blake would surely have known that Reynolds's collection included several Michelangelo drawings, especially as Sir Joshua used to bring works from his collection to show the Royal Academy students. However, Blake's intention is not objective journalism but satire. 'Sketches' is as much of a reductive putdown as 'a Dirty paper scroll' for the rolled-up drawings. In the same vein Blake continues:

> The Florentines said Tis a Dutch English bore
> Michael Angelos Name writ on Rembrandt's door
> The Florentines call it an English Fetch.

One of the meanings of 'fetch' given in the *OED*, with examples both before and after Blake's time, is 'a contrivance, dodge, stratagem, trick; also, a fetch of law, policy, state, and to cast a fetch'. The fetch here is the link Blake sees between Reynolds's self-representations and the art market:

> Tis the trading English Venetian Cant
> To speak Michael Angelo & act Rembrandt.

Blake did not invent the Florentines' hostility. After the self-portrait first arrived, it was 'revered almost as if it were a holy relic', according to the Keeper of the Royal Gallery, Luigi Siries; and in 1776 the Duke sent Reynolds a gold and a silver medal.[27] However, when James Northcote, who had been Reynolds's pupil and assistant, was in Italy – he too accepted the invitation to contribute a self-portrait (1778) to the Royal Gallery – he discovered that Florentine painters were bad-mouthing Reynolds' painting. According to William T. Whitley, Northcote blamed George III's favourite painter, Johan Zoffany, RA, also a member of the

Reale Accademia di Belle Arte, for telling the Florentine artists that 'it will soon fade away and appear quite dreadful'.[28] It is likely that after Northcote returned to London in 1780 his report circulated freely among artists there, and that Blake picked it up there. The fading of the colours of some of Reynolds's portraits was indeed well known in the art world, and Blake wrote in a margin of Reynolds's *Works*:

> When S[r] Joshua Reynolds died
> All Nature was degraded;
> The King dropd a tear into the Queens Ear;
> And all his Pictures Faded.
>
> (E641)

In 'Florentine Ingratitude' Blake presents Reynolds as a charlatan whose pretensions fail to deceive the Florentines.

> But You must not bring in your hand a Lie
> If you mean that Florentines should buy.

Blake reinforces his argument by alluding to two stories about great artists that reinforced his own belief in, as he put it in his *Descriptive Catalogue*, 'the hard and wirey line of rectitude and certainty' (E550).

> Ghiottos Circle or Apelles line
> Were not the work of Sketchers drunk with Wine.

Giotto's circle is from a story made famous in Giorgio Vasari's *Life of Giotto*, which Blake could have been familiar with in William Aglionby's translation, originally published in 1685. Although Blake could have picked up this story somewhere else, that he had read Aglionby's translation of Vasari is suggested by his note to Reynolds's statement that, 'When we read the lives of the most eminent Painters, every page informs us, that no part of their time was spent in dissipation.'[29] Blake objected 'The Lives of Painters say that Rafael died of Dissipation [...] He who has Nothing to Dissipate Cannot Dissipate' (E643). Vasari wrote that Raphael refrained from marrying because he hoped to be made a cardinal:

> In this hope, there, keeping Marriage at a distance, and following secretly other amorous Delights, it happened that he committed once such an Excess that way, that he came Home with a pretty high

Feaver; the Physicians being called, and he concealing the true Cause of his Distemper, which they feared, was an *Inflammation;* they ordered him to be Let Blood. whereas they should have given him *Cordials* and *Restauratives* [...]. He yielded up the Ghost on a *Good Fryday,* in the Seven and Thirtieth Year of his Age, the same day he was Born on.[30]

In Vasari's account, Pope Benedict IX, having heard of Giotto and considering giving him a commission in St Peter's, sends a courtier 'to see what sort of man *Ghiotto* was, and to give him an account of his Painting'.[31] The courtier asks Giotto for a specimen of his work. '*Ghiotto,* who was a pleasant ready man, took a sheet of White-paper, and with a pen dipped in red, setting his Arm close to his Hip to keep it steady, he with one stroke of a Red-lead Pencil, drew a Circle so round, and so equal, that it was wonderful to see it.' Puzzled and annoyed, the courtier nevertheless takes the design to Rome and shows it to the pope, 'telling the *Pope* how he had done it without Compasses, or so much as stirring his Arm from his Side'. As the pope 'understood something of the Art', he 'easily comprehended by this, how much *Giotto* in strength of Design, did Excel over the other Painters of his Time'.[32] As for Apelles's line, the story regarding it originates in Pliny's *Natural History,* but Blake is likely to have known it indirectly through Hogarth's *Analysis of Beauty*:

> Apelles having heard of the fame of Protogenes, went to Rhodes to pay him a visit, but not finding him at home asked for a board, on which he drew a *line,* telling the servant maid, that line would signify to her master who had been to see him; we are not clearly told what sort of a line it was that could so particularly signify one of the first of his profession: if it was only a stroke (tho' as fine as a hair as Pliny seems to think) it could not possibly, by any means, denote the abilities of a great painter. But if we suppose it to be a line of some extraordinary quality, such as the serpentine line will appear to be, Apelles could not have left a more satisfactory signature of the complement he had paid him. Protogenes when he came home took the hint, and drew a finer *or rather more expressive* line within it, to shew Apelles if he came again, that he understood his meaning. He, soon returning, was well-pleased with the answer Protogenes had left for him, by which he was convinced that fame had done him justice, and so correcting the line again, perhaps by making it more precisely elegant, he took his leave.[33]

For Blake the polar opposite of Giotto and Apelles was Rubens, because of his factory methods, his building up paintings by masses of colour rather than outlined forms and his painting central figures that did not conform to the classical or neo-classical ideal. In 'To English Connoisseurs' (E513) Blake says that Rubens portrays Christ as 'a Brewers Servant', no doubt having in mind the muscular Christs of paintings like the *Resurrection of Christ* of the famous Moretus triptych in Antwerp Cathedral, which Blake could have known through engravings. He also accuses Rubens of duplicity: 'I Rubens am a Statesman & a Saint | Deceptions? O no – so I'll learn to Paint' (E513). Rubens had indeed been given important diplomatic commissions. Among others he nego-tiated a treaty between Spain and England, representing Spain in the court of Charles I. His claim to sainthood is puzzling until we consider the original version of line 2: 'he mixd them both & so he Learnd to paint' (E871). Blake is referring to the credit Rubens was given for pre-serving peace between Spain and England, not only as a diplomat but also as an artist. What Blake specifically has in mind here is the picture Rubens painted as a gift for Charles I at the time of his diplomatic visit, *Minerva Protects Pax from Mars or Peace and War* (National Gallery, 46). In it Ceres, as Peace, is shown offering the bountiful fruits of the earth to all, as Minerva drives away Mars and the fury Alecto. At the time Blake was writing these epigrams, the picture had recently been pur-chased by the Duke of Sutherland for 3,000 pounds.[34]

It was inevitable that the 'Petty sneaking Knave' (E509) R. H. Cromek be introduced among these poems. Blake uses Cromek's persona and (as Erdman's notes point out, E869) his Northern accent to produce further double meanings in 'English Encouragement of Art', of which there are two versions in the Notebook. The final one begins:

> If you mean to Please Every body you will
> Menny wouver both Bunglishness & skill.
>
> (E510)

'Menny wouver' = 'maneuver' puns on the name of the much-collected seventeenth-century Dutch painter Philips Wouwermans or Wouverman (1619–1668), here Mynheer Wouwermans, whose paintings almost always feature horses and human figures (a prime example is the Fitzwilliam Museum's *Landscape with a Sporting Party*, part of the original Fitzwilliam bequest of 1816). The nonce-word 'Bunglishness', making a portmanteau of 'bungle' and 'Englishness', is a wonderful Joycean improvement over the 'Ignorance' of the first version, though it is, as

Erdman says, 'too bad to lose from either reading the second and inter-
mediate reading of "great multitude," namely "great Madjority"' (E869).
In an untitled following poem Cromek is refreshingly blunt about the
language of connoisseurship:

> When you look at a picture you always can see
> If a Man of Sense has Painted he
> Then never flinch but keep up a Jaw
> About freedom & jenny suck awa'.
>
> > (E510)

Keeping up a jaw about freedom is, as we know too well, to reapply a
phrase of Dr Johnson's 'the last refuge of a scoundrel', and 'Jenny suck
awa'' is of course *je ne sais quoi*. Cromek has unabashedly laid bare the
devices of the connoisseurs. (Is it possible that 'Jenny suck awa'' is from
a bawdy broadside or ballad?) Cromek of course had little to do with
collecting and connoisseurship, but Blake wants to link the phenomena
of the commodification of the work of art and the exploitative
publisher.

Cromek speaks again in the verses beginning 'I askd my Dear Friend
Orator Prigg' (E515). The name of the speaker suggests not only self-
consciously superior moral fussiness but also, whether spelled with one
'g' or two, stealing and haggling. Tom O' Bedlam sings: 'The palsie
plague these pounces | When I prig your pigs or pullen' (*OED, s.v.*).
Closer to the bone as far as the person Blake called 'Bob Screwmuch' is
concerned is: 'To haggle over the price of something offered for sale.
Chiefly Brit. regional (north.) in later use.' Robert Burns wrote in 'The
Brigs of Ayr' (1787) of 'Men wha grew wise priggin owre hops an' raisins'
(l. 187). Blake also supplies Cromek's Northern dialect in writing 'pant'
for 'paint'.

> So if a Great Panter with Questions you push
> Whats the first Part of Panting hell say a Pant Brush
> And what is the second with most modest blush
> Hell smile like a Cherub & say a pant Brush
> And what is the third hell bow like a rush
> With a lear in his Eye hell reply a Pant Brush.
>
> > (E515)

'Modest blush' is of course a Blakean giveaway, both words being
typically associated with hypocrisy in his writings. It's interesting to

note that while 'pencil' goes back to 1325, the word 'paint brush' does not seem to have been used before the mid-eighteenth century. The *OED*'s earliest example, from a satirical print, is dated ?1762: 'Now my father has left his Paint Brushes'. A little earlier, in *The Cry: A New Dramatic Fable* (1754) by Sarah Fielding and Jane Collier, we find the following example of 'a lucky hit' in the arts: 'The finishing [of] a most famous piece of ancient painting we are told was owing to the rageful despair of the painter, who, by throwing his brush wet with paint, in order to deface what he despaired to compleat, gave that expressive stroke which all his labour before could not effect.'[35] If Blake knew this anecdote, it would have seemed to him appropriate to what he called the 'Blots & Blurs of Rubens & Titian' (*Public Address*, E576).

Blake's satirical poems on art and artists are not polished, to say the least, and they are largely written in verse approximating doggerel. Blake was certainly capable of producing epigrams in the Augustan manner. Referring to Thomas Cook's reengraving of Hogarth's designs in smaller size, for example, Blake writes: 'Tom Cooke cut Hogarth down with his clean graving'. '[C]ut [...] down' richly signifies the style as well as the size of Cook's prints, with perhaps even a suggestion of cutting a corpse down from the gallows, and the second line is very much in the spirit of *The Dunciad*: 'Thousands of Connoisseurs with joy ran raving' (E505). However, for the most part Blake wanted these poems to have a rough texture. He writes in 'Blake's apology for his Catalogue':

> Having given great offence by writing in Prose
> Ill write in Verse as Soft as Bartolloze
> Some blush at what others can see no crime in
> But nobody sees any harm in Rhyming.
>
> (E505)

'Bartolloze' is the commercially successful engraver Francesco Bartolozzi; by wrenching his name and then making the feminine rhyme of the next couplet end colloquially, Blake deflates any 'high' expectations the reader may have. In a similar vein the title of a poem can begin in a 'high' style and then go rapidly downwards, as in 'A Pretty Epigram for the Entertainment of those who have Paid Great Sums in the Venetian & Flemish Ooze' (E513). 'Florentine Ingratitude', the poem on Reynolds's self-portrait, concludes:

These Verses were written by a very Envious Man
Who whatever likeness he may have to Michael Angelo
Never can have any to Sir Jehoshuan.

(E512)

It's as if by using a Hebrew form of 'Joshua' the poet were saying: 'Reader, I wanted to end this poem with a rhyme, but the best I could do was this.' Such sallies into self-referentiality, along with the other rough-and-ready aspects of this group of Notebook poems, may be what have led many readers to place them on the margins of Blake's creativity. Yet, as I hope to have demonstrated, it is these very qualities, along with their mordant wit and satirical thrust, that give Blake's poems on art and artists their claim to our attention.

A closing note in connection with the commodification of the work of art: on 2 May 2006, nineteen of William Blake's twenty original illustrations for Blair's *Grave* were auctioned in New York City. The title page was bought for $650,000, and ten other drawings were sold individually for a total of $5,534,200.[36] (Even so, the sale was not considered a success: fourteen lots did not meet their reserve, and of these eight were bought in.) These drawings had remained intact as a group from 1806, when acquired by R. H. Cromek. They were first sold in 2001, were authenticated by Martin Butlin and were viewed privately in December 2001 by a group of six scholars, of which I was one, and two dealers. 'All these were immediately impressed', as Elizabeth Bentley has written, 'by their authenticity, beauty, importance, and commercial value.'[37] Owing to their being kept together in a portfolio (which was also sold at the auction) since 1836, most of these watercolours were in superbly fresh condition. They might have been sold to a public institution such as Tate Britain, where they could have been studied as a group by scholars and exhibited occasionally to the public (works on paper being so sensitive to light). Instead, these drawings have now been dispersed, and the ownership of four of those sold is unknown, as are the location and future disposition of the eight unsold drawings. Where is the new William Blake to satirize this event?

Notes

1. For dating see *The Notebook of William Blake: A Photographic and Typographic Facsimile*, ed. by David V. Erdman with the assistance of Donald K. Moore (Oxford: Clarendon Press, 1973), pp. 13, 56–7 and 71–2. This edition will be cited as *N*, with the poem's number following.

2. See David Bindman, 'Blake's "Gothicised Imagination" and the History of England', in *William Blake: Essays in Honour of Sir Geoffrey Keynes*, ed. by Morton D. Paley and Michael Phillips (Oxford: Clarendon Press, 1973), pp. 1–28.
3. Letter to William Hayley, 23 October 1804, E756. See my 'The Truchsessian Gallery Revisited', *Studies in Romanticism*, 16 (1977), 217–36.
4. See Gerald Reitlinger, *The Economics of Taste: The Rise and Fall of the Picture Market 1760–1969* (New York: Holt, Rinehart and Winston, 1964), p. 28. The price of admission was one shilling.
5. See William Buchanan, *Memoirs of Painting: with a Chronological History of the Importation of Pictures by the Great Masters into England Since the French Revolution*, 2 vols (London: 1824), i, 189. Buchanan was perhaps the most important art dealer of his day, and his detailed account of the Orléans Sale is invaluable.
6. See Buchanan, *Memoirs*, i, 196, and Reitlinger, *Economics of Taste*, p. 28.
7. See Blake's letter to George Cumberland, 26 August 1799, E704.
8. 'Michael Bryan', in *Grove Art Online*, available at: <http://www.groveart.com> (accessed 7 September 2006).
9. See my *Portraits of Coleridge* (Oxford: Oxford University Press, 1999), p. 29.
10. 'On the Pleasure of Painting', *The Complete Works of William Hazlitt*, ed. by P. P. Howe, 8 vols (London: J. M. Dent, 1931), viii, 14.
11. Buchanan, *Memoirs*, i, 62–3.
12. Letter to the Editor, published in the *Monthly Magazine*, 21 (July 1, 1806), 520–1, E768.
13. Example in the Achenbach Foundation for Graphic Arts, San Francisco, 1963.30.2226.
14. *The Courier*, 26 June 1811; see Samuel Taylor Coleridge, *Essays on His Own Times*, ed. by D. V. Erdman, 3 vols (Princeton, NJ: Princeton University Press, 1978), ii, 195–6; for information on and images of Catalani see the NPG website, available at: <http://www.npg.org.uk/live/search/>
15. *Ibid.*, NPG D2031.
16. For the image, see <http://locutus.ucr.edu/~cathy/bm/BM4–1807.html>
17. Information from 'Louis Ducros', in *Grove Art Online*, available at: <http://www.groveart.com/> (accessed 27 August 2006). For the image of *The Waterfalls of Tivoli*, see *National Gallery of Art*, available at: <http://www.nga.gov/search/index.shtm/>
18. See *BR*, p. 278. The letter is dated 18 December 1808.
19. See Francis Grose, *Classical Dictionary of the Vulgar Tongue* (London: 1811), *s.v.*
20. Morris Eaves, *The Counter-Arts Conspiracy: Art and Industry in the Age* of Blake (Ithaca, NY: Cornell University Press, 1992), p.173. Blake also uses *Poco Piu* in *Public Address* (E581), where it is linked with 'Niggling' or fussing unnecessarily about details (but an earlier meaning, still current in Blake's day, was 'having sexual intercourse').
21. Joshua Reynolds, *Discourses on Art*, ed. by Robert R. Wark, rev. 2nd edn (New Haven, CT: Yale University Press, 1975; repr. 1997), Discourse i, pp. 272–3.
22. *Ibid.*, p. 273.
23. Available at: <http://www.script-o-rama.com/movie_scripts/d/dangerous-minds-script-transcript-pfeiffer.html>

24. The picture is reproduced in *Joshua Reynolds: The Creation of Celebrity*, ed. by Martin Pottle (London: Tate Publishing, 2005), p. 81.
25. Available at: <http://www.tate.org.uk/britain/> (accessed 27 August 2006).
26. 'Design', in *The Oxford Companion to Art* (Oxford: Clarendon Press, 1974).
27. See *The Creation of Celebrity*, p. 80.
28. *Ibid.*
29. Reynolds, Discourse i, p. 18.
30. William Aglionby, *Choice Observations upon the Art of Painting in the Time of Raphael and Michael Angelo* (London: 1719), p. 143.
31. Aglionby, *Choice Observations*, pp. 258–9. I thank Detlef W. Dörrbecker for bringing Blake's probable knowledge of this translation to my attention
32. *Ibid.*, pp. 144, 145.
33. William Hogarth, *The Analysis of Beauty* (London: 1753), pp. xvii–xviii.
34. See Reitlinger, *The Economics of Taste*, p. 442.
35. Sarah Fielding and Jane Collier, *The Cry: A New Dramatic Fable*, 3 vols (London: 1754), ii, 7–8.
36. All figures are from E. B. Bentley, 'Grave Indignities: Greed, Hucksterism, and Oblivion: Blake's Watercolors for Blair's Grave', *BIQ*, 40 (2006), 66–71.
37. *Ibid.*

Index